I0621295

TEACHER'S GUIDE: UNLEASHING GREATNESS —THE KINGDOM OF SHADOWS

Teachers Annotated Guidebook

ROBERT G. WAUGH

MURIEL WAUGH
EDUCATIONAL PRESS

Copyright © 2025 by Robert G. Waugh

All rights reserved.

No part of this book may be reproduced in any form or by any electronic or mechanical means, including information storage and retrieval systems, without written permission from the author, except for the use of brief quotations in a book review.

TABLE OF CONTENTS

TEACHER OVERVIEW: HOW TO USE THIS GUIDE

📖 TEACHER SNAPSHOT PAGE

For *Unleashing Greatness: The Kingdom of Shadows* — Teacher's Annotated Guide

Welcome to the teaching companion for *Unleashing Greatness: The Kingdom of Shadows*, a transformational literacy and leadership curriculum rooted in story, strategy, and student voice.

This Teacher's Guide is designed to help you:
• Implement high-impact, equity-centered literacy instruction
• Strengthen reading, writing, fluency, and SEL
• Embed Science of Reading (SoR) principles into rich, creative lessons
• Guide students through their own journey of reflection, courage, and greatness

To download lesson plans, templates, and the full teacher support suite, scan the QR code or visit: unleashinggreatnessedu.org

🧩 WHAT'S INSIDE THIS GUIDE:

- ✅ 26 Chapter-by-Chapter Instructional Sequences
  - ✅ Standards-Aligned Comprehension & Writing Tasks
    - ✅ ELA Skill Tie-Ins in 25 of 26 Chapters
    - ✅ Science of Reading Primer + Strategies
    - ✅ Differentiated CER Writing Templates & Lessons
    - ✅ SEL Reflection Prompts & Proverb-Based Learning
    - ✅ Reciprocal Teaching Role Cards + Weekly Tracker
    - ✅ Poetry Integration Across 20+ Chapters
    - ✅ Exit Tickets, Anchor Charts, and Creative Extensions
    - ✅ Summative Assessment Ideas + Rubrics
    - ✅ Cross-Curricular & Art Integration Opportunities
    - ✅ Final Chapter-by-Chapter Answer Key

KEY COUNTS AT A GLANCE:

Learning Feature...................Total # Included In Guide

📖 Total Chapters in Novel...........................26

✎ Chapters with ELA Skill Alignment...............25

💬 CER Writing Opportunities.......................26+

📖 Science of Reading Strategies.....................Throughout

🧠 SEL-Integrated Chapters...........................18+

🖼 Visual + Creative Tasks...........................20+

📜 Poetry Packs with Student Activities.............16

📋 Anchor Charts & Planning Tools.................10+

🎟 Exit Tickets / Discussion Prompts...............25+

⏱ Cross-Curricular Extensions
    Yes — ELA, Art, SEL

🛠 INSTRUCTIONAL TOOLS INCLUDED:

• 📝 **Quick-Start Planning Templates**
    • 🧠 **Mini-Lessons & Full Lesson Plans (Sampled & Modeled)**
        • 🎯 **Standards Alignment Reference**
        • 🔄 **Before / During / After Reading Activities**
        • 🗣 **Fluency, Prosody & Reader's Theater Tips**
        • ✏️ **Grammar & Writing Skill Builders**
        • 🖼 **Art Extensions & Performance Options**
        • 🧩 **Token Tracker & Leadership Toolkit Integration**

🌐 EQUITY, ENGAGEMENT, AND DEPTH:

This guide is designed with universal access, equity, and teacher creativity in mind. It includes built-in scaffolds for differentiated instruction, deep reading, culturally relevant pedagogy, and multi-modal learning. Whether your classroom is print-based, digital, blended, or arts-integrated, this guide adapts.

✐ Digital Companion Access

Unleashing Greatness website coming soon! Find digital tools, printable lesson pages, and student resources at:

unleashinggreatnessedu.org

WELCOME TO THE TEACHER'S GUIDE

📚 Welcome to the Teacher's Guide

ABOUT THIS GUIDE

This Teacher's Guide is designed to bring *Unleashing Greatness: The Kingdom of Shadows* to life in your classroom. It works **hand-in-hand** with the **Student Workbook**, guiding you through the story chapter by chapter.

Each lesson provides ready-to-use strategies to deepen comprehension, build vocabulary, strengthen fluency, and inspire emotional growth — all firmly rooted in **Science of Reading (SoR)** practices.

Whether you have a few minutes or a full class period, you'll find **flexible, powerful tools** to meet your students exactly where they are.

🌊 SCIENCE OF READING FOCUS

Throughout this guide, you'll find strategies drawn from the latest **Science of Reading** research:

- **Vocabulary Building** (morphology, root words, context clues)
- **Fluency Development** (prosody, tone, phrasing, expression)
- **Deep Comprehension** (inference, summarizing, cause and effect)
- **Text Structure Awareness** (plot, theme, literary devices)

These strategies are embedded naturally into each chapter's teaching flow — ensuring that students become **confident, capable readers and thinkers**.

⬤ BIG THEMES STUDENTS WILL EXPLORE

Theme	Focus Area
Leadership	Courage, Responsibility, Growth
Unity	Collaboration, Community, Respect
Growth	Resilience, Adaptability, Identity

Students won't just *read* about leadership and change — they'll **practice and reflect** on them through discussions, writing, and creative projects.

▨ HOW THIS GUIDE IS STRUCTURED

Each chapter includes:

☑ **Learning Objectives** — What students will master

☑ **Vocabulary Focus** — Key words + morphology strategies

☑ **Fluency and Prosody Tips** — How to model strong reading

☑ **Comprehension and Literary Focus** — Critical thinking strategies

☑ **Real-World and SEL Connections** — Leadership, empathy, identity

☑ **Differentiation Options** — Supports all levels of learners

☑ **Summary Sheets** - Quick-reference chapter overviews for busy teachers

☑ **Reflection Questions** — Open-ended, leadership-focused prompts for deeper student thinking

☑ **Poetry Activity Pack** — Original poems from the novel paired with ready-to-use literacy and creativity activities

☑ **Standards Alignment** — Matched to 4th Grade Common Core and Science of Reading strategies

☑ **Optional Extensions** — Writing, art, drama, cross-curricular ideas

☑ **Student Reflection Journals** — Found every 4–5 chapters in the Student Workbook, these 2-page spreads encourage students to connect personally to the story, explore themes through writing or art, and reflect on growth. Prompts like "I used to think… but now I think…" help deepen comprehension and build an SEL bridge between school and home.

Student Workbook Alignment Map:

Student Workbook Alignment Map

Chapter	Student Workbook Focus Areas	Leadership/Social Theme
1. Embracing the Unknown	Vocabulary, CER, Reflection, Drawing	Courage, Curiosity
2. Adira's Awakening	Vocabulary, Poem Activity, CER, SEL Prompt	Wisdom, Listening
3. The Wonder Hole	Vocabulary, Prediction, Visualization	Exploration, Instinct
4. Learning to Lead	CER, Dialogue Practice, Art Extension	Leadership Styles
5. The Circle of Belonging	Vocabulary, Reflection Prompt, Theme Tracker	Unity, Inclusion
6. The Tree of Life	Poem Response, CER, Mood Analysis	Growth, Transformation
7–10	Vocab + Poem or CER, Varies by chapter	Trust, Forgiveness, Justice
…	…	…
Final Chapters	Creative Reflections, Character Arc Mapping, Personal Journaling	Resilience, Legacy

Note: Actual workbook content may vary by final design; this guide supports flexible pacing and differentiated use

Special **CER Worksheets** (Claim–Evidence–Reasoning) are included for key chapters, helping students build strong arguments based on text evidence.

LANGUAGE SKILLS EXTENSION UNITS INCLUDING:

• **Language Skills - Grammar Mini Unit**
  • **Sentence Structure Mini Unit**
  • **Literary Elements Mini Unit**
  • **Reciprocal TeachingUnit**

FLEXIBILITY AND SEL ENCOURAGEMENT

This guide is designed to be **adaptable**.

Feel free to **stretch, skip, adjust, or deepen** lessons based on your students' needs.

You'll also find **Social Emotional Learning (SEL)** moments woven throughout — from leadership dilemmas to real-world reflection questions — **and in the Journal Integration pages at key story arcs**. These are perfect for quick formative check-ins, family conversations, or creative expression.

BONUS TOOLS YOU'LL LOVE!

This Teacher's Guide includes powerful extra resources to make planning even easier and student engagement even stronger:

✔ **Summary Sheets** — Chapter-by-chapter quick reference for busy prep days

✔ **Reflection Questions** — SEL prompts to build leadership, empathy, and resilience

✔ **Poetry Activity Pack** — Creative literacy tasks based on the novel's original poems

✔ **CER Worksheets** — Ready-to-use Claim–Evidence–Reasoning organizers for building text-based arguments

✔ **Reciprocal Teaching Materials** — Ready-to-use Reciprocal Teaching Worksheet, Role Cards and Anchor Chart for powerful, student-led discussion collaborative strategies grounded in the Science of Reading.

Everything is flexible, optional, and designed to meet students exactly where they are!

The goal is not just better readers, but stronger leaders, thinkers, and community-builders.

✐ THIS GUIDE BELONGS TO:

(Teacher's Name) _____

(School/Class) _____

◎ FINAL THOUGHT:

Every student has greatness inside them.
Through stories, reflection, and action, we help them unleash it.
Thank you for guiding your students on this important journey.

To download lesson plans, templates, and the full teacher support suite, scan the QR code or visit: unleashinggreatnessedu.org

READING LEVEL & CURRICULUM FIT

📖 Reading Level & Curriculum Fit
  Title: *Unleashing Greatness: The Kingdom of Shadows*
  ISBN: 979-8-9988497-3-2
  Intended Audience: Grades 3–6 (Ideal for Grades 4–5)
  Estimated Lexile Range: 770–850L
  Accelerated Reader (AR) Estimate: 4.7–5.1
  Fountas & Pinnell Estimate: Level T–U
  Interest Level: Upper Elementary / Middle Grade

This story was written especially for upper elementary readers, centering around grade levels 4 and 5. The novel combines rich themes, layered symbolism, and dynamic character arcs with accessible vocabulary, structure, and layered emotional complexity, making it suitable for independent reading, literature circles, guided instruction, book clubs, or social-emotional learning integration. The novel is also appropriate for strong 3rd-grade readers and still resonant for 6th-grade readers who enjoy mythic journeys, shifting friendships, and courageous leadership..

🧠 Core Themes and Literary Skills

Key themes explored in the story include:
- **Leadership and Redemption**
- **Unity and Community Healing**
- **Identity, Forgiveness, and Courage**

Students will practice the following literary and critical thinking skills:
- Understanding and interpreting **figurative language**
- Analyzing **character growth** and **conflict**
- Tracing **cause and effect** relationships
- Making **inferences** and identifying **theme**
- Writing using **Claim–Evidence–Reasoning (CER)** and creative formats like poetry and journals

Curriculum Connections

This novel aligns with the following Common Core ELA Standards (Grades 4–5):
- RL.4.1 / RL.5.1 – Quote accurately and make inferences
- RL.4.2 / RL.5.2 – Determine theme and summarize
- RL.4.3 / RL.5.3 – Describe character, setting, and events
- RL.4.4 / RL.5.4 – Understand words and figurative language in context
- RL.4.5 / RL.5.5 – Analyze structure and story elements
- W.4.1 / W.5.1 – Write opinion pieces with reasons and evidence
- W.4.3 / W.5.3 – Write narratives to develop experiences

Classroom and Enrichment Use

This story is ideal for:
- Whole-class or small-group novel studies
- Thematic units on leadership, community, or identity
- Social-emotional learning (SEL) integration
- Enrichment or independent reading for strong 3rd–5th grade readers
- ELL/ML student support through visual scaffolds and context clues

🔬 Science of Reading Alignment

This novel supports **Science of Reading principles** through:

• **Explicit vocabulary instruction** with context support and sentence modeling

• **Oral reading fluency** practice via poetry and dialogue performance

• **Decoding and morphological awareness** (prefixes, suffixes, compound words)

• **Background knowledge activation** across social studies, science, and SEL themes

• **Structured comprehension routines** including prediction, sequencing, and cause-effect

• **Writing to learn** with CER (Claim–Evidence–Reasoning) strategy for textual analysis

Ideal for balanced literacy classrooms transitioning toward structured literacy practices.

🔬 SCIENCE OF READING IN PRACTICE

🔬 A SIMPLE GUIDE TO THE SCIENCE OF READING

The Science of Reading is a powerful, research-based approach that helps children become strong, confident readers. It brings together decades of studies in education, psychology, and neuroscience — and now, it's guiding how we teach literacy in classrooms, tutoring programs, and at home.

You don't need a teaching degree to use it. This guide uses key SoR strategies in simple, practical ways to support your readers — whether you're a teacher, tutor, or parent.

Here are the four pillars used throughout this guide:

🧩 VOCABULARY BUILDING

What it is: Teaching students how to understand unfamiliar words by breaking them down into meaningful parts (like prefixes, roots, and suffixes) and using context clues.

Why it matters: Students grow stronger in reading and writing when they can unlock meaning from new words on their own.

Example: "Transport" = trans (across) + port (carry) → to carry across

Bonus Tie-In: In some chapters, you'll find a **Morphology Tie-In** — a small list of root-based words *not in the student glossary* but connected to major ideas in the chapter. These extensions are designed to:

• Reinforce decoding and academic vocabulary
• Support cross-curricular word transfer
• Invite mini-lessons or anchor charts on roots, prefixes, and suffixes

Encourage students to create "word webs," build meaning maps, or explore how a root like **tract** (pull) shows up in *distract*, *attract*, or *traction*. Even one-minute explorations grow lifelong word awareness!

🎵 FLUENCY DEVELOPMENT

What it is: Helping students read aloud with accuracy, expression, and natural pacing.

Why it matters: Fluent readers are better able to understand what they read — and enjoy it more.

Includes: Modeling tone, phrasing, and rereading practice

Tip: Try reading a sentence aloud together, then ask the student to read it "like a storyteller."

🔍 DEEP COMPREHENSION

What it is: Teaching students to think about, question, and make connections to what they read.

Why it matters: Strong comprehension builds critical thinking and real-world understanding.

Strategies in this guide: Inference, cause and effect, summarizing, making predictions

TEXT STRUCTURE AWARENESS

What it is: Helping readers recognize how stories are built — including characters, plot, theme, and literary devices.

Why it matters: Knowing how a story works helps readers understand, analyze, and enjoy it.

Look for: Guided questions, story maps, and reflection activities throughout the guide

One Last Thing

Even a few minutes a day using these tools can transform how students read — and how they see themselves as readers. Whether you're a parent or teacher, you're helping unleash the greatness inside them, one page at a time.

TEACHER'S QUICK CHAPTER PLANNING TEMPLATE

**Teacher's Quick Chapter Planning Template
(Unleashing Greatness: The Kingdom of Shadows)**

Chapter Title: _____
   Proverb: _____

Core Focus for This Chapter:
- Vocabulary Words: _____
- Big Theme(s): □ Leadership □ Unity □ Growth □ Other:

Before Reading:
- Introduce Proverb? □ Yes □ No
- Pre-teach Vocabulary? □ Yes □ No
- Anchor Chart Needed? □ Yes □ No
If Yes, Topic: _____

During Reading:
- Fluency Focus:
□ Tone
□ Expression

□ Pacing
• Reading Strategy:
□ Context Clues
□ Inference
□ Visualization
□ Cause & Effect

🧠 After Reading:
• Workbook Activities:
□ Vocabulary Practice
□ Reading Comprehension
□ Sequencing
□ Theme Tracker
□ CER Worksheet (if assigned)
•   Reflection   Question(s):

_____

•   SEL/Leadership   Discussion   Prompt:

_____

🍪 Wrap-Up:
•   Exit   Ticket   Idea:

_____

• Optional Creative Extension:
□ Art
□ Journal Writing
□ Group Discussion
□ Roleplay
□ Anchor Chart Update

🔍 Notes for Next Time:

✅ This can be copied once and reused for every chapter!
It will keep you super organized without feeling overwhelmed.

🙰

✎ SAMPLE CHAPTER PLANNING PAGE

📖 Chapter Title:
Embracing the Unknown: A Day in the Park
🧠 Proverb:

"For tomorrow belongs to those who prepare for it today."

🎯 Core Focus for This Chapter
- **Vocabulary Words:** shimmering, vortex, tremble, resilience
- **Big Theme(s):**
  ☑ Leadership   ☑ Unity   ☑ Growth

📚 Before Reading
- **Introduce Proverb?** ☑ Yes (Discuss how preparation leads to success.)
- **Pre-Teach Vocabulary?** ☑ Yes (Use real-world examples for vortex and resilience.)
- **Anchor Chart Needed?** ☐ No

📖 During Reading
- **Fluency Focus:**
  ☑ Tone (Shift from playful to suspenseful)
  ☑ Expression (Use dramatic voice for warnings)
- **Reading Strategy:**
  ☑ Visualization (The shimmering tear)
  ☑ Cause & Effect (Storm ➔ Portal opens)

🧠 After Reading
- **Workbook Activities:**
  ☑ Vocabulary Practice
  ☑ Reading Comprehension
  ☑ Sequencing (Timeline of events)
- **Reflection Questions:**
  ◦ What might the "Three Tokens" represent?
  ◦ How did the kids show leadership when facing the unknown?
- **SEL/Leadership Discussion Prompt:**

◦ "When have you stepped into something unknown but exciting?"

⌇ Wrap-Up
• Exit Ticket Idea:
"Draw or write about a portal adventure you'd join!"
• Optional Creative Extension:
☑ Create your own Magic Token drawing
☑ Journal Prompt: "If I were chosen to save the world…"

⚲ Notes for Next Time
• Highlight how fear and courage exist side-by-side.
• Remind students: bravery isn't the absence of fear, but action despite it.

☑ Reminder:
This chapter introduces the Hero's Journey concept — circle back to it often!

QUICK START TEACHER'S CHECKLIST

☐ QUICK START TEACHER'S CHECKLIST

Unleashing Greatness: The Kingdom of Shadows

☑ **Before You Begin:**
☐ **Skim the Teacher's Guide Welcome Page**
Quickly review the structure and goals of the guide.
☐ **Gather Materials**
• Student Workbooks
• Pencils/Markers
• Chart Paper or Whiteboard
• (Optional) Visual Vocabulary Cards or Anchor Charts
☐ **Set Your Class Goals**
Decide your focus:
• Literacy Skills
• Leadership and SEL Growth
• Both!

☑ **Each Chapter:**
☐ **Preview the Chapter's Proverb**

Discuss it briefly — set the theme for reading.

☐ **Pre-Teach Key Vocabulary**

Use morphology (prefixes/suffixes), context clues, or a quick Word Wall activity.

☐ **Model Strong Reading (Fluency Focus)**

• Read aloud dramatic parts.

• Practice tone, pacing, and expression.

(Students will mirror your energy!)

☐ **Guide Comprehension Discussion**

Use 2–3 guiding questions from the Teacher's Guide.

Focus on **inference, cause/effect, theme, or symbolism**.

☐ **Complete Student Workbook Activities**

Help students move from literal understanding ➔ deeper thinking.

☐ **Check for a CER Worksheet**

If the chapter has one:

• Guide students through CLAIM → EVIDENCE → REASONING.

• Emphasize text evidence and logical thinking.

☐ **Connect to SEL or Leadership**

Use quick reflection questions like:

• "How would YOU lead in this situation?"

• "What can we learn about unity?"

☐ **Celebrate Progress!**

• Teachers, post a "Wall of Greatness" — a spot for students' inspiring quotes, best work, leadership moments.

(This reinforces SEL + celebrates academic success.)

Acknowledge strong ideas, brave participation, and teamwork.

(End on a positive!)

✅ **Weekly or Unit Wrap-Up:**

☐ **Use Student Goal Tracker (Optional)**

Students reflect on growth in reading skills, leadership, or teamwork.

☐ **Creative Projects (Optional)**

Try art, journal writing, class debates, or murals to deepen engagement.

☐ **Flex and Adapt**

Stretch lessons longer if students are excited — or move quicker if needed.

☐ **Connect Back to the Big Themes**

• Leadership

• Unity

• Growth

Always remind students: the lessons in Wakaduo are lessons for real life, too.

෧෫෯

WEEKLY TRACKER

Teacher Planning & Progress Check

| Week of: _____ | Chapters Covered: _____ |
Class/Section: _____ |

Task...Check ✔

⛛ Chapters Read Aloud or Assigned
✎ Vocabulary Taught
(Morphology/ Word Wall)

⛛ Fluency Modeled
(Pacing, Tone, Expression)

🔍 Comprehension Questions Discussed

💭 Workbook Pages Completed by Students

📝 CER Worksheet Completed (if assigned)

💬 SEL Reflection/Leadership Prompts Discussed

Mini Units or Extensions Used
(Grammar, Plot, etc.)

Student Participation Highlights

"Wall of Greatness" Updates Posted

Creative or Journal Work (if assigned)

Goal Tracker or Personal Growth Moments

Next Week Prep Notes

Teacher Tip: Use this to reflect on what worked well, where students needed more support, and what to adapt in upcoming lessons.

Remember:
This is more than a reading unit — it's a leadership journey.
Your energy, modeling, and encouragement make all the difference!
To download lesson plans, templates, and the full teacher support suite, scan the QR code or visit: unleashinggreatnessedu.org

EMBRACING THE UNKNOWN

Teacher's Annotated Guide

CHAPTER OVERVIEW

In this first chapter, students are introduced to the story's real-world setting and a group of relatable characters. The tone shifts quickly from every-day to fantastical, offering a rich opportunity for thematic exploration, context clue practice, and character analysis.

LEARNING OBJECTIVES

- Analyze setting and mood changes
- Identify cause and effect relationships
- Make predictions using text evidence
- Understand new vocabulary using context
- Develop comprehension strategies using guided reading prompts
- Begin comparing fantasy vs. reality

📚 VOCABULARY FOCUS

Eclipse – Use a visual diagram of a solar eclipse to deepen understanding.

Prophecy – Tie in with the idea of myths and ancient storytelling.

Instinct – Discuss how we "just know" things sometimes—use relatable examples.

Embrace – Highlight courage and change (connect to character choices and themes).

Vocabulary + Morphology Tie-In

Theme Connection: Belonging, Safety, Curiosity

Key Vocabulary Words

These words appear in the narrative or support student understanding of the opening setting and character dynamics.

• **Glen** – a small, narrow valley (setting word; often peaceful or hidden)
• **Wary** – cautious, careful about danger
• **Burrow** – a hole or tunnel dug by an animal
• **Gathering** – a group of animals or people coming together
• **Alert** – watchful, paying attention
• **Murmur** – a soft or quiet sound, often of voices or wind
• **Instinct** – a natural feeling or response, not something learned

🧩 Morphology Tie-In

Use these breakdowns to teach students how word parts help them unlock meaning. For early chapters, we focus on **common prefixes and base words** that appear throughout the novel.

✂️ Word Part Practice

1. Reappear = *re-* (again) + *appear* (to show)

✏️ "Scatter hoped the sun would reappear."

💬 What other "*re-*" words can you find? (*retell, redo, revisit*)

2. Unseen = *un-* (not) + *seen* (visible)

✎ "They followed an unseen path."

☛ What does "unseen" mean? Can you think of other *un-* words?

3. Carefully = *care* (base word) + *-ful* (full of) + *-ly* (in a way that is…)

✎ "She moved carefully through the glen."

☛ What's the base word? What does *-ly* tell us?

⟳ ACTIVITY IDEA

Morphology Match-Up:

Give students word parts (prefixes like *re-*, *un-*, *pre-* and suffixes like *-ly*, *-ful*, *-less*) and ask them to create or identify words from Chapter 1 that use them. Build a running "word wall" as a class!

◆ MINI-LESSON SPOTLIGHT:

Chapter One - Embracing the Unknown

Focus: Setting the Tone, Courage, and Character Insight

◎ **Learning Objective:**

Students will:

• Analyze the shift in tone from peace to tension.

• Identify traits of leadership and empathy.

• Reflect on the role of courage in stepping into the unknown.

🖐 **Quick Teaching Moves:**

• **Intro Hook:** Write the word *Unknown* on the board. Ask: "What feelings come with the unknown?"

• **Vocabulary Burst (3 words):** eclipse, prophecy, instinct – define and connect to real life or natural phenomena.

• **Guided Reading Pause:** Stop when the tear appears — "What would YOU do?"

• **Quick Write Prompt (5–7 min):**

✍ *Describe a moment when you had to make a scary choice. What helped you move forward?*

• **Optional Extension:**

Act out the moment when the voice speaks from the sky. Use music or low lighting for effect.

⚲ COMPREHENSION GUIDE

Before Reading:

- Introduce the chapter's proverb. Invite predictions.
- Preview key vocabulary and ask what students think a "Token" might be.

⟋ Prediction Ladder

What do you think the "Three Tokens of Tariq" are? Why might they be important?

(Use clues from the story to help!)

1   **Clue**   **from**   **the**   **chapter**:

_____

2 My guess: _____

3 I think they will help the heroes because:

_____

During Reading:

- Pause after the tear appears. Ask: "Would you go through?"
- Have students mark or discuss emotional shifts in the tone.

After Reading:

- Use the Theme Tracker to compare bravery vs. teamwork.
- Ask reflective questions like: "Have you ever had to step into the unknown?"

📖 FLUENCY & LITERARY FOCUS

🎨 Fluency & Prosody Tips

Goal: Support expressive, confident oral reading by modeling tone, rhythm, pacing, and character voice. This chapter shifts from calm to chaos, offering rich opportunities for emotional modulation.

🎙 NARRATION TONE SHIFTS

- Begin with a **light, peaceful tone** during the early park scenes ("The day was perfect..."). Use a gentle pace and warm inflection.
- As the **storm approaches**, gradually shift to a **tense, uncertain tone**. Emphasize words like *darkened*, *trembled*, *ominous*, *crackling*.
- During the **tear scene and voice of warning**, model **deep, slow, and resonant delivery**:

"Find the Three Tokens of Tariq..."

Encourage students to read this line aloud using their "epic movie trailer" voice.

🎭 CHARACTER VOICE MODELING

- **Maya**: Calm, thoughtful, slightly cautious. Grows more commanding. Use **firm, centered delivery** when she leads:

"We don't have a choice. If this is real... we have to find the Tokens."

- **JALEN**: PLAYFUL AND SARCASTIC EARLY ON, BECOMING SERIOUS AND brave. Contrast these moods.
- **Malik**: Curious, dreamy, becomes bolder. Encourage students to add wonder to his lines.
- **Zara**: Soft-spoken, uncertain — but gains confidence. Use a **quieter, intentional delivery** that grows stronger by the end.

. . .

FLUENCY PRACTICE MOMENTS
- **Read Maya's opening question aloud**:
"Do you ever wonder if storms are trying to tell us something?"
Model with rising intonation and curiosity.

- **USE ECHO READING** FOR THE BOOMING WARNING VOICE — TEACHER reads, students echo line by line.
  - **Group Performance Tip**: Have each student read a single character's dialogue throughout the scene — then swap and re-read with new voices for comparison.

OPTIONAL DIFFERENTIATION

- For emerging readers, focus on **chunking phrases** and marking pauses in the text with slashes:
The sky / darkened. / Rolling clouds / cast a shadow / over their sunny day.

- For ADVANCED READERS, INTRODUCE **TONE-MATCHING**: ASK students to identify the emotion in a line and match their reading voice accordingly.

CHAPTER SUMMARY SHEET

Chapter Title: Embracing the Unknown
  Main Setting: Inner-city park and the mystical tear in the sky
  Key Themes: Friendship, Empathy, Discovery, Choosing Courage

SHORT SUMMARY:
Four friends—Maya, Jalen, Malik, and Zara—enjoy a playful day at the park when the sky suddenly darkens, revealing a mysterious tear in the air. From the portal, a voice warns them to find the

Three Tokens of Tariq before a coming eclipse. Zara's ancient book supports the voice's prophecy. After saving Malik from the tear's pull, the group realizes they are being called to a grand mission. A drug encounter involving a peer named Jose deepens their sense of purpose and compassion. They decide together: if this adventure is real, they must face it head-on.

🧠 Comprehension Focus:

• What do the Tokens represent?
• Why is Maya's leadership important?
• How do the children respond to fear and responsibility?

💀 Main Characters Introduced/Expanded:

• **Maya**: Insightful and brave leader with strong empathy
• **Jalen**: Confident, loyal, and playful with a protective nature
• **Malik**: Imaginative dreamer and the group's creative spark
• **Zara**: Quiet, intelligent, and guided by stories and intuition
• **Jose**: A troubled boy whose situation sparks social awareness

🧩 Key Vocabulary Words:

• Eclipse – A darkening of the sun
• Intuition – A feeling or instinct without reasoning
• Portal – A doorway to another world
• Compassion – Deep awareness and concern for others
• Courage – Choosing to act bravely despite fear

🧠 SEL Focus

This chapter invites students to explore and reflect on:

• **Empathy** – Seeing others' struggles through Maya's concern for Jose
• **Responsibility** – Choosing to act with courage in the face of fear
• **Teamwork** – Relying on each other to face unknown danger
• **Self-Awareness** – Recognizing inner strengths and moral choices

🖋 NOTABLE QUOTES:

• "Do you ever wonder if storms are trying to tell us something?" — Maya

• "Find the Three Tokens of Tariq... or suffer the eternal darkness." — Mysterious Voice

• "We don't have a choice. If this is real... we have to find the Tokens." — Maya

🔍 **Look For in Illustrations**:

• The shimmering tear in the sky over the playground
• Jose holding a brown paper bag, eyes full of conflict
• Maya's braids flying as she leads the group
• The group's shocked expressions as Malik touches the tear

REFLECTION QUESTIONS

📖 ✎ **Class Discussion / Reflection Prompts**
"Embracing the Unknown: A Day in the Park"

In this chapter, four best friends spend a normal day at the park —until the skies change, a mystical tear opens, and they're called to save the world before the eclipse. Their friendship and choices are tested as they face danger... and destiny.

✎ REFLECTION QUESTIONS:

1. 🌐 **What would you have done if you saw the swirling tear in the sky?**

How do you think you would feel?

2. 💬 **When Maya showed care for Jose, how did it change the group's thinking?**

What would you have done in her place?

3. ⚖ **Do you think the group made the right decision to go into the tear?**

Why or why not?

4. 🕊 **What does this chapter teach us about standing together when things get scary or confusing?**

🌑 TOKEN TRACKER:

Circle the token you think this chapter helped you earn:

● Courage　　● Truth　　● Empathy　　● Friendship

___　　　Draw　　　or　　　explain　　　why:

_____

⚛⚛

STUDENT WORKBOOK ANSWER KEY

☑ **Answer Key (Student Workbook)**
Vocabulary Matching:
1 = B
2 = C
3 = A
4 = D
Fill in the Blank:

1. Prophecy
2. Instinct
3. Embrace
4. Eclipse

Multiple Choice:
1 = B
2 = C
Short Answer (Sample):
3. The storm appeared as a warning and turning point.
4. Answers will vary based on personal response and text support.
Theme Tracker:
Accept a variety of answers—encourage use of text evidence.

🖐 CREATIVE CONNECTIONS

Optional Extension Activities to Spark Imagination & Deepen Engagement
These creative activities allow students to extend their learning

through art, writing, drama, and real-world reflection. Choose one, a few, or invite students to design their own!

✎ WRITING PROMPT

Imagine you turned into an animal hero like Maya and her friends.

💀 What animal would you become? Why?
What would your powers be? What would you protect?

🐾 ART EXTENSION

Comic Strip Challenge:

Draw a 3–4 panel comic showing the moment the characters first saw the swirling tear in the sky.

Include:
• Dialogue
• Sound effects (like *CRACK* or *WHOOOSH*)
• Reactions of the characters

💬 SEL CONNECTION

Class Circle Question:

How did the friends support each other when things got scary — and how can we support each other in real life?

🎭 PERFORMANCE OPTION

Dramatic Reading or Role Play:

Act out the scene where Malik reaches into the tear.
Add music or sound effects for drama!
Then freeze — and have a student narrator share what each character might be *thinking*.

🧠 LEADERSHIP TIE-IN

Ask students:
Which character showed leadership in this chapter?
How?
What kind of leader would *you* like to be?

🧰 TEACHER TOOLS & PLANNING SNAPSHOT

🔁 Quick Recap
Last time...
A brief summary of what happened in the previous chapter.
Example: "The four friends witnessed the tear in the sky and received a mysterious prophecy from a hidden voice."

❓ ESSENTIAL QUESTION
What key life or leadership idea is at the heart of this chapter?
Example: "What does it mean to step into the unknown with courage?"

⏱ TEACHING TIME ESTIMATE / FLEX TIPS
Full lesson: ~40–50 min
Short version (for tight schedules): Focus on vocabulary + 2 discussion questions (~20 min)

🧰 MATERIALS CHECKLIST
• [✔] Student Workbook pages
• [✔] Prediction Ladder
• [✔] CER template (if included)
• [✔] Optional: art supplies, anchor chart paper

🧠 STUDENT SUCCESS SNAPSHOT
Look for signs of understanding:
• Students using vocabulary in conversation or journaling

- Confidently citing evidence from text
- Thoughtful responses in discussion or on reflection prompts

☉ DIFFERENTIATION TIP
For Struggling Readers
Pair students for shared reading and pause often to explain tone or vocabulary. Provide sentence stems for open-ended questions.
For Advanced Readers
Ask them to compare the chapter's theme to another story or current event. Or: Have them draft their own legend or "missing prophecy."

📚 STANDARDS ALIGNMENT

- CCSS.ELA.RL.4.1 / 5.1 – Refer to details and examples when explaining what the text says
- CCSS.ELA.RL.4.3 / 5.3 – Describe characters, setting, and major events
- CCSS.ELA.4.4 / 5.4 - Determine meaning of unknown words using context
- **Science of Reading** – Strong in vocabulary, schema-building, and narrative structure

Vocabulary development (morphology, context)
  Comprehension (inference, theme, cause-effect)
  Fluency and expression (modeled earlier in guide)

📌 FINAL TEACHER NOTES

Chapter One sets the stage for deep classroom engagement. Encourage open-ended discussion, spark imagination, and connect fantasy to real-world choices and values. Let students lead with curiosity. After all—they're preparing for tomorrow, today.

POETRY PACK

Poetry Activity Sheet — Narrative Poem (City Magic & Dreams)

✏ Poem Text:

The Heroes

In the heart of the city, where the trees whisper of mysteries,
Four friends embrace the unknown, with hearts wild and free.
Maya dances with the wind, braids flying like kites,
Jalen dribbles dreams on the court, under the morning light.
Malik draws worlds in the dust, a map to hidden treasures,
While Zara weaves tales of knights, her words are quiet pleasures.

✺ STUDENT POETRY ACTIVITIES

ACTIVITY 1: Dream Catcher Art ✺

☑ Create a *"dream catcher"* poster showing what dreams Maya, Jalen, Malik, and Zara each chase.

☑ Use small drawings or key words ("basketball," "adventure," "stories") around their names!

ACTIVITY 2: MAGIC IN THE CITY ▥

☑ Write 3 sentences describing where *you* find magic in your city or neighborhood.

☑ Bonus: Draw a little scene (park, court, library, tree!) that feels *"magical"* to you.

ACTIVITY 3: WORD WEB

☑ Pick a powerful verb from the poem (examples: *dance, dribble, draw, weave*).

☑ Build a Word Web:

• Put the verb in the center circle.

• Draw lines outward and add 4 more action words you connect to it!

(*Example: dribble → bounce → race → leap → spin!*)

ACTIVITY 4: "HERO THOUGHT BUBBLE" ✎

☑ Pick Maya, Jalen, Malik, or Zara.
☑ Create a "thought bubble" for them:
_"Today, I dream of _____ because _____."

TEACHER TIP (SMALL PRINT)
☑ **Standards Alignment:**
• Personal Response Writing
• Creative Visualization
• Word Association Building
• Story Character Mapping
☑ **Science of Reading Focus:**
• Expressive Language
• Reading-Writing Connection
• Descriptive Vocabulary Expansion

BONUS CHALLENGE:

Perform the Poem! — Each student pretends to be one of the four friends and reads their line with full character voice (Maya = playful, Jalen = energetic, Malik = thoughtful, Zara = dreamy).

2

ADIRA'S AWAKENING

TEACHER'S ANNOTATED GUIDE

**A**dira's Awakening

CHAPTER OVERVIEW

Adira's journey begins in this chapter, blending African natural imagery with fantasy elements. As she steps into her role as Guardian of Wakaduo, students explore key ideas: **bravery**, **transformation**, **leadership**, and the **importance of helping others**.

Adira's story offers young readers a mirror for their own growth, encouraging them to discover their voice, value, and the quiet strength it takes to lead with purpose.

LEARNING OBJECTIVES

- Identify how characters change and grow
- Explore fantasy settings and themes of leadership
- Build vocabulary using context clues

- Analyze story structure (setting → conflict → transformation)
- Interpret a proverb and apply it to character development

📖 VOCABULARY + MORPHOLOGY FOCUS

Chapter 2 – Adira's Awakening

Theme Focus: Transformation, leadership, intuition, magical realism

❄ TIER II & TIER III VOCABULARY WORDS (CONTEXT-BASED)

These are words that appear in the chapter and are important for comprehension, character analysis, and theme development:

1 Guardian – A person who protects or defends others

➤ *Think*: Like a parent, teacher, or superhero

2 Instinct – A natural feeling or reaction that guides action

➤ *Prompt*: "Have you ever felt something was dangerous even before you knew why?"

3 Enchantment – A magical effect or powerful spell

➤ *Prompt*: How is Adira's awakening enchanted in more ways than one?

4 Lurk – To wait or move in a sneaky or hidden way

➤ *Action Idea*: Have students "lurk" around the classroom to act out the word

5 Emergence – The process of coming into view or becoming known

➤ *Related to*: Adira coming into her power

🔍 MORPHOLOGY TIE-INS

Support decoding and word-building skills through analysis of prefixes, roots, and suffixes.

Guardian

guard (watch, protect) + *-ian* (one who)

Meaning: *One who protects or defends*

➤ Invite discussion: "Who are real-life guardians in our world?" (parents, teachers, lifeguards)

Enchantment

en- (to put into) + *chant* (speak or sing with power) + *-ment* (state or condition)

Meaning: *The state of being under a magical spell*

➤ Extension: Compare with "encouragement" or "engagement" to see how *en-* and *-ment* work across meanings.

Instinct

in- (inward) + *stinct* (from Latin *stinguere*, meaning to prick or urge)

Meaning: *An inner feeling or natural urge that guides behavior*

➤ Talk with students about animal instincts (like migration or self-defense) and connect to emotions they might "just feel" without needing to think first.

Lurk

No affix, but useful for exploring root-based meaning.

Possibly related to Old Norse *lurka* (to sneak).

Meaning: *To hide and wait, often in a sneaky or threatening way*

➤ Practice this one with gestures or freeze-frame roleplay to help students "embody" the meaning.

WORD STUDY ACTIVITY SUGGESTIONS

1. Word Trees: Build root-based trees (e.g., *chant* → enchant, chanting, enchantress)

2. Word Sorting: Group words by prefix or suffix (*-ian*, *-ment*, *-tion*)

3. "Power of Words" Discussion:

Ask: Which of these words connects most to Adira's journey—and why?

◆ MINI-LESSON SPOTLIGHT: CHAPTER 2 – *ADIRA'S AWAKENING*

Focus: Leadership, Transformation, and Listening to Instinct

🐚 **Learning Objective:**

Students will:

• Identify how Adira changes and what makes her a leader.

• Explore metaphor and symbolism through magical trans-formation.

• Compare Adira's fears to moments when they themselves have had to be brave.

🐚 **Quick Teaching Moves:**

• **Discussion Spark:** Show the proverb "A single bracelet does not jingle." Ask: "What does this mean about teamwork?"

• **Vocabulary Anchor (3 words):** guardian, instinct, enchant-ment — have students sketch a symbol or emoji for each.

• **Turn & Talk:** Why did Adira risk herself to help someone she didn't know?

• **Quick Sketch + Caption:**

🐚 Draw Adira's moment of transformation. Write one sentence: *"Now, I am someone who…"*

Optional Extension:

Use the haiku as a script — assign each line to a student and perform as a whisper chorus.

🔍 COMPREHENSION GUIDE

Before Reading:

• Review the proverb: *"A single bracelet does not jingle."*
• Ask: "What might this mean about teamwork or interdependence?"

📈 **Prediction Ladder**

"Who do you think Eze is, and why might he be important to Wakaduo?"

. . .

DURING READING:

- Pause after the hut appears. Ask: "Why might this be dangerous?"
- Highlight Adira's emotional state. She feels unsure but still chooses to act. What does that say about her?

After Reading:

- Use the Theme Tracker to connect her actions to bravery and leadership.
- Reflect on how magic is used to represent personal growth and transformation.

✎ FLUENCY & LITERARY FOCUS – CHAPTER TWO

🎏 Fluency Tips

• Model **pausing and phrasing** during the Haiku Sequence — use a slow, rhythmic tone to reflect the natural pacing of the savanna and the poetic mood.

• Practice **intonation** with Adira's internal questions (e.g., "Why me?") to emphasize uncertainty and emerging leadership.

• Use **volume and pacing** to contrast calm scenes with tension moments (e.g., the leopard's attack).

✍ Small Group Idea: Assign students short sections of the haikus to perform aloud with sound effects and "emotional voice."

🎨 Literary Focus

• **Transformation and Initiation** – Students explore how the story structure follows a hero's initiation, where Adira receives magical tools and a new role.

• **Symbolism** – The Essence of the Shell and the sealed boulder represent power, truth, and responsibility.

• **Genre Awareness** – Discuss how this fantasy blends magical elements with realistic character emotions and natural settings.

CHAPTER SUMMARY SHEET

Chapter Title: Adira's Awakening
   Main Setting: African savanna and a mysterious wizard's hut
   Key Themes: Awakening Power, Destiny, Wisdom, Protection
   SEL Focus: *Resilience, Identity, Purpose*
   These values align beautifully with Adira's internal growth, her decision to lead despite fear, and her newfound role as a protector.

SHORT SUMMARY:

In the golden savanna of Wakaduo, Adira, an ancient and wise tortoise, senses a shift in the world. She rescues a captured wizard named Eze from a prowling leopard. In gratitude, Eze gives Adira magical abilities and a new purpose: to protect Wakaduo and lead its creatures in a time of coming danger. Adira gains the power to move objects with her mind, heal others, and perceive deeper truths. As Eze departs, Adira is left as the guardian of the land, now sealed from danger by a giant boulder only she can move. Her transformation from elder to magical protector marks the start of a new era in Wakaduo.

Comprehension Focus:
• What qualities make Adira a worthy leader?
• How does Eze help Adira understand her importance?
• What does the Essence of the Enchanted Shell symbolize?

Main Characters Introduced/Expanded:
• **Adira**: A thoughtful, aging tortoise who becomes a magical guardian
• **Eze**: A wise, elderly wizard who bestows Adira with powers and purpose
• **Charlese**: A dangerous leopard who represents the lurking threat outside Wakaduo

Key Vocabulary Words:
• Essence – The core or defining spirit of something
• Ritual – A formal ceremony often tied to magic or tradition
• Shelter – A safe place or protection from harm

• Wisdom – Knowledge and good judgment from experience
• Guardian – protects or watches over something important

⚑ **Notable Quotes**:

• "You have come at a time of great need. Wakaduo is in danger, and you… you are its new guardians." — Adira
• "Because you are strong. Because you are noble. And because Wakaduo needs you." — Eze
• "There is more magic to learn, Adira. But my time here is done." — Eze

🔍 **Look For in Illustrations**:

• Adira chewing the branch to free Eze above the stream
• The rustic wizard's hut glowing with magical light
• The Essence of the Enchanted Shell in Eze's hands
• Charlese glaring from the shadows as Adira seals the entrance

REFLECTION QUESTIONS

📖✍ **Class Discussion / Reflection Prompts**

A wise tortoise named Adira rescues a stranger from a leopard and gains magical powers from a forest wizard. She is called to lead the animal kingdom of Wakaduo.

✍ **REFLECTION PROMPTS:**

1. 🌙 **Why do you think Adira risked her life to save the stranger?**
What does this say about her character?

2. **What would you do if you were offered magic powers?**
Would you use them to help others?

3. ◔ **Adira didn't believe in herself at first. Have you ever surprised yourself by doing something brave?**
Write about it or draw it.

4. 🌑 **What kind of leader do you think Adira will be—**

and why do you think the animals will (or won't) follow her?

💬 *You may use the Student Workbook reflection question, or select one from this guide for deeper discussion or journaling.*

🌑 **CHOOSE A TOKEN YOU EARNED:**
● Empathy   ● Leadership   ⦾ Courage
(Draw or explain below)

※

💼 TEACHER TOOLS & PLANNING SNAPSHOT

📖 **Chapter Title**: *Adira's Awakening*

📚 **Literacy Skills**: Context clues, character growth, fantasy structure, prosody

💬 **SEL Focus**: *Resilience, Identity, Purpose*

◎ **Teaching Time Estimate**: 1–2 class sessions

🍃 **Differentiation Tip**:

• **Struggling Readers**: Pre-teach "guardian," "ritual," and "enchantment" using visuals and gesture.

• **Advanced Readers**: Ask students to compare Adira's transformation to mythic heroes (e.g., Moana, Gandalf, Simba).

❓ **Essential Question**:

What does it mean to be chosen — and how do we grow into our purpose, even when we're unsure?

💡 **Flex Tip**:

Can be taught as a standalone allegory lesson on leadership, empathy, and identity — even outside the main arc of the novel.

※

💡 **USE THE STUDENT WORKBOOK "REFLECT & RESPOND" PAGE to prompt rich journaling or small group discussion before the CER writing.**

✍ CER WRITING (CLAIM–EVIDENCE–REASONING)

Use this structured writing prompt to support deeper thinking and text-based writing. The CER framework guides students to:
- Form a clear claim
- Support their thinking with specific textual evidence
- Explain how that evidence proves their point
- Practice academic writing sentence starters
- Build argumentative and persuasive thinking
  - *Ideal after discussion, close reading, or as a lead-in to a short response*

CER Worksheet
Title: Chapter 2 — *Adira's Awakening*
Prompt:
Why is Adira's wisdom important to the animals of Wakaduo?

📢 CLAIM
What do you believe?
✏ Starter:
I believe that...

📚 EVIDENCE
Find a quote or describe something from the story.
✏ Starters:
- In the story it says...
- One example is when...
- The author shows that...

REASONING
Explain how the evidence supports your claim.
✏ Starters:
- This shows that...

- This proves that...
- This means...

Quick Checklist
☑ Clear answer?
☑ Strong evidence?
☑ Good explanation?

When to use:
☑ After discussion or reading group
☑ Before writing paragraphs or journal reflections
☑ As a formative assessment
☑ For writing support or enrichment

BONUS (Optional):
Draw Adira standing beneath the stars, holding the enchanted ring.

❈

STUDENT WORKBOOK ANSWER KEY

☑ Answer Key (Student Workbook)

Vocabulary Matching:
1 = C
2 = A
3 = B
4 = D

Fill in the Blank:

1. Lurk
2. Enchantment
3. Instinct

4. Guardian

Multiple Choice:

1 = C

2 = C

Short Answer Examples:

3. She can understand speech, sense hidden truths, and heal others.

4. Answers may vary: Help protect Wakaduo, confront the leopard, find allies.

Theme Tracker Prompt:

Bit through the branch to free Eze.

This shows that Adira is brave and willing to help others, even when it's risky …even when she is afraid or uncertain. She trusts her instincts and puts others first..

🔗 CREATIVE CONNECTIONS – OPTIONAL EXTENSIONS

✏️ Writing Prompt

"A Power With a Purpose"

Imagine you were granted one magical ability like Adira's — but only if you promised to use it to help others.

• What power would you choose?

• How would you use it?

• What rules would you follow?

✎ Write a short personal narrative or create a set of "hero rules" for your power.

🐾 Art Extension – Symbol of Leadership Challenge

Design a **personal "guardian emblem"** like Adira's shell glow or the Essence orb.

• What colors or symbols represent your values as a leader?

• Optional: Add an animal or natural element that reflects you.

🖌️ Create a class mural with everyone's emblem on a shield or banner.

💬 SEL Activity – Circle Reflection

Host a **classroom talking circle** around the prompt:

"What's one way you've had to protect someone — or one time someone stood up for you?"

• Encourage empathy, storytelling, and emotional expression.

• Optional journaling follow-up.

📝 Performance Option – Roleplay the Ritual

Act out the scene where Eze passes the orb to Adira. Assign students to play the narrator, Adira, and Eze. Add sound effects, gestures, and a "magic" effect.

• Great for fluency + prosody practice.

• Discuss: What makes a ritual feel powerful?

🦁 Leadership Tie-In – Build a Hero Code

Work in groups to brainstorm:

• What makes a *wise* leader?

• What should leaders **never** do?

🗑 Students create a class "Code of Leadership" inspired by Adira's example. Add signatures and post in the classroom!

Ask students: *When have you had to make a hard but kind decision?*

📖 STANDARDS ALIGNMENT

- **CCSS.ELA.RL.4.1** – Refer to details and examples when explaining what the text says
- **CCSS.ELA.RL.4.3** – Describe characters, settings, and events using evidence
- **Science of Reading Focus** – Vocabulary development, prosody, cause/effect relationships, inferencing

📌 TEACHER TIPS

- Try a short **role-play activity** where students act out Adira's transformation and bravery.
- Invite comparisons to other wise characters (e.g., **Gandalf**, **Rafiki**, **Moana's grandmother**).
- Provide time for students to draw the **enchanted brew** or the moment Adira's senses awaken.

৬৯৬

POETRY PACK

Poetry Activity Sheet — *Haiku Sequence: Awakening*

✏️ POEM TEXT:

🌾 *Golden savanna,*
Old tortoise stirs, sensing change—
Wind whispers secrets.
👀 *Curious eyes glance,*
Danger prowls, hidden whispers—
Leopard's shadow looms.
🐾 *Branch snaps, river's arms,*
Safety in water's embrace—
Stranger's grateful gaze.
✨ *Magic fills the air,*
Wise words brew, understanding—
New power awakens.

🎯 STUDENT POETRY ACTIVITIES

ACTIVITY 1: Painting the Scene

- Close your eyes and **picture** each haiku.
- Sketch **one scene** from the sequence that stood out the most to you.

. . .

ACTIVITY 2: Haiku Detective!

• **Haiku poems** traditionally have:

　◦ 5 syllables
　◦ 7 syllables
　◦ 5 syllables

• Choose **one** of the haikus above.
• Clap it out!
• Then, write the syllable count beside each line.

Example:

Golden savanna (5)
Old tortoise stirs, sensing change (7)
Wind whispers secrets (5)

ACTIVITY 3: Emotional Vocabulary Hunt

• Find **2 strong feeling words or images** in the haiku sequence.
　• Why do they make the poem feel exciting, scary, or magical?

　1.　Word/Image: _____ → Feeling: _____

　2.　Word/Image: _____ → Feeling: _____

ACTIVITY 4: Tiny but Mighty — Write Your Own Haiku!

　• Pick one topic: "A New Adventure" or "A Hidden Danger."
　• Write your **own** haiku about it! Teacher will supply worksheet.
(Remember 5-7-5 syllables.)

My Haiku:

ACTIVITY 5: Character's Thoughts

• Imagine you are the **old tortoise** or the **stranger by the river**.
   • What would you be *thinking* during this moment?
   • Write a 2–3 sentence **internal thought** as if you were them.
   🍂 Example starter: *"I can feel the winds shifting. Change is near..."*

🦋 TEACHER TIP (SMALL PRINT)
☑ **Standards Alignment:**
   • Syllabication and Fluency
   • Comprehension through Visualization
   • Literary Structure (Haiku Form)
   • Emotional Literacy and Creative Response
☑ **Science of Reading Focus:**
   • Phonological Awareness (syllables)
   • Syntax Awareness
   • Expressive Oral Language
✒ **Quick note:**
You could package several of these "Poetry Activity Sheets" into a **"Poetry & Fluency Booster Pack"** for your website or Teacher Bundle!

$$ꗠ \quad 3 \quad ꗠ$$

THE MYSTERIOUS QUEST

TEACHER'S ANNOTATED GUIDE

 **C**hapter 3: *The Mysterious Quest*
Main Setting: Sacred Grove of Wakaduo
Key Themes: Vision/Doubt, Leadership-tools,
Collective Courage

Short Summary:

The animals of Wakaduo gather to hear Adira's announcement of a mysterious mission. After tasting the enchanted Life-Water given by the Forest Wizard, Adira declares that their journey is not only about a destination, but about discovering who they truly are—together. A symbolic ring and the proverb *"If your only tool is a hammer, you will see every problem as a nail"* encourage the young heroes to think beyond simple solutions and question their own assumptions. Some embrace the quest with excitement, while others respond with fear or skepticism, sparking questions about leadership and belief.

LEARNING OBJECTIVES:

- Interpret symbolism (e.g., ring, tree, animal roles)
- Analyze characters' leadership traits and growth
- Examine skepticism and belief in group settings
- Apply figurative language to real-life problem-solving
- Support comprehension with evidence and discussion

📚 VOCABULARY + MORPHOLOGY FOCUS

Theme Focus: Belief, skepticism, unity, and the beginnings of a larger journey

❄ Tier II & Tier III Vocabulary Words (Context-Based)

1 Quest – A journey made to reach an important goal or truth
➤ *Prompt*: "What's a quest you're on this year—in school or life?"

2 Unity – A state of being joined or working together
➤ *Prompt*: "When do we show unity in our classroom or community?"

3 Skeptical – Doubting that something is true or real
➤ *Prompt*: "If someone says they saw a dragon, how might you respond?"

4 Enigmatic – Mysterious or hard to understand
➤ *Prompt*: "What's something enigmatic about nature or history?"

5 Symbolism – When something stands for something else (like a ring representing leadership)
➤ *Prompt*: "What symbols do we see in stories or real life?"

🔍 Morphology Tie-Ins

Support decoding and vocabulary development by examining each word's meaningful parts.

Word
Morphology Breakdown
Meaning

. . .

QUEST

Latin *quaerere* (to seek)

A mission or journey in search of something important

UNITY

uni- (one) + *-ty* (state of)

The state of being together as one

SKEPTICAL

skept- (Greek *skepsis* = doubt, to reflect) + *-ical* (adjective-forming)

Related to questioning or doubting

ENIGMATIC

enigma (Greek = riddle or puzzle) + *-atic* (relating to)

Something mysterious or puzzling

SYMBOLISM

symbol (sign, mark) + *-ism* (practice or system)

The use of images or objects to represent ideas

WORD STUDY ACTIVITY SUGGESTIONS

1. Real-World Connection Exercise:

Ask students to draw or describe a symbol from their own life (e.g., a team logo, family heirloom, classroom motto).

2. Root Sorting:

Give students roots (*uni, skept, sym, quest*) and have them brainstorm or match words that share the same base.

3. "Mystery Word" Mini-Game:

Write riddles describing one of the new vocabulary words (especially *enigmatic* or *quest*) and let students guess the word.

◆ MINI-LESSON SPOTLIGHT – *THE ENIGMATIC RING*

Focus: Belief, Symbolism, and Leadership Under Doubt

◎ Learning Objective:

Students will:

• Interpret the proverb: "If your only tool is a hammer…"
• Discuss how Scatter steps up as a leader despite skepticism.
• Analyze how belief, symbols, and courage unite a group.

● Quick Teaching Moves:

• **Proverb Anchor:** Write the quote on the board. Ask: "What happens when we only know one way to solve a problem?"
• **Vocabulary Boost (3 words):** quest, skepticism, unity — have students match to images or quick examples.
• **Pair Share Question:**
● "Have you ever believed in something even when others didn't?"
• **Group Activity:**
Create a "Symbol of Hope" as a class. (Draw, describe, or make out of paper.)
Optional Extension:
Read the Villanelle aloud with students — emphasize the refrain. Challenge them to write a mini one of their own.

⚲ COMPREHENSION GUIDE (BEFORE / DURING / AFTER READING)

1. Before Reading (5–7 min):

• Ask: *"What do you think a leader needs to do to earn trust?"*
• Introduce the proverb:

"If your only tool is a hammer, you treat everything like a nail."

33

Discuss how leaders must think flexibly.

2. During Reading (15 -20 min.):
(Reading Aloud or Partner Reading)

- Read **Scatter's speech** aloud with emotion and pauses.
- Ask: *"How does Scatter feel? How does the crowd respond?"*

3. After Reading (15 min):
Comprehension + Vocabulary

- Complete workbook: matching, sequencing, and short responses.
- Pre-teach "enigmatic" and "unity" with images or real-world examples.

Theme & Personal Connection Discussion (10 min):

- Ask: *"Have you ever had to prove you could do something—even if others doubted you?"*

🧠 COMPREHENSION FOCUS:

• What does the proverb suggest about problem-solving and leadership?

• How do the animals respond differently to Adira's announcement?

• What role does the "Life-Water" play in this moment?

🐾 Main Characters Expanded:

• Adira: Transformed into a visionary leader with the aid of Life-Water

• Scatter: Quietly begins to understand her role in the greater journey

• The Elders: Represent tradition, caution, and spiritual authority

🔍 **Teaching Angle**:

This chapter invites students to reflect on how we see the world based on the tools or mindsets we already have. Encourage interpretation of the proverb and the magical transformation scene as metaphors for growth, belief, and stepping into new roles.

📜 FLUENCY & LITERARY FOCUS

Fluency Tips

• Model **prosody and rhythm** by reading the Villanelle aloud, emphasizing repeated lines.

• Encourage **paired reading** of Scatter's speech to build expression, pacing, and confidence.

• Prompt: "How should your voice sound when Scatter speaks with doubt? With pride?"

Literary Focus

• Explore **Symbolism**: What does the Sacred Ring stand for? Why is it trusted by some and doubted by others?

• Focus on **Refrain Use** in poetry (Villanelle) — how repetition builds mood and theme.

• Discuss **Foreshadowing**: "What clues suggest there's danger watching beyond the valley?"

📋 CHAPTER SUMMARY SHEET

Chapter Title: The Mysterious Quest – The Enigmatic Ring

Main Setting: Valley of Wakaduo, beneath the Council Tree

Key Themes: Trust, Legacy, Destiny, Community Leadership

SEL Focus: Courage, Belief in Self, Building Consensus

📜 SHORT SUMMARY:

In the valley beneath the mighty Council Tree, Scatter, a small pouched mouse, reveals the Sacred Ring of Journeys to the animals of Wakaduo. Found deep within the Hollow Tree of Elders, the ring glows with ancient magic and bears the symbols of unity and past leaders. Though met with skepticism from some animals, Scatter bravely defends the ring's importance and the vision of a new home it presents. Adira, still watchful, supports Scatter's potential, and Henry the honey badger steps in to affirm their trust. By nightfall, the valley shifts from doubt to hope as the animals prepare to follow Scatter into the unknown, their faith ignited by courage and shared purpose.

Comprehension Focus:
- How does Scatter convince others to trust her?
- Why is the ring an important symbol in the story?
- What does leadership look like in a time of uncertainty?

Main Characters Introduced/Expanded:
- **Scatter**: Small but brave mouse chosen by fate, bearer of the Sacred Ring
- **Adira**: Continues as wise observer and cautious supporter
- **Henry**: Courageous, loyal honey badger who defends Scatter
- **Sally**: Sharp-witted mandrill who voices skepticism
- **The Animal Council**: Represents Wakaduo's diverse community, both doubtful and hopeful

Key Vocabulary Words:
- Enigmatic – Mysterious and hard to understand
- Sacred – Treasured and honored as special or spiritual
- Legacy – Something valuable passed down through generations
- Skepticism – Doubt or disbelief, especially without proof
- Unity – Being joined together with others as one

Notable Quotes:
- "It's not just a ring. It was a message. A sign that the time had come for us to move forward." — Scatter
- "True strength comes from surprising places." — Adira

Look For in Illustrations:
- Scatter holding up the ring as lightning crackles in the background

• The crowd of animals with mixed expressions—doubt, hope, wonder
    • Sally the mandrill raising a skeptical eyebrow
    • The Majestic Hollow Tree of Elders in the distance

REFLECTION QUESTIONS

📖 ✍ Class Discussion / Reflection Prompts

Scatter finds a legendary ring that could lead everyone to safety—but not everyone believes her. She has to decide whether to step up as a leader, even while being doubted.

✍ REFLECTION PROMPTS:

1.   **Why do you think Scatter decided to show the ring, even when she wasn't sure anyone would believe her?**

2. 🔍 **Have you ever had to prove something you believed in?**
What was that like?

3. 🐾 **What do you think the ring symbolizes in this story?** (Hint: it's more than just magic…)

4. 👁 **How did Henry's and Adira's support/ help Scatter? What does that tell us about leadership and trust?**

🌑 CHOOSE A TOKEN YOU EARNED:
  🔴 Truth   🔴 Friendship   ⚪ Self-Worth
  (Draw or explain below)

📊 TEACHER TOOLS & PLANNING SNAPSHOT

⏳ Essential Question:

How do leaders build trust, even when others doubt them?

⏳ Teaching Time Estimate:

45–60 minutes

(15–20 for reading, 15 for discussion, 10–15 for extension or writing)

🧠 Differentiation Tips:

• **For struggling readers:** Use real objects (ring, roots, tree) to act out the scene.

• **For advanced readers:** Rewrite Scatter's speech using elevated language or poetic metaphor.

Flex Teaching Tips:

• Use the poem's refrain for quick fluency practice.

• Allow "council votes" in the classroom to simulate group decision-making.

USE THE STUDENT WORKBOOK "REFLECT & RESPOND" PAGE to prompt rich journaling or small group discussion before the CER writing.

✍️ CER WRITING (CLAIM–EVIDENCE–REASONING)

Use this structured writing prompt to support deeper thinking and text-based writing. The CER framework guides students to:

• Form a clear claim

• Support their thinking with specific textual evidence

• Explain how that evidence proves their point

• Practice academic writing sentence starters

• Build argumentative and persuasive thinking

  Ideal after discussion, close reading, or as a lead-in to a short response

✍️ CER WRITING PROMPT:

Prompt: Why does the Sacred Ring become a symbol of leadership for Scatter?

CLAIM STARTER: I BELIEVE THE RING BECOMES A SYMBOL OF leadership for Scatter because…

EVIDENCE STARTERS:
- In the story it says…
- One example is when Scatter…

REASONING STARTERS:
- This shows that…
- This proves…
- This means…

BONUS EXTENSION: WRITE A SHORT JOURNAL REFLECTION: "IF I found a sacred ring in my neighborhood, how would I use it for good?"

 Quick Checklist

✅ Did I make a clear claim?
✅ Did I support it with evidence from the story?
✅ Did I explain how my evidence proves my claim?

✺✦✺

✿ STUDENT WORKBOOK ANSWER KEY

Vocabulary Matching:
1 = C
2 = A
3 = B
4 = D

Fill in the Blank:

1. Quest
2. Skeptical
3. Enigmatic
4. Unity

Multiple Choice:
1 = C
2 = A

Short Answer Samples:
3. She shares its origin and how she felt a deep truth when she found it.

4. It means if we only know one way to solve problems, we might miss better solutions. Scatter shows them they need each other's ideas.

Sequencing Order:

1. The animals gather under the Council Tree
2. Scatter introduces the Sacred Ring
3. Scatter found it in the Hollow Tree
4. Sally questions the ring
5. Henry supports Scatter
6. Adira announces the journey

CHARACTER TRAITS CHART – SAMPLE ANSWERS:

- **Scatter** – *Brave*: Presents the ring despite doubt
- **Sally** – *Skeptical*: Questions the ring's power
- **Henry** – *Supportive*: Publicly backs Scatter
- **Adira** – *Wise*: Confirms Scatter's call to lead

◉ DIFFERENTIATION IDEAS

- **Struggling Readers** – Show real objects (a ring, ancient-looking box) to bring the story to life.
- **Advanced Learners** – Write a persuasive speech as Scatter convincing the crowd.
- **Kinesthetic Learners** – Act out the Council Tree gathering!

◉ STANDARDS ALIGNMENT

- **CCSS.ELA.RL.4.1 & RL.4.3** – Use details to describe characters and events
- **Science of Reading Integration:**
- *Vocabulary Acquisition:* Root study ("mystical," "unity")
- *Fluency:* Choral reading of Scatter's speech
- *Inferencing/Prediction:* Use the *Prediction Ladder* to track ideas

◉ CREATIVE CONNECTIONS

1. Writing Prompt – Leadership Letter

Write a letter from Scatter to the future leader of Wakaduo. What advice would she give? What fears did she overcome?

2. Art Extension – Comic Strip Challenge

Draw a 3–4 panel comic showing Sally's doubt and Scatter's courage. Caption each with dialogue or thoughts.

3. SEL Connection – Group Circle

Discuss: "When have you had to speak up even though it was scary?" Create a "Courage Wall" of anonymous stories.

4. Performance Option – Council Debate

Role-play the animal council! Have some students support Scatter's plan, others question it. Use evidence from the story to argue.

5. Leadership Tie-In – Toolbelt of a Leader

Proverb connection: "If your only tool is a hammer…"

Create a leader's "toolbelt" with traits like *listening*, *compromise*, *creativity*, and *vision*. Label tools with real-life actions!

POETRY PACK

Poetry Focus Activity Sheet — *Villanelle: The Enigmatic Quest* (this poetry form includes "refrains" for fluency focus)

🖊 POEM TEXT:

In the heart of the valley, beneath skies wide and vast,
Little Scatter stood brave, the Sacred Ring held fast.
If your only tool is a hammer, you see each problem as a nail.
Hope and worry mingled, as thunderclouds amassed,
Magic whispered of journeys, of legends from the past.
In the heart of the valley, beneath skies wide and vast.
"The ring speaks of safety," Scatter's voice cast,
Promises of shelter, from dangers so vast.
If your only tool is a hammer, you see each problem as a nail.
Adira questioned the truth, her tone overcast,
Is this ring true, will its guidance last?
In the heart of the valley, beneath skies wide and vast.
With a tale of old fires and paths long surpassed,
Scatter's faith in the ring, a contrast so vast.
If your only tool is a hammer, you see each problem as a nail.
Under starlit whispers, their fates forecast,
Together they'd journey, no doubts to outlast.
In the heart of the valley, beneath skies wide and vast,
If your only tool is a hammer, you see each problem as a nail.

🌀 STUDENT POETRY ACTIVITIES

ACTIVITY 1: Explore the Refrain

• A **villanelle** repeats certain lines multiple times.

• Find the **two lines** that are repeated throughout the poem.

• Write them below and explain why you think they are important:

1.

2.

QUESTION: WHY DO YOU THINK THE AUTHOR CHOSE TO REPEAT these two lines?

ACTIVITY 2: FEELING THE RHYTHM

• Read the poem aloud with a partner.

• **Underline** words that feel powerful, musical, or emotional.

• Circle **any words** that feel like they "pound" or "echo" like a drumbeat. (Insert space for underlined/circled words.)

ACTIVITY 3: FAMOUS QUOTE FOCUS

• The line: *"If your only tool is a hammer, you see each problem as a nail."* is a famous saying about problem-solving!

◦ What do you think it **means**?

◦ Have you ever seen someone (or yourself!) approach a problem the wrong way?

Write 2–3 sentences about it:

ACTIVITY 4: FIND THE MOOD

• Does the mood of the poem feel: **Hopeful**, **Mysterious**, or **Worried**?

• Circle one word — and then **prove it** by copying one phrase from the poem that shows that feeling.

Mood: _____

Phrase   that   proves   it:

ACTIVITY 5: Your Own Mini Villanelle
• Try writing a **3-stanza mini-villanelle!**
• Pick **2 lines** you want to repeat.
• Make up your own short poem about a quest or journey.
First   repeated   line:

Second   repeated   line:

My Mini Villanelle:

POETRY PACK BONUS SUGGESTION:
Invite students to try a "choral reading" of the Villanelle. Emphasize the repeated lines for rhythm and tone building (supports fluency goals in Science of Reading).

TEACHER TIP (SMALL PRINT)
✅ **Standards Alignment:**
• Reading Fluency through Recitation
• Literary Analysis (Refrain Use)
• Interpretation of Symbolic Phrases (Famous Quotes)
• Creative Writing (Structured Poetry)
✅ **Science of Reading Focus:**
• Prosody (reading with feeling and rhythm)
• Syntax Structure in Repetitive Poetry Forms

PROVERB TEACHING TIP:
"If your only tool is a hammer…" → Ask students to list 3 different "tools" leaders need (e.g., listening, planning, courage). This builds on the proverb and encourages flexible thinking.

. . .

DIFFERENTIATION TIP:

"Have students create a mini-poster or comic strip showing Scatter convincing Sally or the crowd — great for visual learners and reluctant writers."

▮▮ ANCHOR CHART

"What Makes a Leader?" – Lessons from Scatter
Title: What Makes a Leader?
Learning from Scatter in Chapter 3
Sections of the Chart:

Scatter's Action	What It Shows	What We Learn
She found the Sacred Ring and brought it to the Council.	She takes initiative, even when unsure.	Leaders act, even when afraid.
She stands tall and speaks up, even when Sally doubts her.	She stays calm and brave under pressure.	Leaders believe in themselves and their mission.
She listens to Adira and accepts help from Henry.	She respects others' wisdom and builds trust.	Leaders build unity by working with others.

✐ Leadership Words to Remember:
Brave • Humble • Trustworthy • Visionary • Kind • Courageous
Exit Question (written at the bottom or on the whiteboard):

What's one way YOU could show leadership in our classroom today?

BONUS IDEA:

Later, you could offer a **"Villanelle Challenge"** to see if students can create a full 6-stanza villanelle using their own repeated lines!

❧ 4 ❧

SCATTER'S STORY

TEACHER'S ANNOTATED GUIDE

Chapter Four : Scatter's Story

◷ CHAPTER OVERVIEW

This chapter gives students the opportunity to analyze how personal hardship can be transformed into leadership. Scatter's journey invites reflection on belonging, voice, and the power of being underestimated. The proverb encourages students to think about the outsized impact of small, courageous actions.

◎ Learning Objectives

- Analyze character growth through personal storytelling
- Explore symbolism and metaphor, especially the Sacred Ring and Scatter's transformation
- Practice fluency with rhythm and emotional expression via poetry
- Connect theme to real life through leadership, self-worth, and perseverance

📖 VOCABULARY + MORPHOLOGY FOCUS

Chapter 4 – Scatter's Story

Theme Focus: Identity, belonging, transformation, and unseen potential

✴ Tier II & Tier III Vocabulary Words (Context-Based)

1 Legacy – Something passed down from the past, especially values or accomplishments

➤ *Prompt*: "What kind of legacy would you like to leave behind someday?"

2 Symbol – An object, image, or word that stands for something else (often abstract)

➤ *Prompt*: "What does the Sacred Ring represent in this story? What about Scatter's tail?"

3 Self-Worth – The belief that you have value, even when others don't see it

➤ *Prompt*: "How do you show yourself respect, especially when things are hard?"

4 Destiny – A future that feels planned or meant to be

➤ *Prompt*: "Is destiny something you wait for—or something you build?"

5 Belonging – Feeling accepted and connected to a group or community

➤ *Prompt*: "What places or people make you feel like you belong?"

🔍 Morphology Tie-Ins

Legacy

Definition: Something passed down from the past, especially values or accomplishments.

Morphology: Comes from the Latin root *legare*, meaning "to bequeath" or "to send."

➤ Use in context: "Scatter's legacy isn't just her past—it's what she dares to become."

➤ Prompt: "What kind of legacy would you like to leave behind someday?"

SYMBOL

Definition: An object or image that represents something deeper or abstract.

Morphology: Derived from the Greek *sym-* meaning "together" and *ballein* meaning "to throw."

➤ Use in context: "The Sacred Ring is more than a ring—it's a symbol of leadership."

➤ Prompt: "What everyday symbols do you notice that carry deeper meaning?"

SELF-WORTH

Definition: The belief that you are valuable, no matter what others say.

Morphology: Made up of *self* (one's own being) and *worth* (value or importance).

➤ Use in context: "Scatter's self-worth grows as she realizes her voice matters."

➤ Prompt: "What helps you feel proud of who you are?"

DESTINY

Definition: A future that feels meant to be or strongly guided.

Morphology: From the Latin *destinare*, meaning "to make firm or establish."

➤ Use in context: "Some believe destiny chooses them. Scatter chooses hers."

➤ Prompt: "Is destiny fixed—or can we shape it?"

. . .

BELONGING

Definition: The feeling of being accepted, included, or valued by a group.

Morphology: From *be-* (to make) and *long* (to be a part of).

➤ Use in context: "Wakaduo gives the forgotten creatures a place of true belonging."

➤ Prompt: "Why is belonging so powerful—and what creates it?"

WORD STUDY ACTIVITY SUGGESTIONS

1. Symbol Mapping:

Create a "Symbol Web" showing items from the story (e.g., Sacred Ring, Scatter's tail) and what they represent. Then let students add personal or cultural symbols they know.

2. Word Journals – "What's My Worth?"

Students reflect in writing or drawing: What are three things that make you feel proud of yourself?

3. Morphology Match:

Break apart "legacy," "self-worth," and "destiny" into root parts. Ask students to build new words using similar roots (*self-care, worthless, predestined*).

4. Belonging Gallery Walk:

Students draw or describe a space where they feel they belong. Then walk around to observe classmates' answers, finding patterns.

◆ MINI-LESSON SPOTLIGHT: CHAPTER 4

Chapter Title: Scatter's Story

Essential Focus: Transforming pain into pride through storytelling

📖 Learning Objective

Students will explore how sharing personal history can shift others' perceptions, build leadership, and foster belonging.

📜 Vocabulary in Context

1. Legacy – "Scatter's legacy isn't just her past—it's what she dares to become."

2. Symbol – "The Sacred Ring is more than a ring—it's a symbol of leadership."

3. Self-Worth – "Scatter's self-worth grows as she realizes her voice matters."

4. Belonging – "Wakaduo gives the forgotten creatures a place of true belonging."

5. Destiny – "Some believe destiny chooses them. Scatter chooses hers."

🌰 Read-Aloud Guidance

Choose a strong reader (or model read) to deliver Scatter's monologue about her name:

"The name Scatter was once a joke... but now I'm proud of it."

Pause to ask:

🐾 "What changed in Scatter's thinking? What gave her power over her name?"

💬 Discussion Prompts

• Why did some animals doubt Scatter at first?

• What did Scatter do or say that changed their minds?

• How can symbols (like a ring or a tail marking) communicate meaning?

✍ Student Activity

Symbol Mapping

Draw the Sacred Ring and add words or pictures that show what it represents (unity, courage, destiny). Add your own personal "symbol" beside it—something that shows your strength or story.

Optional Extension

Poetry & Performance:

Read aloud the sonnet *"Tiny Feet on a Giant Path."* Assign groups to each quatrain and perform it with gestures or tone.

Prompt: "Which line do you think would make someone feel strong? Why?"

🔍 COMPREHENSION GUIDE

Before Reading:
• Introduce the proverb: *"If you think you are too small to make a difference, you haven't spent the night with a mosquito."*
 – Ask: "What does this mean to you?"
 – Prompt a quick-pair discussion: "Can small things have big power? What's a time you made a difference, even in a small way?"
• Preview vocabulary: *legacy, destiny, self-worth, symbol*
 – Ask: "What do you think it means to *belong* somewhere?"
 – Encourage students to connect to the theme of "being underestimated."

DURING READING:
• Pause when the animals begin to doubt Scatter.
 – Ask: "How would you feel if everyone laughed or whispered while you were speaking? What would you do?"
 – Highlight the different reactions from the crowd (doubt, hope, respect) and track their shift as Scatter shares more of her story.
• As Scatter shares her past, ask:
 – "What parts of her story show leadership?"
 – "Why might her name, *Scatter*, feel painful—and later, powerful?"
• After Adira and Ernie speak up:
 – Ask: "How do their voices affect the crowd's feelings about Scatter?"

AFTER READING:
• Discuss how Scatter uses storytelling to gain trust.
 – Ask: "What changed the crowd's mind—facts, feelings, or both?"

• Connect the symbol of the ring and Scatter's tail marking.

– Ask: "What do symbols like these represent in real life? (e.g., flags, team logos, medals)"

– Let students brainstorm a symbol that represents something *they* value.

• Theme Reflection:

– "What does this chapter teach us about turning struggle into strength?"

– "Who do you think was the most influential character in this chapter—Scatter, Adira, or Ernie? Why?"

TEACHING PLAN – *SCATTER'S STORY*

Warm-Up (5–7 minutes)

• Begin with the proverb: *"If you think you are too small to make a difference, you haven't spent the night with a mosquito."*

• Ask students: *"What do you think this means?"*

• Optional Quick-Write: *"Have you ever felt small but made a big impact?"*

Read-Aloud or Partner Reading (10–15 minutes)

• Teacher reads Scatter's speech aloud, modeling courage and tone.

• Ask students to highlight or underline moments where Scatter shows emotional growth.

• Optional Performance: Have volunteers act out lines to practice expressive reading and fluency.

Workbook Activities (20–25 minutes)

• Guide students through vocabulary, sequencing, comprehension, and character activities.

• Support emerging readers with sentence starters or paraphrased prompts.

• Encourage students to use evidence when responding.

Group Discussion (10 minutes)

• *"How does Scatter grow as a leader?"*

• *"Why do symbols like the Sacred Ring matter in stories—and in real life?"*

- *"How do the animals' doubts turn into belief?"*

🪶 Creative Extension (Optional)

- Students create personal "Unity Symbols" inspired by Scatter's ring.
- Display their designs under a class banner titled: **Small Voices, Big Leaders**.

෫෪ඁ

📖 FLUENCY & LITERARY FOCUS

Fluency Tips

- Model **intonation and pacing** using Scatter's speech and the sonnet; use pauses to emphasize emotional turning points.
- Encourage **group choral reading** of the sonnet to practice rhythm and collective voice.
- Suggested line to practice: *"The name Scatter was once a joke… but now I'm proud of it."* — cue for emphasis and tone of transformation.

Literary Focus

- **Symbolism**: The Sacred Ring and the symbol on Scatter's tail serve as layered metaphors for legacy, identity, and leadership.
- **Theme**: Belief in self, courage in the face of doubt, redefining one's own story.
- **Characterization**: Use Scatter's transformation to explore indirect characterization (actions, dialogue, others' reactions).

📑 CHAPTER SUMMARY SHEET

Main Setting: Wakaduo Valley at night under the stars

Key Themes: Self-Worth, Overcoming Doubt, Belonging, Inner Strength

SEL Focus: Self-Worth, Belonging, Courage, Identity

📜 SHORT SUMMARY:

Under a star-filled sky, Scatter—the once-mocked pouched

mouse—shares her truth with the animals of Wakaduo. Holding the Sacred Ring high, she tells of her difficult past: abandoned as a baby, raised by Ernie the owl, and once ridiculed for her name. Yet, it was this same "Scatter" who was chosen by destiny. Though doubted by many, including the skeptical Ms. Guinea Fowl and others, Scatter stands firm, transforming ridicule into power and loneliness into leadership. As animals listen, her words stir hearts, and even doubters begin to believe. Adira and Ernie speak on Scatter's behalf, helping unify the animals behind her vision of a brave, shared future. Wakaduo is buzzing with hope—and ready for the journey ahead.

COMPREHENSION FOCUS:

• How does Scatter turn her pain into power?
  • Why do the animals begin to trust her?
  • What makes a leader—even one who's small?
  ### Main Characters Introduced/Expanded:
  • **Scatter**: Small mouse with a giant heart, rises as a symbol of unity and strength
  • **Ernie**: The wise eagle-owl, loving guardian to Scatter and keeper of stories
  • **Ms. Guinea Fowl**: Vocal skeptic who questions Scatter's ability to lead
  • **Adira**: Adds her voice of wisdom to support Scatter
  • **Various Animal Doubters**: Including monkeys, mongooses, porcupines, and zebras—representing community concern and change

NOTABLE QUOTES:

  • "The name Scatter was once a joke… but now I'm proud of it." — Scatter
  • "True strength comes from surprising places." — Adira
  • "Scatter's bravery should inspire us all to rise above our doubts and fears." — Ernie

🔍 **Look For in Illustrations**:

- Scatter holding the ring before a crowd under a glowing sky
- The skeptical animals whispering in the background
- A Colubus monkey jumping in alarm
- The enigmatic Ring of Journeys

⬛ ANCHOR CHART

Title: 🐭 Small Voice, Big Power — What Makes a Leader?

Create a class anchor chart with a large image of Scatter in the center (or a silhouette of a small mouse). Around her, students help you add words, phrases, or examples from the text to describe leadership qualities she shows.

CHART STRUCTURE:

- 💬 **Words That Describe Scatter**

(e.g., "Brave," "Truthful," "Determined," "Wise in her own way")

- **What Leaders DO**

(e.g., "Speak their truth," "Stand up even when scared," "Inspire others with stories")

- 🗨 **Class Contributions: "Times I Showed Leadership"**

Students can write sticky notes or short reflections that start with:

"I led when…" or "I spoke up even though…"

REFLECTION QUESTIONS

📖 ✍ **Class Discussion / Reflection Prompts**

. . .

CHAPTER 4 – SCATTER'S STORY

Scatter tells the animals about her past and how she came to have the ring. She transforms pain into pride, and some animals begin to believe in her leadership.

REFLECTION PROMPTS:

1. 🐨 Scatter says her name was once a joke—but now it gives her strength. Can you think of something about yourself you've grown proud of over time?

2. 🐘 Why do you think it was hard for the other animals to trust Scatter at first?

3. 💜 Ernie helped raise Scatter, even though they were very different. What does that teach us about family and friendship?

4. 🔥 Have you ever had to speak up when you were nervous? What helped you find your voice?

CHOOSE A TOKEN YOU EARNED:

Self-Worth   ● Friendship   ● Empathy
(Draw or explain below)

৩৯৩

✒ TEACHER TOOLS & PLANNING SNAPSHOT

A quick, actionable guide at a glance.

⏲ Essential Question:

How can sharing our story help others see our strength?

⏳ Teaching Time Estimate:

45–60 minutes

(10–15 min for read-aloud, 15–20 min workbook + discussion, 10+ for poetry or role-play)

🐘 Differentiation Tips:

• For emerging readers: Break Scatter's speech into speech bubbles and explore it through role-play.

• For advanced learners: Have students write a companion monologue from Adira or Ms. Guinea Fowl's perspective.

• For visual learners: Ask students to illustrate the Sacred Ring with symbols representing their own personal strengths.

Flex Teaching Tips:

• Start or end class with students adding to a **"Small Voices, Big Power" Wall** — one way they used their voice for good.

• Use the proverb as a journal or quote-of-the-week activity.

✍ CER PROMPT

Prompt: Why does Scatter's personal story help others see her as a leader?

Claim Starter: I believe Scatter's story helped others see her as a leader because…

EVIDENCE STARTERS:
• In the story, Scatter says…
• One example is when…
• The animals reacted by…

REASONING STARTERS:
• This shows that…
• It proves that…
• Her story helped them feel…

BONUS: DRAW A COMIC PANEL SHOWING THE MOMENT THE ANIMALS start to believe in Scatter.

STUDENT WORKBOOK ANSWER KEY

☑ Answer Key

Vocabulary Matching:

1 = C, 2 = A, 3 = B, 4 = D

Fill in the Blanks:

1. mosquito
2. destiny
3. ancestors
4. unity

Multiple Choice:

1 = C, 2 = B

Short Answers (Examples):

3. Scatter shares how she was abandoned and once hated her name, but now wears it with pride.

4. She uses her story to help others understand that her strength comes from experience—not size.

Sequencing:

1. Scatter stands with the ring
2. Doubts rise from Ms. Guinea Fowl
3. Scatter explains the ring
4. Scatter shares her story
5. Adira speaks up
6. The animals prepare for the journey

Character Chart (Examples):

- **Scatter** – Brave, wise – Shares her story and stands tall despite doubt
- **Adira** – Supportive – Encourages belief in Scatter
- **Ms. Guinea Fowl** – Skeptical, fearful – Begins to soften after hearing Scatter's truth

📚 Standards Alignment

- **RL.4.1** – Citing evidence from Scatter's speech
- **RL.4.3** – Character development through action and dialogue
- **RL.4.4** – Understanding key terms like "destiny" and "unity"

🔍 Differentiation Strategies

- Use speech bubbles to break down Scatter's monologue
- Have advanced students write a companion poem from Adira's POV
- ESL support: bilingual visuals and vocabulary cards for "destiny," "unity," and "ancestor"

🪨 Bonus Activities

- **Mini Debate:** "Do you need to be big to be a strong leader?"
- **Role Play:** Act out the moment Scatter is doubted—then reverse it to show support
- **Art Extension:** Collaborative *Mural of Unity* featuring all Wakaduo animals and their leadership traits

POETRY PACK

Poetry Activity Sheet — *Sonnet: Scatter's Courage*

✏️ Poem Text:

In Wakaduo's night, a small mouse stands tall,
Holding high a ring, ancient tales recall.
"If you think you're too small to change the flow,

Spend a night with the mosquito's echo."
Brave Scatter speaks beneath the stars that light,
Her voice a whisper against the cool night.
Every creature listens, hope does swell,
In her tiny paws, a world's story she'll tell.
"Though small, our might combined can shift fate's weight,
This ring, our guide to a future we create.
Let doubters hear, let skeptics see the sign,
In unity, our strength, together we align."
From the smallest mouse to the tallest tree,
Every heart beats to the sound of unity.
Scatter's tale, a new legend we compose,
In her story, a giant's heart enclosed.

STUDENT POETRY ACTIVITIES

ACTIVITY 1: Sonnet Structure Detective
• A **sonnet** usually has **14 lines** and a special rhythm.
• Count the lines — how many are there? _____
• Find two rhyming pairs of lines and write them here:
1. _____ rhymes with _____
2. _____ rhymes with _____

ACTIVITY 2: SMALL BUT MIGHTY
• The line: *"If you think you're too small to change the flow, Spend a night with the mosquito's echo."* is a metaphor for **small actions making a big impact**.
Think about it:
• Have you ever seen a small thing (or person) make a big difference?
• Write a short example from your life below:

ACTIVITY 3: THEME TRACKER
• What do you think is the **main message** (theme) of this

poem? Circle ONE:

    A) **Bravery can come from small places**

    B) **Only strong creatures succeed**

    C) **Legends are forgotten quickly**

Prove your answer: Copy a line from the poem that shows your choice:

ACTIVITY 4: PICTURE THE POEM

• Draw (or describe in words) what you imagine when you hear:

"In her tiny paws, a world's story she'll tell."

Your Drawing or Description:

ACTIVITY 5: WRITE YOUR OWN LINE OF HOPE

• Imagine you are Scatter.

• Write ONE powerful line you might say to inspire others:

"My words to inspire:

"

_____

TEACHER TIP (SMALL PRINT)

☑ **Standards Alignment:**

• Understanding Poetic Forms (Sonnet)

• Identifying Theme and Literary Devices

• Connecting Personal Experience to Text

• Creative Writing (Imagining Character Voice)

☑ **Science of Reading Focus:**

• Reading Fluency through Rhythm and Meter

• Building Comprehension through Theme Analysis

BONUS IDEA:

Later, you could create a *"Small But Mighty"* wall where students post their one-line inspirations!

❦ 5 ❦

THE GATHERING

TEACHER'S ANNOTATED GUIDE

☑ OVERVIEW OF CHAPTER 5: *THE GATHERING*

Main **Setting**: Council Glade at the edge of the Wakaduo wilds

Key Themes: Decision-Making, Loyalty, Stepping Into the Unknown

▧ SHORT SUMMARY:

In a solemn and suspenseful chapter, the chosen heroes must decide whether to accept the mission and leave the safety of Wakaduo. They stand at the edge of something larger than themselves—facing the unknown, bonded by purpose. Elders speak, doubts emerge, and friendships begin to deepen. The moment becomes not just about leaving home, but about crossing the threshold into courage.

. . .

☉ LEARNING OBJECTIVES

- Examine how characters respond to risk and leadership decisions
- Expand vocabulary through contextual learning
- Strengthen inferencing, sequencing, and cause-effect reasoning
- Make real-life connections about courage and decision-making

≋ VOCABULARY + MORPHOLOGY FOCUS

Chapter 5 – The Gathering

Theme Focus: Decision-Making, Unity, and the First Steps of a Brave Journey

✱ VOCABULARY WORDS (WITH MORPHOLOGY TIE-INS)

Threshold

Definition: The beginning of a new stage or a literal doorway to another space.

Morphology: From Old English *þrescold*, meaning "door-sill" or "place of entering."

➤ Use in context: "Crossing the threshold meant there was no turning back."

➤ Prompt: "Have you ever stepped into something new that changed your life?"

Allegiance

Definition: Loyalty or devotion to a person, group, or cause.

Morphology: From Latin *ligare*, meaning "to bind," and the prefix *al-* (toward).

➤ Use in context: "The animals showed their allegiance to Wakaduo by standing together."

➤ Prompt: "To whom or what do you feel allegiance in your life?"

Mirage

Definition: An optical illusion often seen in the desert, something that looks real but isn't.

Morphology: From French *mirer*, meaning "to look at" or "to reflect."

➤ Use in context: "Was the path ahead real—or just a mirage of their hope?"

➤ Prompt: "Can people sometimes chase mirages in real life, too?"

Pledge

Definition: A serious promise or vow, often spoken aloud.

Morphology: From Latin *plegere*, meaning "to vow" or "commit."

➤ Use in context: "They made a pledge to protect each other no matter what."

➤ Prompt: "What's something you've pledged—or promised—to do?"

◆ MINI-LESSON SPOTLIGHT: CHAPTER 5

Chapter Title: The Gathering

Essential Focus: Making brave choices—even when the future is uncertain

▌ **Learning Objective**

Students will analyze how fear, loyalty, and courage shape decisions during a turning point.

▧ VOCABULARY IN CONTEXT

1. Threshold – "Crossing the threshold meant there was no turning back."

2. Allegiance – "The animals showed their allegiance to Wakaduo by standing together."

3. Mirage – "Was the path ahead real—or just a mirage of their hope?"

4. Pledge – "They made a pledge to protect each other no matter what."

5. Journey – "Their journey had only just begun, but their hearts were already tested."

🐚 READ-ALOUD GUIDANCE

Focus on Adira's speech about the **Desert of No Return**. Use a slow, steady tone to model gravity.

Ask:

🌵 "What do the mirages in the desert represent, besides just heat?"

🐚 "Why is it important to listen to legends or old stories before making a decision?"

💬 DISCUSSION PROMPTS

• Would you have stepped forward like Henry? Why/why not?

• What does "crossing a threshold" mean in real life?

• How did Scatter grow in this chapter—even though she was still unsure?

✏️ STUDENT ACTIVITY
Team Tracker Map

Draw a visual map of the Council Tree gathering. Add arrows or speech bubbles showing which characters supported the journey and which hesitated. Label emotions like doubt, courage, and loyalty.

🔍 COMPREHENSION GUIDANCE

Before Reading:

• Introduce the proverb: *"When a needle falls into a deep well, many will look in, but few will go down after it."*

• Ask: "What does this suggest about courage and commitment?"

• Have students predict: "What risks might the animals face in this chapter?"

During Reading:

• Pause when Adira tells Kabora's story. Ask: "Why do legends matter in decision-making?"

• Highlight the emotional tones of Polly (skepticism), Henry (bravery), and Scatter (doubt).

• Ask: "What do you think Scatter is feeling right now?"

After Reading:

• Ask students to summarize why each animal chose to join—or not join—the journey.

• Use a Theme Tracker to log moments of courage, fear, and leadership.

• Discuss: "What does it mean to lead even when you're unsure?"

⚲ TEACHING ANGLE:

This chapter pairs well with lessons on symbolism, especially the use of "thresholds" and "pledges." Highlight the emotional tone shift as the heroes take a collective first step beyond safety—and into challenge.

⚙ SUGGESTED LESSON PLAN: OPENING DISCUSSION (5–7 MIN)

Proverb: *"When a needle falls into a deep well, many will look in, but few will go down after it."*

Ask: What does this mean? When have you seen this happen in real life?

READ-ALOUD OR PAIRED READING (10–15 MIN)

Focus on key moments: Adira's tale of Kabora, Henry's boldness, Polly's doubt.

Model tone: calm (Adira), bold (Henry), skeptical (Polly), reflective (Scatter).

· · ·

WORKBOOK ACTIVITIES (20–30 MIN)

- Vocabulary
- Cause-effect and sequencing
- Character reflections

Differentiation Tip:

- Use sentence frames and prediction charts for support
- Let visual learners map alliances or illustrate events

♣ FLUENCY & LITERARY FOCUS

Fluency Tips
- Model shifts in tone: calm for Adira, skeptical for Polly, bold for Henry, hesitant for Scatter.
- Use the repeated *chorus* in the ballad as a choral reading activity to build oral fluency.
- Practice expressive phrasing by reading Adira's warning aloud with a slow, weighty tone.

Literary Focus
- **Symbolism** – The Sacred Ring represents unity and destiny; the Tree of Life foreshadows wisdom.
- **Tone and Mood** – Analyze how tone shifts from doubt to determination.
- **Poetic Device** – Explore how the *chorus* in a ballad builds rhythm and emotional emphasis.

☑ SUMMARY SHEET FOR CHAPTER 5: THE GATHERING

Main Setting: Council Tree, Wakaduo borderlands
   Key Themes: Unity, Responsibility, Courage to Begin

· · ·

▓ SHORT SUMMARY:

As night falls on Wakaduo, a secret gathering of animals takes place at the Council Tree to decide who will brave the Desert of No Return in search of a new home. Adira the wise tortoise warns of dangers in the desert: mirages, thirst, and vanishing paths. Scatter, still unsure of herself, is chosen to lead the expedition. Tusker, Ernie, and Henry step forward to join her, forming the core of the hero team. Doubts, fears, and hope swirl among the gathered animals, but a shared promise binds them: *they will move forward together.*

◔ COMPREHENSION FOCUS:
- What makes a good leader?
- Why is Adira's warning important?
- How do the heroes show bravery?

☺ MAIN CHARACTERS INTRODUCED / EXPANDED:
- **Adira:** Wise tortoise, keeper of legends and warnings
- **Scatter:** Chosen leader, uncertain but courageous
- **Tusker:** Strength and wisdom, maternal and protective
- **Ernie:** Strategic, vigilant, and deeply loyal
- **Henry:** Bold honey badger, spirited and comic relief

❁ KEY VOCABULARY WORDS:
- *Council Tree* – A sacred place of animal meetings
- *Mirage* – A trick of the eyes, like seeing water that isn't there
- *Leadership* – Guiding others with care, courage, and choices
- *Journey* – A long trip filled with adventure and challenges
- *Pledge* – A promise made with intention and honor

✒ NOTABLE QUOTES:
"We move forward together." — Scatter

"The Desert of No Return is not just sand... It's a place that tests the soul." — Adira

"Every great journey begins with a choice." — Ernie

🔍 LOOK FOR IN ILLUSTRATIONS:
• The ring glowing in Scatter's paw
• The baboons nervously chattering
• The Four Heroes, Quest ready
• Polly the skeptical Grey Parrot

🧠 SEL FOCUS:
• **Decision-Making** – Understanding consequences and weighing fear against duty
• **Teamwork** – Recognizing how trust and group courage shape leadership
• **Overcoming Self-Doubt** – How Scatter learns to lead despite uncertainty

۞

📖 ✍ REFLECTION QUESTIONS

The animals of Wakaduo gather to decide whether to follow Scatter into the unknown. Doubts arise, stories of danger are shared, and the first team of brave explorers steps forward.

✍ REFLECTION PROMPTS:
1. 💬 **If you were in the crowd at The Gathering, would you raise your paw/wing/voice to join the journey? Why or why not?**

2. 🪶 **What lessons can we learn from Adira's story about Kabora and the Desert of No Return?**

3. ⏱ **Scatter wasn't sure she was ready—but her friends stood with her. How do friends help us be braver?**

4. 🔍 **What do you think makes a good team? What do you think each character brings to this quest?**

5. 🎥 **Have you ever made a brave decision that others didn't understand at first?**

Write 3–4 sentences about how you felt before and after.

🌑 **Choose a Token You Earned:**
  🔴 Leadership   ⚪ Courage   🔵 Friendship
  ⬜ (Draw or explain below)

⚜

📊 **Anchor Chart: "What Makes a Brave Decision?"**

Title: 🐾 *"Brave Choices, Big Impact"*
  Subtitle: What makes a decision brave—even when it's scary?

Chart Format:

Brave Decision	Why It's Brave	What Helped the Character Decide
Scatter accepts the journey	She's unsure of herself	Friends stand beside her
Henry speaks up first	Risk of being wrong or alone	Belief in Scatter
Adira shares Kabora's story	It might scare the animals	She wants them prepared
Ernie pledges to help	Fear of danger	Loyalty and wisdom

Follow-Up Class Questions:
  • What's the difference between a *brave* decision and a *reckless* one?
  • Can asking for help also be a brave decision?

TEACHER TOOLS & PLANNING SNAPSHOT

Teaching Time Estimate
- **Total Duration**: ~60 minutes
- **Suggested Breakdown**:
- 5–7 min: Warm-up Proverb + Discussion
- 15–20 min: Read-Aloud (with roleplay or tone modeling)
- 20–25 min: Workbook Activities (Vocabulary, Comprehension, Cause/Effect)
- 10–15 min: Reflection Discussion + Anchor Chart or Writing Extension

Differentiation Tip
- **For Struggling Readers**:
- Use a visual timeline of the Gathering's key moments (Adira's warning, Polly's doubt, Henry's decision).
- Pre-teach key vocabulary with icons or images.
- Break text into chunks with sentence starters for journal writing.
- **For Advanced Learners**:
- Challenge them to write a monologue from Polly's point of view defending her skepticism.
- Compare Adira's leadership style with another literary or historical leader (e.g., Harriet Tubman, Moses, Moana's grandmother, etc.).

Essential Question
What makes someone brave enough to lead others—even when they're scared or doubted?

Use this to frame the chapter before and after reading. It ties to the core SEL themes and can drive journal responses or group debate.

 **Use the Student Workbook "Reflect & Respond" page to prompt rich journaling or small group discussion before the CER writing.**

✍ CER WRITING (CLAIM–EVIDENCE–REASONING)

Use this structured writing prompt to support deeper thinking and text-based writing. The CER framework guides students to:
- Form a clear claim
- Support their thinking with specific textual evidence
- Explain how that evidence proves their point
- Practice academic writing sentence starters
- Build argumentative and persuasive thinking
    - *Ideal after discussion, close reading, or as a lead-in to a short response*

✍ CER Writing Prompt
Chapter 5 — *The Gathering*

Prompt: *Why is it important to make brave decisions even when others doubt you?*

 **CLAIM**

✎ Starter:

I believe that making brave decisions—even when others don't believe in you—is important because...

📖 **EVIDENCE**

✎ Starters:
- In the story it says...
- One example is when...
- The author shows that...

(Use examples such as Scatter gripping the ring, Henry stepping up, or Adira sharing Kabora's story.)

 **REASONING**

✎ Starters:
- This shows that...
- This proves that...
- This means that brave choices can...

. . .

☑ Quick Checklist

- ☑ Do I explain my main idea clearly?
- ☑ Did I include at least one piece of strong evidence from the text?
- ☑ Did I explain how the evidence supports my idea?

BONUS Activity (Optional):

Design a "Courage Crest" for Scatter or another character.

- Include a symbol, color, or quote that represents their bravery.

☉ Quick Checklist

☑ Is my answer connected to a real part of the story?

☑ Did I explain the lesson clearly?

☑ Does my explanation match my evidence?

☁ STUDENT WORKBOOK ANSWER KEY

Vocabulary Matching:

- Threshold = C
- Allegiance = A
- Mirage = B
- Seriousness = D

Cause & Effect:

- Adira warns… = B
- Polly doubts… = A
- Henry supports… = C
- Scatter doubts… = D

Sequencing:

1. Adira shares Kabora's story
2. The group debates
3. Polly questions the journey
4. Henry steps up
5. Scatter holds the ring and reflects
6. Ernie and Tusker join
7. The group sets out

Character Reflection:

- **Adira** – Wise – Warns but lets them choose
- **Scatter** – Courageous – Leads despite self-doubt
- **Henry** – Bold – Speaks up first
- **Polly** – Skeptical – Needs proof before belief

📚 Standards Alignment

- **RL.4.1** – Text evidence
- **RL.4.3** – Deep character analysis
- **RL.4.4** – Vocabulary: allegiance, mirage

📖 Fluency Extension
Readers' Theater Activity
Assign roles: Adira, Henry, Scatter, Polly
Focus on emotion, pacing, tone shifts
Optional Enrichment
Real-World Connection:

- Watch a short video on mirages
- Discuss how illusions appear in real life (e.g., peer pressure)

Mapping Activity:

- Create a visual map from Wakaduo to the Tree of Life

Writing Prompt:

- Write a journal entry from Ernie the night before departure

✖ Differentiation & Support

- Use graphic organizers for struggling readers
- Provide visuals + sentence starters for ELL students
- Challenge advanced students to link the story to real-life leaders or historical events

ꙮ

POETRY PACK FOCUS ACTIVITY FOR CHAPTER FOUR:

Poetry Activity Sheet — *Ballad: The Call of Wakaduo*

✎ POEM TEXT:

In the land where the shadows blend with light,
The creatures of Wakaduo gather at night.
Beneath the Council Tree's broad span,
They spoke of a journey, a perilous plan.
🎵 **Chorus:**
Oh, hear the whisper of the sand,
The Gathering's tale, so grand.
With courage pooled and fears to withstand,
Together they'll traverse the no-return land.
 Adira stood firm, her voice a deep call,
Warning of the desert where many might fall.
"The tales of old, of Kabora's pride,
Should guide us well, as we decide."

♫ **Chorus Repeat**

Baboons fretted, their voices loud,
While the wise old elephant seemed so proud.
Each animal spoke from heart and mind,
Searching for answers they hoped to find.
The night grew heavy, the air so still,
As they pondered the ring, its power and will.
Would Scatter's small form and the ancient band,
Lead them safe to a promised land?

♫ **Chorus Repeat**

☞ STUDENT POETRY ACTIVITIES

ACTIVITY 1: BALLAD BUILDING BLOCKS

• A **ballad** usually tells a **story** and uses a **chorus**.
• **Find and underline** the chorus every time it appears in the poem.
• How many verses (story parts) are there? _____

ACTIVITY 2: COMPARE AND REFLECT

Think about it:
• The animals must **make a hard decision**.
Answer this:
• Have you ever had to make a tough decision with a group?
• What made it easier or harder?
Write a few lines about your experience:

ACTIVITY 3: FEELING THE MUSIC

• Ballads often have a **musical feel**.
Circle the words that sound musical or sing-songy when you read them out loud:
• Whisper

- Gathering
- Traverse
- Heavy
- Council

(Hint: Many musical words have strong rhythm or vivid sound!)

ACTIVITY 4: CREATE YOUR OWN CHORUS

- Write **your own new chorus** for "The Call of Wakaduo"!

Think about courage, unity, and facing fears.

Start with:

"Oh, hear the call of _____,

The journey's _____ and _____..."

(Complete the lines with your own words!)

ACTIVITY 5: ILLUSTRATE THE COUNCIL MEETING

- Draw the Council Tree at night.

Show some animals debating what to do!

Your Sketch or Description:

TEACHER TIP (SMALL PRINT)

✅ **Standards Alignment:**

- Understanding Poetry Forms (Ballad and Chorus Structure)
- Text-to-Self Connection (Reflecting on Decision-Making)
- Sound and Rhythm Awareness

✅ **Science of Reading Focus:**

- Fluency (through Chorus Repetition)
- Deep Comprehension (narrative structure in poetry)

BONUS IDEA:

Students could **sing the chorus** together in small groups for fun! 🎤🎶 (Helps oral fluency and builds classroom energy!)

✿ 6 ❀

THE TREE OF LIFE

📖 CHAPTER 6 OVERVIEW

In this chapter, Scatter and her friends arrive at the majestic Tree of Life—an ancient symbol of unity and wisdom. As they approach, each character must offer a token of personal significance to unlock the tree's guidance. Through these offerings, we learn about their individual growth and the collective strength of their unity.

Inside the tree, Scatter is chosen to face the Queen Bee. In a powerful dialogue about purpose and belonging, Scatter earns the Queen's respect and receives a magical potion—a gift that will help them on their journey to the Mountain of Dreams. The chapter ends with the group renewed in purpose, bracing for the unknown desert ahead.

Proverb Focus: "If you want to go quickly, go alone. If you want to go far, go together."

Themes: Unity • Wisdom • Courage • Self-Discovery • Ritual and Transformation

. . .

◎ LEARNING OBJECTIVES

By the end of this chapter, students will:

• Analyze character motivation and internal growth

• Explore the symbolism of the Tree, the offerings, and the Queen Bee

• Identify and interpret figurative language (e.g., limericks, metaphor)

• Use context clues to define new vocabulary

• Compare leadership traits through character dialogue and decisions

🧠 VOCABULARY DEVELOPMENT

Key Words: *Charged, Sacred, Resilience, Majestic, Summon*

This chapter introduces powerful vocabulary connected to emotional depth, ritual, and transformation. These words reflect not only the action of the story but also its symbolic weight. Each term ties directly to character growth and the larger themes of unity, courage, and wisdom.

Charged

This word refers to something full of emotional or spiritual energy. In this chapter, the atmosphere around the Tree of Life is described as "charged" with meaning. Discuss with students how emotions or settings can feel *charged* during important moments.

– Morphology Tie-In: Comes from the Latin *carricare*, meaning "to load or burden." Connect this to the idea that emotion can "load" a scene or moment with significance.

Sacred

Often associated with religion or ancient tradition, *sacred* means something deeply respected or holy. Students should understand that the Tree of Life is not just magical—it is *sacred* to the animals of Wakaduo.

– Morphology Tie-In: From Latin *sacer* meaning "holy." Connect to similar words like *sacrifice* or *sacrament*, helping students see the shared root and deepen meaning.

Resilience

79

This is a critical vocabulary term, especially for SEL (Social Emotional Learning). In the story, Tusker's offering and Scatter's challenge show their growing *resilience*—the ability to recover and stay strong.

– Morphology Tie-In: From Latin *resilire*, meaning "to jump back." Help students visualize how resilience means bouncing back from difficulty, not just surviving it.

Majestic

Used to describe the Tree of Life, *majestic* evokes a sense of awe and grandeur. It's a great word to explore mood and tone. Ask: "What makes something *majestic* to you?"

– Morphology Tie-In: Comes from Latin *majestas*, meaning "greatness." Related to the word *majesty*, used for kings and queens.

Summon

To *summon* is to call upon someone or something with authority or purpose. The bees summon Scatter for her challenge—a moment of great symbolic importance.

– Morphology Tie-In: From Latin *summonere* (sub- = under + monere = to warn/call). Relate this to other "-mon" words like *admonish* or *premonition*, which deal with calls or warnings.

✎ Instructional Tip

Use these morphology connections to deepen meaning, not just memorize roots. Invite students to "play with the pieces" of words and predict meanings of unfamiliar terms they might encounter later, such as *majesticness*, *resiliently*, or *summoner*.

Student Activity Idea:

Have students draw or define one vocabulary word using a scene from the chapter (e.g., "Resilience" – Tusker offering old skin).

❋ Figurative Language & Symbolism
• **Tree of Life** = Wisdom, community, tradition

- **The offerings** = Growth through past experiences
- **The bees** = Collective action, protection, knowledge
- **The potion** = Newfound purpose and leadership

Class Discussion Prompt:

"What does each character's gift say about who they are becoming?"

◆ MINI-LESSON SPOTLIGHT: THE TREE OF LIFE

Essential Focus: Personal growth through sacrifice and unity

📖 Learning Objective

Students will interpret symbolic offerings and analyze how unity is built through empathy, courage, and shared purpose.

📚 VOCABULARY IN CONTEXT

1. Charged – "The air around them seemed charged, as if the land sensed their quest."

2. Sacred – "The Tree of Life was sacred—respected by all creatures."

3. Resilience – "Tusker's old skin showed her resilience through hard times."

4. Majestic – "The Tree stood tall, majestic against the sky."

5. Summon – "Scatter could summon bees when needed most."

🐾 READ-ALOUD GUIDANCE

Read Scatter's speech to the Queen Bee aloud as a performance piece. Use soft volume at first, building confidence as she speaks about belonging.

Ask:

🐝 "How does Scatter's tone change as she speaks to the Queen Bee? What helps her feel strong?"

. . .

💬 Discussion Prompts
• What made each character's offering meaningful?
• Why did Scatter's tiny pebble matter just as much as the others?
• What does the Queen Bee mean when she says: "You speak of belonging... perhaps you are worthy."

✏ Student Activity
Offering Reflection

Students draw or write about something small that's helped them feel strong—like Scatter's pebble.

Prompt: "What's something that helped you get through a hard time? If you had to offer it to the Tree of Life, what would it show about you?"

Optional Extension
Limerick Writing

Have students write a limerick about one character's offering.
Example:
There once was a pebble so small,
That helped a mouse stand proud and tall...

📖 READING COMPREHENSION STRATEGIES

Before Reading:
• What do you think the Tree of Life might represent?
• Why might it require a personal offering?
• What kinds of things do people give or share when something is important to them?

During Reading:
• How do the limericks at the start frame the tone of the chapter?

• Why do you think Scatter was chosen to meet the Queen Bee?

• Pause when the characters offer their tokens. Ask: "What does this gift reveal about this character?"

• Highlight Henry's honey moment: What is he learning about self-control and teamwork?

AFTER READING:

• What does the Queen Bee's test teach Scatter about leadership?

• Why does the tree glow when the offerings are given?

• Why did the Queen Bee change her mind about Scatter?

• What is the real "power" of the potion—and does it come only from magic?

✎ CHARACTER ANALYSIS

Scatter – Faces fear with quiet bravery; earns respect through sincerity.

Tusker – A symbol of strength and wisdom; shares a story of transformation.

Henry – Adds humor but struggles with temptation (honey); learns discipline.

Ernie – Guides the group with calm insight and ritual knowledge.

Mini-Reflection Prompt:

"Which character are you most like in this chapter? Why?"

⟳ CAUSE AND EFFECT

Cause: The heroes give meaningful offerings.

Effect: The Tree of Life responds with warmth and light.

Cause: Scatter respectfully pleads with the Queen Bee.

Effect: She is given a potion that grants aid in future trials.

Cause: Henry jokes about honey, nearly disrupting the group.

Effect: He learns self-control and respect for the mission.

. . .

🕮 LITERARY ELEMENTS TO TEACH
- **Mood:** Awe, reverence, wonder
- **Foreshadowing:** "The mountain remembers all who come to it..."
- **Narrative Structure:** This is a moment of *transformation*, preparing for the *climax* in the upcoming chapters.

✍ FLUENCY & LITERARY FOCUS – CHAPTER 6: *THE TREE OF LIFE*

📖 Fluency Tips:
- Practice reading Scatter's dialogue aloud where she addresses the Queen Bee. Emphasize nervousness that grows into courage.
- Choral read the limericks with rhythm and rhyme, encouraging playful tone but with thoughtful reflection on the journey's gravity.

🔍 Literary Focus:
- **Symbolism** – The tree, pebble, honey, and potion all represent internal growth, struggle, and transformation.
- **Allegory** – The Tree of Life scene serves as a metaphor for earning wisdom through sacrifice and self-knowledge.

📖 ELA STANDARDS ALIGNMENT (GRADE 4)
- **RL.4.1** – Refer to details when explaining character growth
- **RL.4.2** – Identify theme (unity, growth, leadership)
- **RL.4.3** – Describe character reactions and decisions
- **RL.4.4** – Understand figurative language and vocabulary in context
- **RL.4.5** – Analyze chapter's role in story arc

☑ SUMMARY SHEET

Main Setting: Sacred Tree of Life, Edge of the Desert
Key Themes: Wisdom, Sacrifice, Trust, Growth

📜 **SHORT SUMMARY:

Scatter and her team journey to the legendary Tree of Life before crossing the desert. The tree holds ancient wisdom and only shares its secrets with those who prove themselves. The heroes each offer a personal item—representing their fears, memories, or strength. Scatter, unsure of her worth, presents a small pebble that once comforted her in loneliness, and it is accepted with a soft glow. Later, she enters the tree to meet the Queen Bee, who grants her a potion to help guide them. The tree reveals their next destination: the Mountain of Dreams. Their bond as a team deepens.

🐌 Comprehension Focus:
- Why does each hero's offering matter?
- What does the Tree of Life symbolize?
- How does Scatter grow during this chapter?

🐾 MAIN CHARACTERS EXPANDED:
- **Queen Bee:** Guardian of the Tree, grants magical wisdom
- **Scatter:** Learns courage comes from vulnerability
- **Tusker:** Shares a token of resilience (old skin)
- **Henry:** Reveals bravery isn't about fearlessness
- **Ernie:** Shows growth through music and memory

🧩 KEY VOCABULARY WORDS:
- *Offering* – A meaningful gift given to earn trust or favor
- *Hive* – Home of the bees, guarded and sacred
- *Instinct* – Natural reaction or behavior without thinking
- *Unity* – The strength of being together with others

· · ·

✒ Notable Quotes:

"Our different strengths light up the tree." — Scatter

"A leader who speaks not just of survival, but of belonging… perhaps you are worthy after all." — Queen Bee

"Every family deserves a home, brave little mouse." — Queen Bee

⚲ Look For in Illustrations:

- The glowing pebble, Scatter's offering
- The Queen Bee in her throne within the tree
- The vial of golden potion
- The heroes circled around the tree, offerings in hand
- Sticky honey-covered Scatter!

✿✿✿

📖 ✎ REFLECTION PROMPTS / CLASS DISCUSSION

The heroes reach the ancient Tree of Life, where each must offer something deeply personal. Scatter earns the trust of the Queen Bee and gains wisdom to guide the group forward.

✎ Reflection Prompts:

1. **Each character gave up something meaningful. What would you offer if the Tree of Life asked you to share a symbol of your journey?**

2. 🐝 **Why do you think the Queen Bee trusted Scatter? What did Scatter say or do that showed she was a good leader?**

3. ✒ **The potion Scatter drank gave her special insight. If you could receive a magical gift from the Tree, what power would you want—and why?**

4. 🍵 **Henry struggled with temptation. Have you ever wanted something so badly it distracted you from your goals? How did you handle it?**

🌑 **Token Earned:**

● Wisdom ● Empathy ○ Courage
(Draw or explain your token below)

❦

✗ TEACHER TOOLS & PLANNING SNAPSHOT – CHAPTER 6

☉ Teaching Time Estimate
• 60–75 minutes (split into two sessions recommended)
? Essential Question
• How do personal sacrifices and shared purpose create a strong community?
↻ Flex Tip
• If short on time, focus only on the offering scene and Queen Bee dialogue—save the potion and Tree voice for next session.
▮ Differentiation Tip
• Use token illustrations (visual support) for struggling readers.
• Challenge advanced students to write their own "ritual offering" scene with a new character.

✑ CER WRITING (CLAIM–EVIDENCE–REASONING):

Use this structured writing prompt to support deeper thinking and text-based writing. The **CER** framework guides students to:
• Form a clear claim
• Support their thinking with specific textual evidence
• Explain how that evidence proves their point
• Practice academic writing sentence starters
• Build argumentative and persuasive thinking
  Ideal after discussion, close reading, or as a response lead-in.
�CER Worksheet
Prompt/Question:
What lesson did Scatter and her friends learn from the Tree of Life?

· · ·

1. ✾ CLAIM
✎ Starter: *I believe that...*

2. ▤ EVIDENCE
✎ Starters:
- *In the story it says...*
- *One example is when...*
- *The author shows that...*

3. REASONING
✎ Starters:
- *This shows that...*
- *This proves that...*
- *This means...*

◉ QUICK CHECKLIST
☑ Clear answer? ☑ Strong evidence? ☑ Good explanation?

WHEN TO USE:
☑ After discussion or reading group
☑ Before writing paragraphs or journal reflections
☑ As a formative assessment
☑ For writing support or enrichment

BONUS (OPTIONAL):
Draw the Tree of Life glowing with magic.

DIFFERENTIATED CER WORKSHEET – CHAPTER 6: *THE TREE of Life*
Prompt: *What lesson did Scatter and her friends learn from the Tree of*

Life?

    This version is scaffolded for emerging writers and ELL students, with sentence starters directly built into the response lines.

📣 CLAIM (WHAT DO YOU BELIEVE?)

✎ I believe that Scatter and her friends learned that

BECAUSE

📜 EVIDENCE (WHAT PART OF THE STORY SUPPORTS YOUR answer?)

✎ In the story it says,

WHICH SHOWS THAT

ANOTHER EXAMPLE IS WHEN

REASONING (WHY DOES THAT PROVE YOUR ANSWER IS true?)

✎ This shows that
because

IT MEANS THAT

☑ QUICK CHECKLIST:

✓ I made a strong **claim**.
✓ I found **evidence** from the story.
✓ I **explained** my thinking clearly.

. . .

BONUS ACTIVITY: DESIGN THE TREE OF LIFE

Draw the Tree glowing with magic.
• Add each hero's offering around the roots
• Include bees, leaves, or symbols of unity and growth
✏ My drawing:
[Blank space for art]
🖊 My Tree Teaches:

🖼 TEACHER ANSWER KEY – CHAPTER 6 CER EXAMPLE
📢 CLAIM:

I believe Scatter and her friends learned that unity and personal sacrifice help unlock true strength and guidance.

📚 EVIDENCE:

In the story it says the Tree of Life glowed only after each character gave a meaningful offering.

One example is when Scatter offered a small pebble from her childhood, and the tree accepted it with a warm light.

REASONING:

This shows that the Tree valued their honesty and teamwork, not just power or size.

It means the heroes learned that working together—and being vulnerable—makes them stronger as a group.

☙❧

POETRY PACK: CHAPTER 6 – *THE TREE OF LIFE'S CALL*

Poem Form: *Limerick Sequence*

Great for building fluency and exploring rhythm and rhyme.

◎ Student Activities
ACTIVITY 1: Find the Pattern

• Count the lines and syllables in one limerick.

• Clap out the rhythm. What makes it feel playful or lyrical?

ACTIVITY 2: Symbol Spotting

• Choose one limerick. What symbol appears (the tree, ring, friends)?

• What does it stand for?

ACTIVITY 3: Write a "Token Limerick"

Write a limerick about one character's offering.

Example Starter:

There once was a flute from a storm...

It played as the tree took its form...

ACTIVITY 4: Compare Poetic Tone

• How does the tone of these limericks differ from the more serious poetry (like the sonnet in Chapter 4)?

ANCHOR CHART

What Makes a Gift Meaningful?

Character	What They Gave	Why It Mattered
Scatter	A small pebble	It reminded her she wasn't alone
Tusker	Shed skin	Showed she had grown and endured
Ernie	A note from a lost friend	Honored memory and connection
Henry	His favorite treat (eventually!)	Showed he could overcome temptation

Mini Discussion Prompt:

What would YOU give to show who you are becoming?

EXIT TICKET PROMPTS

• "What did Scatter learn about leadership today?"

• "What is one lesson the Tree of Life teaches all of them?"

• "If you could ask the Queen Bee one question, what would it be?"

7

THE DESERT OF NO RETURN

🔥 TEACHER'S ANNOTATED GUIDE

📖 CHAPTER OVERVIEW – CHAPTER 7: *THE DESERT OF NO RETURN*

In this chapter, the heroes step into the unforgiving terrain of the Desert of No Return—a vast and blistering expanse where illusion threatens truth, and resilience is tested at every step. With each mile under the scorching sun, the group's unity begins to fray. The desert plays tricks on their senses, leading them toward danger disguised as salvation.

Henry's disappearance after chasing what he believes is a cooling oasis strikes a devastating blow to morale, underscoring the harsh reality of their journey. Yet even in grief, the remaining heroes press on, carrying with them the weight of loss and the determination to fulfill their quest. The chapter emphasizes how legends become legacy, and how survival is as much a battle of the mind as it is of the body.

Proverb Focus: "The Sun is the King of Torches."

Themes: Survival • Loss • Resilience • Illusion vs. Reality • Legacy

☞ LEARNING OBJECTIVES

By the end of this chapter, students will:
• Visualize setting and tone using descriptive language
• Analyze how characters face internal and external challenges
• Explore symbolism and figurative language (e.g., mirage, sentinels)
• Interpret metaphor and mood to deepen theme understanding
• Use sequence and cause-and-effect to track events

📖 VOCABULARY + MORPHOLOGY TIE-IN – CHAPTER 7

These words reinforce key emotional and environmental elements of the desert setting and the characters' mental and physical struggles. Use the breakdowns below to support decoding, word-building, and deeper understanding.

Mirage
From Latin *mirari* ("to wonder at" or "to look at")
Definition: An optical illusion, often appearing as water in the distance.
Tie-In: Talk about times when something looked real but wasn't. Why might the desert play tricks?

Scorching
Root: *scorch* (to burn) + Suffix: *-ing* (ongoing action)
Definition: Extremely hot or burning
Class Activity: Ask students to act out or describe "scorching heat" using body language and sensory words.

Treacherous
Root: *treach* (betray) + Suffix: *-erous* (full of)
Definition: Full of hidden danger; not to be trusted
Connection: Compare to the predators' deceptive plans in previous chapters.

Vanished

Root: *vanish* (to disappear) + Suffix: *-ed* (past tense)

Definition: Disappeared suddenly or mysteriously

Prompt: "What's the difference between someone who *left* and someone who *vanished*?"

Sentinels

Root: *sentire* (Latin: "to watch or feel") → *sentinel* (a guard)

Definition: Watchers or guards (here, used metaphorically to describe trees)

Imagery Prompt: "If a tree is a sentinel, what might it be guarding?"

ACTIVITY:

Use a "Desert Word Wall" to illustrate each word with an image and quote from the text.

◆ MINI-LESSON SPOTLIGHT: CHAPTER 7

Chapter Title: The Desert of No Return

Essential Focus: Perseverance, illusions, and emotional resilience

LEARNING OBJECTIVE

Students will explore how physical hardship mirrors emotional struggle, and how internal strength, unity, and storytelling help characters overcome loss.

VOCABULARY IN CONTEXT

1. Mirage – "Henry chased the water, but it was a mirage—only sand."

2. Scorching – "The scorching heat made every step feel like a trial."

3. Sentinel – "Dead trees stood like sentinels, silent and still."

4. Vanished – "Henry vanished into the dunes—gone, without a trace."

5. Treacherous – "The desert's beauty was treacherous, masking danger."

🐘 READ-ALOUD GUIDANCE

Read Tusker's story of the **Silent Caravan** aloud with a slow, mysterious tone. Emphasize phrases like:

"The desert is alive…"

Discussion Pause:

💬 "What do you think Tusker means by that?"

🎤 "How do her words prepare the others—and us—for Henry's fate?"

💬 DISCUSSION PROMPTS

• Why do you think Henry chased the mirage?

• How do Ernie and Scatter react to his disappearance?

• What's the role of storytelling in surviving a place like the desert?

📢 STUDENT ACTIVITY
"Dear Henry" Letter Writing

Write a letter from Scatter to Henry after his disappearance. What would she say? How does she feel? Students can write from Ernie's or Tusker's point of view if they choose.

OPTIONAL EXTENSION
Create Your Own Cinquain

After analyzing the provided cinquains, students create their own to express a moment in the desert (e.g., seeing a mirage, facing a storm, comforting a friend).

Use this pattern:

1. Noun
2. 2 Adjectives
3. 3 Verbs
4. A phrase
5. Final noun (synonym or reflection)

READING COMPREHENSION STRATEGIES

Before Reading:
• What dangers might a desert hold for travelers?
• What does it mean when something is "too good to be true"?
• What is a mirage? Have you ever *thought* you saw or believed something that turned out to be untrue?

During Reading:
• How does the desert test the group's trust in each other?
• What role does music and storytelling play in their survival?
• Pause after Henry first jokes about the mirages. Ask: "Why do you think he's laughing?"
• As Tusker tells the legend of the Silent Caravan, ask: "How does this story help the team understand the desert?"

After Reading:
• Why does Henry disappear? What does this teach the group?
• What do the "Red Dunes of Time" symbolize in the story?
• What do the heroes learn about themselves—and their limits?

CHARACTER ANALYSIS

Scatter – Leads through heartbreak; refuses to lose hope.

Henry – Brave and funny, but vulnerable to desire and distraction.

Ernie – Watchful and wise, provides warnings and guidance.

Tusker – Shares ancestral knowledge, inspires with stories and calm leadership.

Prompt:
"What did each character learn about themselves in the desert?"

· · ·

⟳ CAUSE AND EFFECT

Cause: The heroes remember the Tree of Life's lessons.
Effect: They find strength in unity and adapt through hardship.
Cause: Henry chases a mirage.
Effect: He vanishes, showing the power of illusion and distraction.
Cause: Tusker shares her personal story.
Effect: The team gains emotional insight and guidance.

✦ FIGURATIVE LANGUAGE & SYMBOLISM

- **The Desert** – Trials of the unknown, internal fears
- **The Mirage** – False hope, distraction from purpose
- **Red Dunes of Time** – Memory, legacy, the weight of history

Discussion Prompt:
"What does it mean that 'the desert is alive'?"

▤ LITERARY ELEMENTS TO HIGHLIGHT

- **Mood Shifts:** From hopeful → tense → grieving → determined
- **Foreshadowing:** "We must be like the desert—always adapting."
- **Setting as Character:** The desert influences every moment of the plot

▥ ELA STANDARDS ALIGNMENT (GRADE 4)

- **RL.4.1** – Explain character decisions with evidence
- **RL.4.2** – Identify theme and summarize
- **RL.4.3** – Describe setting and its influence on plot
- **RL.4.4** – Interpret metaphor and figurative vocabulary
- **RL.4.6** – Explore different points of view

❧ EXTENSION IDEAS

97

• Creative Writing:

Write a letter from Scatter to Henry after his disappearance. What would she say?

• Science Tie-In:

Study mirages, survival in desert ecosystems, or the behaviors of real animals like honey badgers and elephants.

• Drama/Performance:

Act out Tusker's story of the Silent Caravan using shadow puppets or dramatic reading.

EXIT TICKET PROMPTS

• "What did the desert teach the heroes?"
• "Why do you think Henry ran toward the mirage?"
• "How will the group change after losing Henry?"

✍ FLUENCY & LITERARY FOCUS – *CHAPTER 7: THE DESERT OF NO RETURN*

📖 Fluency Tips

• Select students to read the section where Henry disappears as a dramatic reading. Practice pausing and pacing to reflect tension.

• Use echo reading for the opening cinquains to build rhythm and tone.

📚 Literary Focus

• **Symbolism** – The desert becomes a living character: unpredictable, unforgiving, and wise.

• **Mood & Tone** – Help students notice how tone shifts from awe to fear to sorrow.

• **Foreshadowing** – Tusker's story and Ernie's warnings build anticipation for Henry's fate.

SUMMARY SHEET

☑ **Chapter 7: The Desert of No Return — One-Page Summary Sheet**

CHAPTER TITLE: THE DESERT OF NO RETURN

Main Setting: Shifting sands, ancient dunes, blazing sun

Key Themes: Illusion vs. Truth, Endurance, Loss, Memory

▧ SHORT SUMMARY:

Scatter and her companions enter the scorching *Desert of No Return*, where mirages test their minds and survival instincts. With guidance from Ernie and stories from Adira, they push forward, singing to keep their spirits high. Along the way, Tusker tells stories of ancient wanderers and shares her wisdom from the *Caverns of the Ancients*. The sands shift, illusions form, and Henry tragically chases a mirage—vanishing before their eyes. Despite heartbreak and exhaustion, the remaining trio continues, fueled by love, memory, and purpose. As they pass the Red Dunes of Time, they know the Mountains of the Moon await.

◕ COMPREHENSION FOCUS:
- What do the mirages symbolize?
- How does the desert test their beliefs and resolve?
- How do legends and past wisdom help them survive?

◔ MAIN CHARACTERS EXPANDED:
- **Tusker:** Shares the "Silent Caravan" legend and her own childhood rite
  - **Henry:** Lost to a mirage, symbolizing the cost of distraction

- **Scatter:** Endures pain and guilt but shows true leadership
- **Ernie:** Balances hope and caution while navigating by air

KEY VOCABULARY WORDS:
- *Mirage* – An illusion caused by heat, often mistaken for water
- *Whirlwind* – A sudden, spiraling wind, symbolic of chaos
- *Endurance* – The ability to keep going despite hardship
- *Wanderers' Whirl* – Mythic desert storm said to be caused by spirits
- *Instinct* – Natural internal guidance (used symbolically in this chapter)

NOTABLE QUOTES:
"The desert changes to protect its secrets." — Tusker

"Each grain of sand reminds me of those who didn't make it back." — Scatter

"We must be like the desert—always adapting." — Tusker

LOOK FOR IN ILLUSTRATIONS:
- Tusker under the desert moon, recalling ancient wisdom
- The mirage Henry runs toward—beautiful but false
- The glowing red dunes marking the passage of time
- The heroes' silhouettes shrinking against the endless desert horizon

REFLECTION QUESTIONS

Class Discussion / Reflection Prompts

CHAPTER 7 – THE DESERT OF NO RETURN

The team journeys through the harsh, magical desert. They learn about illusions, memories, and loss. Henry is taken by a mirage, leaving the team heartbroken but determined.

Reflection Prompts:

1. **What do the mirages in the desert represent in the story? Have you ever believed something that wasn't really true?**

2. **Tusker says, "To survive, we must understand the desert's mysteries." What does this mean, and how can it apply to real life?**

3. **Henry is lost to the mirage. What do you think he learned during his time away from the group?**

4. **Scatter promised, "We will survive." What keeps people strong even when something sad or scary happens?**

Token Earned:

Truth   Courage   Self-Worth

(Draw or explain your token below)

ANCHOR CHART: *WHAT TESTS A HERO?*

Create a classroom visual titled:

What Tests a Hero?

Subtitle: Facing the Desert Within

Chart Sections:

- **Physical Challenges** (heat, exhaustion, mirages)
- **Mental Challenges** (fear, doubt, illusions)
- **Emotional Challenges** (loss, guilt, leadership under grief)

At the bottom, a reflective box:

"What challenge in your life tested your courage most?" (Students add sticky notes)

✂ TEACHER TOOLS & PLANNING SNAPSHOT – CHAPTER 7

❓ Essential Question
What does the desert teach us about resilience and illusion?

⏳ Teaching Time Estimate
• 60–75 minutes (ideal across 2 sessions)

🔄 Flex Tip
• If short on time, focus on the mirage scene and Tusker's flashback—these carry the emotional and symbolic weight of the chapter.

📙 Differentiation Tip
• Provide a *mirage vs. reality* graphic organizer for ELL or visual learners.

• For advanced students: Write a monologue as Henry from "inside the mirage"—what might he see or think?

✍ CER WRITING (CLAIM–EVIDENCE–REASONING)

📝 Differentiated CER Worksheet – Chapter 7
Title: *The Desert of No Return*

Prompt: *What lesson did Scatter and her friends learn from their journey through the desert?*

📣 CLAIM
✏ I believe that Scatter and her friends learned that

BECAUSE

📚 EVIDENCE
✏ In the story it says,

. . .

WHICH SHOWS THAT

ANOTHER EXAMPLE IS WHEN

REASONING
✎ This shows that

BECAUSE

IT MEANS THAT

✅ CHECKLIST
✓ I made a clear **claim**
✓ I gave **evidence** from the text
✓ I **explained** how my evidence supports my answer

BONUS CHALLENGE
Draw the Mirage:
Illustrate the moment Henry saw the mirage.
• What did it look like?
• What emotions do you think Henry felt?
✐ My sketch:
[Blank space]
✎ Caption:

🖼 TEACHER ANSWER KEY – CER SAMPLE (CHAPTER 7)
📣 CLAIM:
I believe Scatter and her friends learned that they must rely on each other and not give in to illusions or fear.

📚 EVIDENCE:

In the story it says, "Henry ran toward what he thought was water—but it was just a mirage, and then he vanished."

Another example is when Tusker says, "The desert is alive. We must adapt to it and to ourselves."

REASONING:

This shows that they learned how dangerous it is to act on false hope and how important it is to think clearly and stay together.

It means that unity, focus, and trusting their instincts helped them survive even after losing someone they cared about.

POETRY PACK FOCUS ACTIVITY FOR CHAPTER SEVEN:

✏️ Poem Text:

🏔️ Cinquain 1:

Desert,
Vast, harsh,
Whispering, shifting, testing,
Hides its deep secrets,
Expanse.

🐍 Cinquain 2:

Sand dunes,
Endless, red,
Rolling, towering, daunting,
Challenge the bravest hearts,
Silence.

🏹 Cinquain 3:

Journey,
Tough, long,
Walking, enduring, hoping,
Seeking paths never found,
Quest.

🐾 Cinquain 4:

Heroes,
United, strong,
Supporting, believing, striving,
Facing fears together,
Band.

STUDENT POETRY ACTIVITIES

ACTIVITY 1: CINQUAIN SHAPE DETECTIVES

• A **cinquain** has **5 lines** and a special rhythm of words.
Label each line in one cinquain:

1. _____ (One noun)
2. _____ (Two describing words)
3. _____ (Three action words)
4. _____ (A sentence or strong phrase)
5. _____ (One synonym or final word)

Try this for *Cinquain 1*!

ACTIVITY 2: PICTURE IT!

Pick your favorite **Cinquain** and **draw** what it describes.
• What do you see?
• What colors, shapes, or feelings come to mind?
Sketch or describe it here:

ACTIVITY 3: SECRET MESSAGE

Each Cinquain hides a deeper **feeling** or **lesson**.
• What lesson about bravery or teamwork does Cinquain 4 (Heroes) teach?
Write your answer:

. . .

ACTIVITY 4: CREATE YOUR OWN DESERT CINQUAIN

• Write a brand-new **cinquain** about a desert, a challenge, or a feeling from an adventure.

Use this guide:

1. One noun (topic)
2. Two adjectives (describing)
3. Three action verbs (doing)
4. A short phrase about it
5. A synonym or new word for your topic

Start yours here:

ACTIVITY 5: WORD POWER!

Circle powerful words from the original poem that show:

• **Movement:**
• **Feeling:**
• **Bravery:**

(Hint: Look at action verbs like *whispering, enduring* and feeling words like *daunting, striving*.)

TEACHER TIP (SMALL PRINT)

☑ **Standards Alignment:**

• Structure and Pattern in Poetry (Cinquain Rules)
• Inferencing (finding hidden meanings)
• Descriptive Language Practice

☑ **Science of Reading Focus:**

• Vocabulary Development (adjectives, verbs)
• Written Expression (original cinquains)

BONUS IDEA:

Create a **Cinquain Chain** — every student writes one cinquain, and you connect them in order to form a giant class "Journey Through the Desert" poem! 🌵

✵ 8 ✵
THE MOUNTAINS OF
THE MOON

📖 TEACHER'S ANNOTATED GUIDE

Chapter Overview – *The Mountains of the Moon*
As the heroes ascend the Mountains of the Moon, the physical climb mirrors their emotional and spiritual journeys. The thin air, breathtaking views, and dreamlike visions challenge them to reflect on who they are becoming and what truly drives their quest. The mountain is more than a setting—it's a metaphor for transformation, identity, and purpose.

At this midpoint in the novel, inner growth becomes as important as outer action. Dreams and exhaustion blur the line between magic and memory. Each character confronts their past and future as the journey reaches a turning point.

Themes: Transformation • Identity • Reflection • Resilience • Inner Vision

Proverb Connection: *Not all who wander are lost... especially when climbing.*

☾ **LEARNING OBJECTIVES**

- Decode multisyllabic vocabulary through morphology
- Read aloud with emotion and phrasing
- Infer character growth through dream symbolism
- Connect personal experiences to narrative themes
- Analyze metaphor and figurative meaning

📖 VOCABULARY + MORPHOLOGY TIE-IN – CHAPTER 8

These vocabulary words support comprehension of symbolic and emotional elements in the mountain setting. Morphology connections help students decode meaning from root parts and relate words to character experience.

Majestic

Root: *maj* (Latin *magnus*, meaning "great") + Suffix: *-estic* (adjective, possessing the quality of)

Definition: Grand, awe-inspiring in beauty or presence

Prompt: "What places or people feel *majestic* to you?"

Resilient

Root: *re-* (again) + *silire* (Latin, "to leap or spring")

Definition: Able to recover quickly from difficulty; bouncing back

Discussion Prompt: "When have you had to be resilient, even when you felt tired or afraid?"

Enchantment

Prefix: *en-* (to cause or put into) + Root: *chant* (to sing/speak with power) + Suffix: *-ment* (state or condition)

Definition: The state of being under a magical or emotional spell

Activity: Compare "enchantment" in magical stories vs. the feeling of being enchanted by a place or memory.

Breathtaking

Root: *breath* + Verb: *take* + Suffix: *-ing* (continuous action)

Definition: So beautiful or powerful that it takes your breath away

Partner Prompt: "Describe the most breathtaking thing you've ever seen."

◆ MINI-LESSON SPOTLIGHT: CHAPTER 8

Chapter Title: The Mountains of the Moon
Essential Focus: Identity, transformation, and inner strength through dream trials

▨ LEARNING OBJECTIVE

Students will analyze how symbolic dreams reveal character growth and connect personal strengths to leadership and resilience.

▧ VOCABULARY IN CONTEXT

1. Majestic – "The Mountains of the Moon stood majestic, cloaked in silver mist."
2. Enchantment – "The mist curled around them like a soft enchantment."
3. Resilient – "Even after climbing for days, they remained resilient."
4. Ascend – "To ascend the Mountain of Dreams is to climb inward as well as up."
5. Trial – "Each dream was a trial—one they had to pass to understand themselves."

▨ READ-ALOUD GUIDANCE

Choose one dream scene to read dramatically (Scatter in the library is a great pick for modeling voice, pacing, and tone). Encourage students to close their eyes and visualize as they listen.
Prompt:
　◥ "How does this dream help Scatter understand herself better?"

. . .

💬 Discussion Prompts
- What did each hero learn from their dream?
- How do the dreams blend their animal and human selves?
- Why do you think they had these dreams after climbing?

✏️ Student Activity
Dream Reflection Map

Students create a split-page reflection: one side shows the dream (drawn or described), the other shows what it teaches about the character's strengths.

Optional Extension
Mini-Monologue Writing

Write a short "I learned…" speech from the perspective of Scatter, Ernie, or Tusker after waking from the dream. Encourage use of metaphor and emotional tone.

🌙 COMPREHENSION GUIDE – *THE MOUNTAINS OF THE MOON*

📖 Before Reading
- What do mountains usually represent in stories or legends?
- What do you expect a "Mountain of Dreams" to be like?

📖 During Reading
- Pause when each character begins to dream—ask: *"What might this dream be showing them?"*
- Highlight sensory language: What do they feel, see, hear in the mountain air and mist?

🌄 After Reading
- What do the heroes learn from their dreams?

. . .

• WHY IS THIS PLACE CALLED THE *VALLEY OF DREAMS*? WHAT DOES it mean to each hero?

  • Why does the mountain affect each character differently?

  ✒ Activity: *Dream Match* – Students pair each dream to a character insight.

🎙 FLUENCY & LITERARY FOCUS

• **Fluency Target**: Practice reading with expressive tone, especially during dream scenes and reflective narration.

  • **Literary Focus**: Metaphor, symbolism, and character interiority are central in this chapter.

  • **Dramatic Reading Idea**: Assign roles for dream dialogue (Scatter, Tusker, Ernie, Narrator). Encourage dreamlike pacing, whispering tones, and pauses to mirror the mysterious mood.

  • **Mini-Workshop**: Explore how authors use **setting as mood**—discuss how the mist, stars, and mountain wind affect the characters' feelings.

  • **Challenge Option**: Have students write a **mini-monologue** from one character's dream point-of-view.

🎙 FLUENCY PRACTICE

- Assign roles for dream sequences: Scatter, Ernie, Tusker, Narrator
- Practice dreamlike tone: slower pacing, whispering intonation
- Reader's Theater with a fluency rubric that includes tone, emphasis, and post-reading comprehension

🌐 SCHEMA BUILDING

- Discuss mountain symbolism in literature (e.g. *The Alchemist, Lord of the Rings*)
- Show photos of the Rwenzori Mountains
- Talk about sacred mountains in Indigenous and African cultures

Formative Assessment Ideas

- Exit Ticket: "One thing I learned from a dream was..."
- Think-Pair-Share: "Who grew the most on the mountain?"
- Interactive Journal: "Write or draw your own 'mountain moment.'"

Differentiation Ideas

- Emerging Readers: Use visual aids and sentence starters
- Mid-Level: Guided story maps for emotional arc tracking
- Advanced: Students write dream sequences for new characters

SoR Integration Summary

- Vocabulary: Word-building and morphology
- Fluency: Dreamlike prosody practice
- Comprehension: Inferring emotional arcs
- Schema: Parallels to real-world symbolism
- Text Structure: Identifying metaphors and foreshadowing

TEACHER TIP

Model how fiction reveals truths through dreams and metaphor. Invite students to reflect on a time their thoughts or dreams helped them grow—just like the heroes.

❦

CHAPTER SUMMARY SHEET

Main Setting: Misty peaks, star-filled summits, rugged cliffs

Key Themes: Self-discovery, Dreams, Unity, Ancestral Guidance

SHORT SUMMARY:

After surviving the Desert of No Return, Scatter, Ernie, and Tusker reach the mystical *Mountains of the Moon*. Exhausted but hopeful, they scale steep paths where the air is thin, the wind is fierce, and the stars feel close enough to touch. That night, at the summit, they fall into a magical sleep. Each of them experiences a powerful **Dream Trial**, blending their human and animal selves. Through visions of past struggles, future hopes, and ancestral echoes, they gain clarity about their identities and destinies. They awake wiser, stronger, and more united, ready to continue their journey to Ugalla.

COMPREHENSION FOCUS:

• How do dreams reflect their inner struggles and growth?
• What do the mountain's trials teach about identity & unity?
• What role does memory and culture play in their trans-formation?

. . .

MAIN CHARACTERS EXPANDED:

- **Scatter/Zara:** Learns that her quiet nature and intelligence are her superpowers
- **Tusker/Maya:** Discovers true leadership lies in nurturing others, not control
- **Ernie/Malik:** Embraces his vision and creativity as strengths in guiding others
- **Henry/Jalen:** In a separate dream, finds resilience through both athletic skill and emotional growth

KEY VOCABULARY WORDS:

- *Ascend* – To climb or rise upward, especially physically or spiritually
- *Trial* – A challenge or test of one's abilities or beliefs
- *Dual nature* – A combination of two identities (human/animal)
- *Enlightenment* – Gaining deep insight or understanding
- *Dream Trial* – A vision quest that reveals deep personal truths

NOTABLE QUOTES:

"The mountain didn't call us here just to quit." — Scatter

"It showed us who we are. What we can become." — Tusker

"My dreams felt so real… I think the mountain was teaching us something." — Ernie

LOOK FOR IN ILLUSTRATIONS:

- The winding climb to the summit, lit by starlight
- Animal-human blended forms revealing their deeper selves
- The Mountains of the Moon Token
- The tranquil *Valley of Dreams* appearing as they descend

📖 ✎ REFLECTION QUESTIONS

The heroes reach the Mountain of Dreams. They each experience a magical dream revealing their inner strengths and deepest fears.

✎ REFLECTION PROMPTS:

1. ᶻᶻ **Each hero had a dream showing their human and animal forms. What would your dream show about your greatest strength?**

2. 📖 **Scatter realizes her quietness is a strength. Have you ever discovered something about yourself that you didn't see as special at first—but later did?**

3. 🏔 **Why do you think the Mountain of Dreams waited until the top to give them their dreams? What does this say about hard journeys?**

4. **Ernie says, "It showed us who we are. What we can become." What do you think this means?**

🌑 **Token Earned:**

🔴 Friendship   Self-Worth   🔴 Leadership

(Draw or explain your token below)

✗ TEACHER SNAPSHOT – CHAPTER 8

? Essential Question

What do our dreams and challenges teach us about who we are becoming?

⏳ Teaching Time Estimate

60–80 minutes (spread over two days is ideal)

📖 Differentiation Tip

Let students rewrite a dream sequence in comic form for visual learners.

Advanced: Compare the dreams to vision quests or spiritual journeys in world cultures.

ANCHOR CHART – "WHAT MOUNTAINS TEACH US"

Title: *What Mountains Teach Us*
  Subtitle: *Climbing Up = Growing Inside*
  Chart Sections:
  Physical Climb
• Exhaustion
• Cold
• Wind
• Steep trails
  Inner Climb
• Doubt
• Loss (Henry)
• Dreams of identity
• Letting go of fear
  Lessons Gained
• Unity
• Purpose
• Discovery
• Wisdom
  Prompt: "What's a 'mountain' in your life that taught you something important?" Add sticky notes. Create a wall of learning!

CER WRITING – THE MOUNTAINS OF THE MOON

Prompt: What lesson did the heroes learn from their dreams on the Mountain of Dreams?

CLAIM

  I believe the heroes learned that understanding their strengths and emotions helps them become true leaders...

EVIDENCE

  In the story, Scatter dreams of a giant library and realizes that her quietness is a strength.

Another example is when Ernie learns that his creative vision can guide others like an artist.

REASONING

This shows that the mountain helped each of them embrace who they really are.

It means that leadership doesn't always look the same—it can be quiet, creative, strong, or wise.

✅ Checklist

✔ I made a strong claim

✔ I used two examples from the text

✔ I explained how the dream taught them something

DIFFERENTIATED CER VERSION (WRITERS NEEDING SUPPORT)

Prompt: What did the heroes learn from the Mountain of Dreams?

CLAIM

I believe the heroes learned that_____

because_____

EVIDENCE

One example is when_____

ANOTHER EXAMPLE IS_____

REASONING

This shows that _____

IT MEANS THAT _____

POETRY PACK ACTIVITY SHEET - ACROSTIC POEM

✏ Poem Text:
🏔 Acrostic Poem: MOUNTAINS

Majestic peaks touch the sky,
Offering challenges, high and dry.
Under stars, they whisper old tales,
Navigating through their rugged trails.
Trails that twist, turn, and ascend,
Above the world, they seem to suspend.
Inspiring those who dare to climb,
Nurturing dreams, transcending time.
Secrets held in their misty embrace, beckoning the brave to chase.

⊚ STUDENT POETRY ACTIVITIES

ACTIVITY 1: Find the Hidden Word!

An **acrostic** poem spells a word vertically.
• What hidden word does this poem spell?
• Write it here: _____

ACTIVITY 2: POETRY DETECTIVE

Look at each line.
• **Which line** describes the feeling of adventure?
• **Which line** describes nature and beauty?
Write your answers:
Adventure line:

NATURE/BEAUTY LINE:

ACTIVITY 3: DRAW YOUR MOUNTAIN

Using words from the poem (*majestic, twist, ascend, misty*), **draw** a mountain scene.

• Include stars, trails, and anything else from the poem!

Sketch here or describe your drawing:

ACTIVITY 4: Write Your Own Acrostic!

Pick a new adventure word (like **Courage**, **Climber**, or **Summit**) and write your own **acrostic poem**.

Here's your frame:

C _____

O _____

U _____

R _____

A _____

G _____

E _____

(*Choose your own word if you want! Creative points!*)

ACTIVITY 5: Word Hunt!

Circle powerful words that show:

• **Movement:**

• **Feeling:**

• **Nature:**

Teacher Tip (Small Print)

☑ **Standards Alignment:**

• Poetry Structure (Acrostic form)

• Visualization and Descriptive Language

☑ **Science of Reading Focus:**

• Vocabulary Expansion (adventure and nature terms)

• Comprehension and Creative Writing

Bonus Idea:

Have students **build a class "Mountain of Words"** — each person writes one line describing a mountain adventure, and you "stack" them on the wall into a giant paper mountain! 🏔️🖐️

❊ 9 ❊
UGALLA

 TEACHER'S ANNOTATED GUIDE

CHAPTER OVERVIEW:

This chapter is intentionally brief and transitional. It introduces *Ugalla* as a new home and sets a tone of relief and arrival. Thematically, it offers a moment of reflection. Teachers may use this moment to:

- Reinforce themes of perseverance and journey
- Revisit character growth so far
- Ask: "What have the characters earned by this point?"

Optional activity: Create a class "travel map" tracing their journey from Wakaduo to Ugalla.

❦

Chapter Title: The Kingdom of Ugalla

Main Setting: The lush Valley of Dreams within Ugalla, surrounded by cliffs and forests

Key Themes: Homecoming, Leadership, Secrets, Broken Trust, New Alliances

◆ MINI-LESSON SPOTLIGHT: CHAPTER 9

Chapter Title: The Kingdom of Ugalla

Essential Focus: Leadership, betrayal, and the cost of survival

📖 LEARNING OBJECTIVE

Students will examine themes of broken trust and the tension between instinct and loyalty, while exploring complex emotions like guilt and forgiveness.

📚 VOCABULARY IN CONTEXT

1. Alliance – "An alliance between Wakaduo and Ugalla could restore peace."

2. Betrayal – "Scatter's heart broke when she learned of Ernie's betrayal."

3. Reconvene – "Gurr called the predators to reconvene under moonlight."

4. Instinct – "Ernie's predator instinct had returned—without warning."

5. Forgiveness – "Forgiveness would not come easily—perhaps never."

🐾 READ-ALOUD GUIDANCE

Dramatically read Scatter's confrontation with Ernie:

"How could you eat my parents and pretend to be my friend?"

Then ask:

◌ "How would you feel if you were Scatter? Or Ernie?"

· · ·

⏤ DISCUSSION PROMPTS

• Can someone still be trusted after a big mistake? Why or why not?

• What do you think Ernie is feeling in this chapter?

• How does Gurr's leadership compare to Tusker's or Scatter's?

✎ STUDENT ACTIVITY

CER: Can Ernie Still Be Trusted?

Use the provided CER graphic organizer. Students will make a claim, support it with evidence from the text, and explain their reasoning.

ꞏ OPTIONAL EXTENSION

Class Debate

Split the class into two groups. One side argues "Ernie can still be trusted," the other says, "He can't." Use respectful dialogue and evidence to support claims.

ꞏ COMPREHENSION FOCUS:

• What does leadership look like when faced with betrayal?

• How do characters rebuild trust after it is broken?

• What does it mean to belong to a home or community?

ꞏ MAIN CHARACTERS EXPANDED:

• **Scatter:** Her heart is broken by Ernie's betrayal, but she remains determined to lead

• **Ernie:** Revealed to have relapsed into predator instinct—his guilt is overwhelming

• **Tusker:** Voices concern about Ugalla's eerie stillness; her wisdom continues to anchor the group

• **Gurr:** Majestic lion leader torn between past loyalty and future survival

• **Undavu:** Strong lioness who questions Gurr's bold plan and references Tau's power

✦ KEY VOCABULARY WORDS:

• *Alliance* – A formal agreement or friendship between groups for mutual benefit
• *Betrayal* – Breaking someone's trust or confidence
• *Reconvene* – To come together again for a purpose
• *Predator instinct* – The natural impulse to hunt or feed on other animals
• *Ruaha* – A distant kingdom, mysterious and ruled by the legendary lion, Tau

✦ NOTABLE QUOTES:

"Nothing has come back from Ruaha." – Gurr
"How could you eat my parents and pretend to be my friend?" – Scatter
"We must be clever, brave, and outsmart Tau." – Gurr
"This valley should be teeming with life." – Tusker

✦ LOOK FOR IN ILLUSTRATIONS:

• The tranquil but eerie Valley of Dreams
• Tusker spraying Scatter with soil

☑ SUMMARY SHEET

Main Setting: The lush Valley of Dreams within Ugalla, surrounded by cliffs and forests
Key Themes: Homecoming, Leadership, Secrets, Broken Trust, New Alliances
▨ Short Summary:

After surviving the Mountains of the Moon, the heroes arrive in *Ugalla*, a serene and lush valley filled with waterfalls, green meadows, and ancient trees. They are welcomed by **Gurr**, a noble lion chief with scars of wisdom and regret. While Gurr speaks of restoring lost unity between their lands, a deeper problem is revealed—**the land is too quiet**, and **the animals are missing**.

When Scatter investigates, she uncovers a tragic betrayal: **Ernie has eaten a fellow mouse**. Her faith in him is shattered. Meanwhile, Gurr secretly gathers the **remaining predators** of Ugalla, forming a plan to reconnect with Wakaduo and outmaneuver the feared ruler of Ruaha, **Tau the Mighty**. Two missions now run in parallel: one group heading back to Wakaduo with urgent news, the other toward Ruaha. Unity will be tested, and secrets will force hard choices.

▉ ⚖ REFLECTION QUESTIONS

The group arrives in Ugalla, believing they've found paradise—but something is wrong. Shadows stir, and trust is tested.

⚖ REFLECTION PROMPTS:

1. 🐚 **Scatter feels something is wrong in Ugalla. Have you ever had a feeling that something wasn't right, even if it looked perfect on the outside? What did you do?**

2. 🦉 **Ernie breaks Scatter's trust. Can someone still be good if they make a mistake? What would you say to Scatter or Ernie right now?**

3. 🐾 **Gurr tells the group about past connections and broken friendships. Why is it important to heal old wounds between groups?**

4. 🐾 **What makes someone a real leader? Gurr is wise, but his land is struggling. What kind of leader would you be in his place?**

🌑 **Token Earned:**

● Empathy   ● Wisdom   ● Forgiveness
(Draw or explain your token below)

ॐ

CER. CLAIM—EVIDENCE—REASONING ACTIVITY

Prompt: *Can Ernie still be trusted after his mistake?*

CLAIM
What do you believe?
✎ Sentence starter:
I believe that Ernie (**can / cannot**) still be trusted because...

EVIDENCE
Find something from the story that supports your thinking.
✎ Sentence starters:
• In the chapter, it says...
• One example is when...
• The author shows that...

REASONING
Explain how your evidence proves your claim.
✎ Sentence starters:
• This shows that...
• This proves that...
• This means...

QUICK CHECKLIST
☑ Did I answer the question clearly?
☑ Did I use a quote or detail from the story?
☑ Did I explain why that detail matters?

· · ·

☑ Teacher Answer Key – Sample Responses

📣 Sample CLAIM:

I believe that Ernie **can still be trusted** because he felt truly sorry and didn't try to hide what he had done.

—or—

I believe that Ernie **cannot be trusted again** because he broke a sacred bond and hurt someone who believed in him.

📚 Sample EVIDENCE:

In the chapter, Scatter finds out that Ernie ate another mouse, and he doesn't deny it. He says, "I didn't mean for it to happen."

—or—

The author shows that Ernie looks away in shame when Scatter confronts him. He stays silent and does not fight back.

Sample REASONING:

This shows that Ernie is aware of his mistake and feels guilty, which means he might learn and change.

—or—

This proves that his predator instinct is still too strong. It means he could hurt others again, even without meaning to.

10

GURR

▣ TEACHER'S ANNOTATED GUIDE

CHAPTER OVERVIEW

As the group reaches Ugalla, a place of ancient wisdom and emotional reckoning, the story shifts again. Betrayal, silence, and heavy truths challenge the group's bond. Ernie's actions lead to questions about trust and forgiveness. Gurr's presence is powerful, yet quiet—a lesson in leadership without dominance.

LEARNING OBJECTIVES
- Analyze mood, conflict, and theme
- Use morphology to decode vocabulary (e.g. betrayal, alliance)
- Infer motivation and predict consequences
- Connect to proverbs about trust and leadership
- Practice expressive reading of dialogue

▉ VOCABULARY AND MORPHOLOGY TIE-IN FOR CHAPTER 10

Vocabulary Focus

- **Challenge** – A test of strength or ability.

  Ask: "What kind of challenges push us to grow?"

- **Instinct** – A natural feeling or reaction.

  Use animal behavior examples: "Why do birds fly south?"

- **Courage** – The ability to do something brave, even when afraid.

  Prompt: "How is courage different from fearlessness?"

- **Confront** – To face something directly, especially a fear or enemy.

  Use a roleplay: "What does it feel like to confront someone?"

Morphology Tie-In

- **Challenge**

  Root: *calx* (Latin, meaning "to compete or strive")

  Suffix: *-enge* (forms a noun from a verb or adjective)

  → A thing that invites competition or demands effort.

- **Instinct**

  Prefix: *in-* (within)

  Root: *stinguere* (Latin: "to prick" or "to incite")

  → A feeling or urge that arises from within.

- **Courage**

  Root: *cor* (Latin: "heart")

  Suffix: *-age* (forming abstract nouns)

  → From the heart; bravery.

- **Confront**

  Prefix: *con-* (together, face-to-face)

  Root: *front* (Latin *frons*: "forehead" or "face")

  → To face directly, often with intensity.

📘 VOCABULARY FOCUS WITH ROOT WORK

- *Sentinel* – Root: "sent" (to watch)
- *Alliance* – Root: "alli" (to bind)
- *Betrayal* – Root: "tray" (to hand over)

📌 Mini Activity: Word sort into "trust" and "betrayal" categories with context clue definitions.

◆ MINI-LESSON SPOTLIGHT: CHAPTER 10 - GURR

Theme: *Trust, Leadership, and Hidden Truths*

✒ *Objective:*

Students will analyze how trust is built and broken in relationships. They'll explore symbolism and interpret Gurr's character through text evidence and poetic tone.

📖 *Quick Teach: Symbolism + Inference*

1. Opening Quote Discussion:

"Wisdom is like a baobab tree; no one individual can embrace it."

➤ *Prompt:* What do you think this proverb means? How does Gurr represent this idea?

2. Symbol Focus:

- ○ **Gurr's scars** = experience and past pain
- ○ **The silent valley** = loss, mystery, broken bonds
- ○ **Scatter's twitching tail** = intuition, warning, foreshadowing

3. Mini Text Analysis Prompt:

"Scatter's breath caught in her throat... Her stomach twisted. 'No… no, this can't be right.'"

➤ What has just happened? What does this moment show about betrayal?

4. Short Write Activity:

✎ *Write a short journal entry from Scatter's point of view after seeing Ernie. Include how her feelings have changed and what she thinks of leadership now.*

▌ FULL COMPREHENSION GUIDE FOR CHAPTER 10 – *GURR*

Before Reading

• Preview the setting: Ask students what kind of places feel "forbidden" or off-limits.

• Introduce the concept of fear vs. respect in wild environments.

• Ask: "What might make a creature both terrifying and respected at the same time?"

During Reading

• Pay attention to the group's reactions to the unknown sounds and sights.

• Track the descriptive language used for Gurr. What words or phrases create suspense?

• Highlight how the group sticks together — or splits — under pressure.

After Reading

• Discuss what Gurr represents symbolically — is it just a creature or something more?

• Ask: "How did the heroes face fear in this chapter?"

• Reflect: How do stories use mythical creatures to teach courage?

⚲ COMPREHENSION PROMPTS

- Inference: What do Gurr's scars tell us?
- Prediction: Will Ernie be forgiven?
- Visualization: Describe Ugalla's eerie quiet.
- Assessment: Write a paragraph predicting how Tau will respond next.

▌ FLUENCY & LITERARY FOCUS

• **Narrative Fluency**: This chapter's poem, "The Tale of Gurr," is a narrative poem rich in pacing, emotion, and dialogue. Assign verses to students to practice reading with expression and rhythm.

• **Tone Practice**: Focus on Gurr's solemn yet inspiring tone, Scatter's heartbreak, and Ernie's guilt. Use choral reading to contrast the beginning's peace with the ending's tension.

• **Literary Craft Focus**:

– **Foreshadowing**: "No one has returned from Ruaha..."

– **Metaphor**: "Wisdom is like a baobab tree; no one individual can embrace it."

– **Symbolism**: The ring's twitching, the quiet valley, and the scarred lion represent unspoken danger and deep history.

• **Optional Performance**: Readers' Theater script adapted from Gurr's speech and Scatter's confrontation with Ernie.

⌀ DIFFERENTIATION IDEAS

- Struggling Readers: Use simplified summaries and cause/effect visuals
- ELL Students: Use labeled images for key terms (baobab, betrayal)
- Advanced Readers: Debate—Should Ernie be forgiven or exiled?
- Artistic Learners: Create an emotion map for Scatter's evolving trust

🧠 SKILLS TRACKING (SCIENCE OF READING)

• Fluency: Reader's Theater with emotional range
• Vocabulary: Morphology quizzes and sentence writing
• Comprehension: Plot diagramming
• Schema: Compare leadership styles (Gurr vs. Tau)
• Literary Structure: Setting shift and foreshadowing

• • •

🌐 CROSS-CURRICULAR CONNECTIONS
- Science: Baobab trees and African ecosystems
- History/Social Studies: Study Nelson Mandela or Wangari Maathai's leadership
- Writing: Journal entry from Ernie's perspective

📌 ASSESSMENT IDEAS
- Exit Ticket: "What does the proverb teach us about Gurr's leadership?"
- Debate Reflection: Should Ernie be trusted again?
- Think-Pair-Share: How do emotions impact leadership?

🔁 CAUSE & EFFECT

• **Cause**: The heroes arrive in Ugalla after a long journey.
  Effect: They are welcomed by Gurr and learn about the kingdom's past and current struggles.
  • **Cause**: Scatter senses something wrong and follows her instincts.
  Effect: She discovers Ernie eating a mouse, shattering her trust in him.
  • **Cause**: Gurr gathers the remaining predators of Ugalla.
  Effect: He reveals a secret plan to rejoin Wakaduo and resist Tau's growing influence.
  • **Cause**: The group is shaken by Ernie's betrayal.
  Effect: Their unity falters, and tension builds as two missions begin—one returning to Wakaduo, the other venturing toward Ruaha.

📜 SUMMARY SHEET - GURR

Main Setting: The lush Valley of Dreams within Ugalla, surrounded by cliffs and forests

Key Themes: Homecoming, Leadership, Secrets, Broken Trust, New Alliances

📖 SHORT SUMMARY:

After surviving the Mountains of the Moon, the heroes arrive in *Ugalla*, a serene and lush valley filled with waterfalls, green meadows, and ancient trees. They are welcomed by **Gurr**, a noble lion chief with scars of wisdom and regret. While Gurr speaks of restoring lost unity between their lands, a deeper problem is revealed—**the land is too quiet**, and **the animals are missing**.

When Scatter investigates, she uncovers a tragic betrayal: **Ernie has eaten a fellow mouse**. Her faith in him is shattered. Meanwhile, Gurr secretly gathers the **remaining predators** of Ugalla, forming a plan to reconnect with Wakaduo and outmaneuver the feared ruler of Ruaha, **Tau the Mighty**.

Two missions now run in parallel: one group heading back to Wakaduo with urgent news, the other journeying toward Ruaha. Unity will be tested, and secrets will force hard choices.

🐚 COMPREHENSION FOCUS:
- What does leadership look like when faced with betrayal?
- How do characters rebuild trust after it is broken?
- What does it mean to belong to a home or community?

🐾 MAIN CHARACTERS EXPANDED:
- **Scatter:** Her heart is broken by Ernie's betrayal, but she remains determined to lead
- **Ernie:** Revealed to have relapsed into predator instinct—his guilt is overwhelming
- **Tusker:** Voices concern about Ugalla's eerie stillness; her wisdom continues to anchor the group
- **Gurr:** Majestic lion leader torn between past loyalty and

future survival

• **Undavu:** Strong lioness who questions Gurr's bold plan and references Tau's power

✾ Key Vocabulary Words:

• *Alliance* – A formal agreement or friendship between groups for mutual benefit
• *Betrayal* – Breaking someone's trust or confidence
• *Reconvene* – To come together again for a purpose
• *Predator instinct* – The natural impulse to hunt or feed on other animals
• *Ruaha* – A distant kingdom, mysterious and ruled by the legendary lion, Tau

✐ Notable Quotes:

"Nothing has come back from Ruaha." – Gurr
"How could you eat my parents and pretend to be my friend?" – Scatter
"We must be clever, brave, and outsmart Tau." – Gurr
"This valley should be teeming with life." – Tusker

⚲ Look For in Illustrations:

• Gurr: a lion with silver in his mane and eyes full of story
• The tranquil but eerie Valley of Dreams
• Scatter discovering Ernie's shocking act
• Undavu, a fierce lioness, raised her concerns

📖 ⚴ REFLECTION QUESTIONS / PROMPTS

The heroes speak with Gurr, the leader of Ugalla. They learn about Ruaha, an ancient rival land, and Gurr's plan to reconnect the broken kingdoms—even if it means risking everything.

✍ REFLECTION PROMPTS:

1. 💀 **Gurr speaks of Tau the Mighty. What makes a ruler strong—fear, wisdom, or kindness? Why?**

2. 🔄 SCATTER'S TAIL SENSES CHANGE. **WHAT DO YOU THINK IT means? Have you ever felt a strong instinct or "gut feeling"? What did it tell you?**

3. 💔 WHAT SHOULD SCATTER DO NOW THAT HER TRUST IN ERNIE **is broken? Can friends repair trust after it's been lost? How?**

4. 🛶 GURR PLANS TO TAKE A DANGEROUS RIVER ROUTE BACK TO **Wakaduo. What would YOU do if you had to choose between safety and a bold mission to help others?**

🌑 TOKEN EARNED:
⚫ Leadership   ⚫ Wisdom   ⚫ Forgiveness
(Draw or explain your token below)

৩✕৩

POETRY PACK ACTIVITY - NARRATIVE POEM

🖊 **Poem Text:**
📜 **Narrative Poem: The Tale of Gurr**
In the heart of lush Ugalla's land,
Where trees like sentinels proudly stand,
Came heroes weary, their journey grand,

To meet Gurr, the leader, whose presence was planned.
Gurr, with mane like the silver night,
Scars from battles, old plights,
His voice deep, eyes alight,
Welcomed friends to share their sight.
They spoke of travels, of fears they quelled,
Of deserts crossed and mountains felled,
Gurr listened close, his heart swelled,
Stories of unity, a future upheld.
But as night's cloak drew ever near,
Gurr's tales of sorrow bore a tear,
"Hard times have found us, year to year,
Together, perhaps, we'll conquer fear."
Scatter stepped forward, heart aglow,
"Teach us, Gurr, so we too may know,
How together, stronger we grow,
And from this land, let kindness show."
Gurr nodded, wisdom in his gaze,
Spoke of old ties, in brighter days,
"Hardships shared, and friendly ways,
Let's weave anew our alliance's rays."
As moonlight danced on leaves above,
Gurr and heroes pledged their love,
To blend their strengths, push and shove,
And rise united, like stars above.

STUDENT POETRY ACTIVITIES

ACTIVITY 1: STORY STARTER
This poem tells a **story**.
- Who is the main character?

_____

- What is Gurr's main problem?

_____

- How does the group decide to solve it?

ACTIVITY 2: FEEL THE MOOD

How does the **mood** of the poem change from beginning to end?

Beginning   mood:

Ending   mood:

ACTIVITY 3: GURR'S WISDOM

If Gurr could give the heroes **one piece of advice** for the future, what would it be?

Write it in a speech bubble!

Gurr   **says:**

ACTIVITY 4: WORD PLAY

Find **powerful words** that show:
- **Strength** _____
- **Friendship**

_____

- **Challenge**

_____

Now use one of these words to write your own sentence about teamwork!

TEACHER TIP (SMALL PRINT)

✅ **Science of Reading Focus:**
- Text Comprehension (story elements through poetry)
- Vocabulary and Fluency Building

THE RETURNING HEROES

Teacher's Annotated Guide
📖 Chapter 11 – The Returning Heroes
Proverb Focus: *"Patience is the mother of a beautiful child."*

📖 CHAPTER OVERVIEW

This transitional chapter reveals the heroes not arriving home, but beginning their *return*—a return filled with deeper internal growth, continued threats, and critical decisions. Tau and his predators lie in wait, and Henry's dramatic return foreshadows the importance of listening to instinct, trusting visions, and choosing the harder—but wiser—path. The Swamp of Mists becomes a metaphorical and literal turning point.

◎ LEARNING OBJECTIVES

Students will:
- Define unfamiliar words using context and morphology
- Analyze character growth and motivation

• Interpret literary symbolism and foreshadowing
• Connect the chapter's themes to real-life dilemmas
• Engage in structured response writing using text evidence

📚 VOCABULARY + MORPHOLOGY FOCUS

Tier II Vocabulary Words

1. Honor – Respect earned through good actions
➤ Prompt: "What's something someone did that earned your respect?"

2. Journey – A long trip with meaningful personal change
➤ Prompt: "Have you ever changed during a personal journey—even if it wasn't physical?"

3. Loyalty – Staying faithful to someone or something
➤ Prompt: "What does loyalty look like in friendship or teamwork?"

4. Pride – A sense of satisfaction or dignity in oneself or others.
➤ Prompt: "When is pride helpful? When might it cause problems?"

Morphology Tie-In
• **Honor**
Root: *honor* (Latin, meaning "esteem, respect")
→ A timeless value, often tied to character and integrity.
• **Journey**
Root: *diurnum* (Latin for "daily") → *jour* (Old French "a day")
→ Originally a day's travel; now, a long or meaningful trip.
• **Loyalty**
Root: *loyal* (Old French *loial*, Latin *legalis*: lawful)
Suffix: *-ty* (forms nouns)
→ The state of being lawful or devoted.
• **Pride**
Root: *prūd* (Old English *prūd*, "brave, gallant")
→ A strong sense of self-worth or achievement.

🪨 Vocabulary Focus

- *Resonate* – re + sonare (to sound)
- *Guile* – trickery, from French
- *Resolve* – re + solv (to loosen or decide)

📌 Strategy: Students create "antonym cards" for words like guile/honesty, resonate/silence.

◆ MINI-LESSON SPOTLIGHT: THE RETURN BEGINS

Theme Focus: Redemption, Facing the Unknown, Leadership Growth

🎯 Lesson Goal:

Students will evaluate what it means to lead during uncertain times. They will analyze how Henry's return and Scatter's vision symbolize redemption and resolve.

Teaching Moves:

• *Proverb Analysis*: "Patience is the mother of a beautiful child."

➤ Ask: How does this connect to Henry's long return and the group choosing the harder path?

• *Character Comparison*

○ **Henry**: From isolation → loyalty, urgency, belonging

○ **Scatter**: From witty follower → intuitive, bold leader

• *Turn & Talk*:

➤ "What would you do if a safer path might hurt more people in the long run?"

♫ FLUENCY & LITERARY FOCUS

🎤 Fluency Practice

• Free verse poem: *Echoes of the Wild*

➤ Assign by stanza for choral performance

• Tone modeling:

○ **Henry**: Breathless, emotional and urgent

○ **Tau**: Measured and threatening

○ **Scatter**: Calm but commanding

🎙 Fluency Practice:

Free verse is meant to sound natural and emotive. Encourage students to use:
- · ∘ Pauses for effect
- · ∘ Rising tone in lines with hope or fear
- · ∘ Slower pacing for mystery and danger

📖 LITERARY CRAFT FOCUS

• Symbolism
- ∘ *Swamp of Mists* → fear of the unknown, testing courage
- ∘ *Wonder Hole* → unavoidable confrontation before transformation
- ∘ *Tau's silence* → deceptive calm

• Foreshadowing Lines
- ∘ "Let them believe they are safe." – Tau
- ∘ "The mist whispers to you." – Ernie

• Free Verse Features
- ∘ Imagery and rhythm: "Laughter weaves through the trees"
- ∘ Repetition of mood changes through nature metaphors: "The earth speaks in soft murmurs"

🔍 FULL COMPREHENSION GUIDE

Before Reading
- • Ask: *"What does it take to return a hero—not just to survive, but to be welcomed back?"*
- • Introduce: The idea of *re-entry* and emotional reintegration.
- • Prompt: "What might it feel like to return to your home after a big challenge?"

During Reading
- • Track how each character reacts to danger and change.
- • Highlight Henry's transformation.
- • Use guided questions:

➤ "Why is the group hesitant about the swamp?"
➤ "What does Henry's return say about loyalty?"

After Reading

• Ask: *"Do you think the group made the right choice by taking the harder path?"*

• Discuss: *"What personal challenges lie ahead based on this chapter?"*

COMPREHENSION MINI-LESSONS

- Inference: What do Henry's actions tell us about loyalty?
- Prediction: What might the swamp symbolize?
- Summarization: Track Henry's return and Scatter's leadership development

Strategy Tip: Support with sentence frames; challenge with metaphor analysis.

SCHEMA CONNECTIONS

- Compare the "Dance of the Wild" to predator-prey behavior in nature
- Explore stories of personal change, forgiveness, or emotional growth

Optional: Read African folktales about returning heroes and wisdom earned.

SYMBOLISM & STRUCTURE

- Symbol: Swamp = uncertainty, hidden truth
- Foreshadowing: Tau's patience + ghost voice = trouble ahead
- Setting Contrast: Peaceful return vs. looming danger

📌 Anchor Chart: Draw and label the symbolic meanings in the swamp and "Dance of the Wild."

🔄 CAUSE & EFFECT

• **Cause**: Ernie spots predators hidden near the river route.

Effect: The heroes abandon their original plan and consider a riskier path.

• **Cause**: Scatter has a dream that shows the Swamp of Mists as an alternative.

Effect: The group decides to take the swamp route despite its dangers.

• **Cause**: Tau instructs his predators to wait and observe.

Effect: The heroes unknowingly walk into deeper peril, giving Tau time to strike.

• **Cause**: Henry reunites with the group and confirms the threat is real.

Effect: The group is reassured in their decision to avoid Tau and take the longer way home.

• **Cause**: The Wonder Hole blocks the only passage to the swamp.

Effect: The heroes must face Grootslang, the ancient guardian, to continue their journey.

📊 ASSESSMENTS

- Exit Ticket: "Why did Scatter choose the harder path?"
- Journal: "What will happen in the Swamp of Mists?"
- Vocabulary Match: Word → Root → Context Sentence

🧩 DIFFERENTIATION STRATEGIES

- Emerging Readers: Audio support, sentence frames
- On-Level: Role-play scenes

- Advanced: Thematic essays on change, redemption, or resilience

Cross-Curricular Extensions
- Science: Wetland ecosystems and adaptation
- Drama: Voice tone in readers' theater
- Writing: Letter or journal entry from Henry to Scatter

REFLECTION QUESTIONS

- How does patience shape leadership?
- What does it mean to return as a hero—not just once, but again?

☑ THIS LESSON SUPPORTS RL.4.1, RL.4.3, RL.4.4, AND RF.4.4 and integrates all SoR domains through expressive reading, vocabulary development, and theme analysis.

❧

📖 SUMMARY SHEET - THE RETURNING HEROES

Main Setting: Traveling near the Ruaha Wetlands and Wonder Hole
Key Themes:
- Loyalty and Redemption
- Leadership Through Instinct
- Courage in Choosing the Unknown
Short Summary:
The heroes begin their journey home but face new threats—Tau's predators lie in wait, and the Ugalla River route is no longer

safe. Scatter leads the group toward the mysterious Swamp of Mists after receiving a dream-vision. Meanwhile, Henry returns just in time to warn the group. Their emotional reunion strengthens their resolve. As they near the Wonder Hole, the team prepares to face the legendary Grootslang to reach their new path.

COMPREHENSION FOCUS:
- How do individuals grow through hardship and forgiveness?
- What does it mean to earn back someone's trust?
- Why is choosing a hard path sometimes the right thing to do?

MAIN CHARACTERS EXPANDED:
- **Scatter:** Leads with quiet strength, still recovering emotionally from Ernie's betrayal
- **Ernie:** Tries to regain the group's trust by protecting them and using his sharp senses
- **Henry:** Returns as a stronger, more loyal version of himself after being separated
- **Tusker:** Serves as emotional support and wisdom-keeper for the group
- **Tau the Mighty (off-screen):** A looming threat whose forces are hunting silently

KEY VOCABULARY WORDS:
- *Reconvene* – To gather again after being apart
- *Loyalty* – Being faithful to a person, group, or cause
- *Reconnaissance* – Secret scouting to gather information
- *Treason* – Betraying trust or loyalty, esp. to a leader or group
- *Pathfinder* – Someone who finds or chooses a new way forward.
Notable Quotes:
"I followed the voice... and it led me back to you." – Henry

"Trust is like water in the desert. Hard to find. Easy to spill." – Ernie

"We can't run forever. The swamp is waiting... and so is the truth." – Scatter

"Home isn't just a place. It's the people we fight for." – Tusker

🌲 Look For in Illustrations:

• The group huddled near Lake Nyasa, mist rising around them

• Ernie flying above, spotting predators in the jungle

• Henry sprinting through the brush, eyes wide with relief

• A fork in the path showing the decision to enter the **Swamp of Mists**

• Tau's glowing eyes watching silently from the forest shadows

• The heroes silhouetted against the swamp fog, stepping forward into the unknown

📖 ✍ REFLECTION QUESTIONS

Theme: Loyalty, Trust, and Choosing the Harder Path

🗨 *"Patience is the mother of a beautiful child."*

Reflection Prompts:

1. Henry came back to warn the others, even though he feared they might not accept him. When have *you* had to be brave even when you weren't sure people would understand?

2. The group decides to take the Swamp of Mists instead of the river, even though it's harder. Why is doing the right thing sometimes more difficult?

3. Tau said, "Let them believe they are safe." What makes false safety dangerous? Can you think of a time you trusted something or someone that wasn't what it seemed?

4. How do you think the heroes are changing—not just physically, but emotionally?

🌑 **Token Earned:**

🔴 Bravery in Uncertainty

Draw or describe a moment when you had to take the hard path:

۞

✍ CER WRITING CHALLENGE

Prompt: Why did Scatter choose the Swamp of Mists over the river path?

🗣 **Claim**

✎ I think Scatter chose the Swamp of Mists because...

📚 **Evidence**

✎ One example is when she says...

✎ In the story it says...

Reasoning

✎ This shows that...

Because...

✎ THIS PROVES SHE...

☑ Checklist

✔ I made a clear claim

✔ I used specific evidence

✔ I explained my reasoning

📜 POETRY PACK

Title: *Echoes of the Wild*

Poetry Type: Free Verse

Poem Text:

Whispers on the wind,
Echoes of footsteps in the wild,
Heroes return, hearts bound,
With tales of courage, woven and compiled.
In the silence of their march,
A rhythm of resilience beats,

Under starry skies they arch,
Each step towards home, hope meets.
The earth speaks in soft murmurs,
A mother's lullaby to the weary,
They carry dreams, draped in fervor,
In their eyes, the light of query.
Their laughter weaves through the trees,
A tapestry rich with newfound ties,
They move with the grace of the evening breeze,
Under the watchful stars' guise.
Yet danger lurks, veiled in shadow,
Predators wait with bated breath,
The heroes' journey, far from shallow,
Tests their spirit, a dance with death.
Henry's return, a ripple in the calm,
His warning a thread in their woven fate,
Together they stand, a soothing balm,
United, they challenge the hands of fate.

POETRY ACTIVITIES
ACTIVITY 1: Visualize the Poem
Sketch the heroes' path through the wild.
Label: expressions, nature, emotions.
ACTIVITY 2: Feeling the Rhythm
List 3 emotional words from the poem's beginning, middle, and end.
 • Beginning: _____
 • Middle: _____
 • End: _____
ACTIVITY 3: Image Translation
Describe two vivid images from the poem in your own words.
 • Example: "Dance with death" = facing danger together
 • "Echoes of footsteps" = shared journey
ACTIVITY 4: Echoes of Courage Journal
Prompt: "Today we crossed the wild once more..."

Write 3–4 sentences from the POV of a returning hero.

ACTIVITY 5: Your Own Free Verse

Write 4–6 lines about a time you were brave or made a hard decision.

Starter: "The path was unclear, but I..."

TEACHER TIP (SMALL PRINT)
✅ Standards Alignment:

- Visualization and Mental Imagery
- Emotional Interpretation
- Creative Writing (Free Verse Structure)

✅ SCIENCE OF READING FOCUS:

- Deepening Text Comprehension
- Building Oral and Written Expression

BONUS IDEA:

🎧 Soundscape Challenge — Have students listen to natural sounds (wind, forest, water) and **create a mini "Echoes of the Wild" soundscape** to match the poem's mood!

❀ 12 ❀

THE WONDER HOLE

⬚ TEACHER'S ANNOTATED GUIDE

Proverb: "Do not stand in a place of danger trusting in miracles."

A call to action—courage, cleverness, and preparation, not blind hope, will guide the way.

CHAPTER OVERVIEW

The heroes encounter Grootslang, a mythic gatekeeper who tests their wisdom with a riddle. This moment pushes character development forward while establishing the Wonder Hole as a symbolic entry into the unknown. Scatter's insight and Grootslang's challenge prepare readers for the psychological terrain of the Swamp of Mists.

◉ LEARNING OBJECTIVES

• Analyze mythical motifs and character responses
  • Decode new vocabulary using morphological strategies

- Practice expressive reading through Reader's Theater
- Predict and infer using evidence from character interactions
- Reflect on wisdom vs. force as a central theme

▦ VOCABULARY AND MORPHOLOGY TIE-IN FOR CHAPTER 12: *THE WONDER HOLE*

Vocabulary Focus

- **Mystery** – Something that is unknown or hard to explain.
Use examples: "What's a mystery you'd like to solve?"
- **Depth** – Greatness in dimension or meaning (literal or symbolic).
Prompt: "Can feelings have depth?"
- **Discovery** – The act of finding something for the first time.
Ask: "What's something surprising you've discovered before?"
- **Ancient** – Very old or from long ago.
Use visuals: images of fossils, pyramids, etc.

Morphology Tie-In

- **Mystery**
Root: *mysterion* (Greek: "secret rite or doctrine")
→ Something hidden or not yet understood.
- **Depth**
Root: *deep* (Old English *dēop*)
Suffix: *-th* (forms abstract nouns)
→ The quality or state of being deep.
- **Discovery**
Prefix: *dis-* (opposite of, away)
Root: *cover* (from Latin *cooperire*, "to cover")
→ To uncover what was hidden.
- **Ancient**
Root: *ante* (Latin: "before")
Suffix: *-ent* (forms adjectives)
→ Belonging to a time long before now.

VOCABULARY FOCUS

Key Words: *ferocious, coiling, tremor, lurking, gleam*
  Strategies:
  • Use prefixes/suffixes to break down meanings
  • Create synonym webs
  • Fill-in-the-blank activities using student-constructed definitions

MINI-LESSON SPOTLIGHT: CHAPTER 12 - THE WONDER HOLE

Theme: *Cleverness Over Strength, Facing the Unknown*
  Objective:
Students will examine how riddles and myths reveal character values. They will interpret ballad structure and explore how Scatter's cleverness saves the group.
  Quick Teach: Riddles & Symbolism
  1. Essential Question:
Why did Grootslang test them with a riddle and not a battle? What does that say about her values?
  2. Close Read Line:
"A bottle! You look into a bottle's neck with one eye, but never two."
  ➤ What past moment helped Scatter solve this? What does this teach us about problem-solving?
  3. Riddle Craft Challenge:
  ➤ Students write their own mythical-style riddle using metaphor or personification.
  "I never speak, but you hear me every day. I'm loud in storms, quiet in shade. What am I?"
  4. Partner Talk:
  ➤ Do you think Grootslang was just a monster, or something more? What might she symbolize?
  5. Short Poem Response:
  Write 2 rhyming couplets about courage in a dark place.
  Example:

Beneath the rocks, where shadows creep,
We found our strength, not just to weep.

▌ FULL COMPREHENSION GUIDE FOR CHAPTER 12 – *THE WONDER HOLE*

Before Reading
• Activate curiosity: "What do you think a place called the Wonder Hole might be like?"
• Prompt students to imagine a magical place that shows people their truth.
• Ask: "What would you want to see if a place could show you something about yourself?"

During Reading
• Track each character's reaction to what they see in the Wonder Hole.
• Highlight descriptions of the space — how does the author create wonder and mystery?
• Ask: "Does the Wonder Hole give each character what they want or what they need?"

After Reading
• Discuss how the Wonder Hole helps each hero grow.
• Reflect: "What lesson would the Wonder Hole give *you*?"
• Extension: Create a short description of your own Wonder Hole — what it looks like and what it shows.

▌ FLUENCY & LITERARY FOCUS

Fluency Practice Tips:
• **Grootslang's voice**: Low, slow, menacing. Practice pauses between hisses or threats.
• **Scatter's speech**: Hesitant but determined—build volume and confidence as she finds the riddle's answer.
• **Group Reading Exercise**:
  ◦ Echo read key lines of the ballad ("Scatter stepped with a trembling heart...")

○ Reader's Theater for the riddle scene: Grootslang, Scatter, Henry, Ernie

LITERARY FOCUS TOPICS:
- **Genre**: *Ballad Poetry*—story in verse with rhyme and rhythm
- **Symbolism**:
  ○ *Grootslang* = Fear of the unknown / inner test
  ○ *The riddle* = The test of insight over strength
  ○ *Scroll of Mists* = Symbolic guide for emotional and mental growth
- **Foreshadowing**:
  ○ Grootslang's warning: "Remember the lessons learned here"
  ○ The mist waiting beyond: "Even bravery might not be enough"

FLUENCY PROMPTS
- Model Grootslang's voice—low, slow, eerie
- Pause dramatically after the riddle
- Practice emotional emphasis on key lines ("A bottle!")
- Group echo-read final scene for tone control

COMPREHENSION STRATEGY PROMPTS
- What does Grootslang value most?
- Why test instead of attack?
- What might the Swamp of Mists "change" in them?

Activity: *Riddle Writing & Symbol Mapping*

Students invent their own riddle that tests a moral trait.

SCHEMA CONNECTIONS
- Mythical guardians: Grootslang, Sphinx, Anansi
- Caves as metaphor: transformation, descent into the unknown
- Cultural comparisons to global legends

. . .

📚 LITERARY ANALYSIS FOCUS

• Wonder Hole = threshold into psychological and emotional testing
• Scroll of Mists = symbolic map of inner knowledge
• Grootslang = gatekeeper archetype

📊 ASSESSMENT IDEAS

Formative:
• Vocabulary sorting
• Fluency performance rubrics
• Predictive journals: "What will the Swamp of Mists do to the group?"

Summative:
• Written response: Wisdom vs. force
• Creative project: Design a guardian and riddle

🧩 DIFFERENTIATION STRATEGIES

• Visual: Annotated creature sketches
• Auditory: Partner reading with character voices
• Kinesthetic: Act out the riddle scene
• ELL: Word banks with visuals + sentence stems

🌐 CROSS-CURRICULAR CONNECTIONS

• Science: Cave systems and ecosystems
• Social Studies: Global riddle traditions
• SEL: Pressure, quick thinking, bravery under challenge

▥ SUMMARY SHEET

Chapter Title: The Wonder Hole

Main Setting: The cavernous Wonder Hole leading to the Swamp of Mists

Key Themes: Riddles and Wit, Courage Under Pressure, Teamwork, Respecting Power

▥ SHORT SUMMARY:

As the heroes enter the ominous Wonder Hole, they face Grootslang, an ancient and massive serpent who guards the way to the Swamp of Mists. With bravery, humor, and trust in each other, they navigate the dark cavern. When Grootslang challenges them with a riddle, the group's fate hinges on Scatter's ability to solve it. With a flash of insight, Scatter correctly answers: "A bottle." Impressed, Grootslang grants them passage and reluctantly surrenders the Scroll of Mists. The heroes emerge with new confidence and a sense of unity—just as a deeper threat, Gurr, moves closer to Wakaduo.

🧠 Comprehension Focus:

• Why is solving Grootslang's riddle important?

• How do the heroes use teamwork to overcome fear?

• What does the Scroll of Mists represent?

💀 Main Characters Introduced/Expanded:

• **Grootslang**: Ancient, intelligent guardian of the Wonder Hole, powerful and terrifying

• **Scatter**: Shows quick thinking and leadership under pressure

• **Tusker, Henry, Ernie**: Supportive allies with unique strengths and growing bonds

• **Gurr**: Foreshadowed as a looming rival, traveling toward Wakaduo

🧩 Key Vocabulary Words:

• Riddle – A tricky question or puzzle to test cleverness

• Scroll – A rolled-up piece of writing, often containing secret or ancient knowledge

• Courage – Bravery when facing fear

• Passage – A safe way through a dangerous place
• Guardian – A powerful being who protects a location or secret
✒ **Notable Quotes**:
• "Since time forgotten... What do you look in with one eye, but never with two?" — Grootslang
• "It's a bottle!" — Scatter
• "Go forth with the knowledge you seek, and remember the lessons learned here." — Grootslang
🔍 **Look For in Illustrations**:
• The glowing eyes of Grootslang in the cave's darkness
• Scatter solving the riddle with a memory of the potion bottle
• The Scroll of Mists glowing with a future promise

📖 ✍ REFLECTION QUESTIONS

Theme: Wit, Courage, and Facing the Unseen
🗣 *"Do not stand in a place of danger trusting in miracles."*
Reflection Prompts:
1. Grootslang challenges the heroes with a riddle. What does this moment teach us about the power of words, riddles, and clever thinking?
2. Scatter solves the riddle, but only by remembering her past. When has a memory helped you figure out something hard?
3. Even when afraid, the group jokes and teases each other. How can humor help in tough situations?
4. Grootslang gives them a warning: "Remember the lessons learned here." What lessons did the group learn in the Wonder Hole?

🌑 **TOKEN EARNED:**
⚫ Wisdom Under Pressure
What is one riddle or life lesson you'll never forget?

CAUSE & EFFECT

• **Cause**: The heroes approach the Wonder Hole to reach the Swamp of Mists.

Effect: They encounter Grootslang, a powerful guardian who blocks their path.

• **Cause**: Grootslang challenges the group with a riddle instead of attacking.

Effect: The heroes must rely on wit, not strength, to survive and continue.

• **Cause**: Scatter remembers the Queen Bee's potion and how she looked through the bottle.

Effect: She correctly solves the riddle and earns safe passage for the group.

• **Cause**: Henry teases Grootslang, demanding the Scroll of Mists.

Effect: Grootslang angrily tosses the scroll to them before disappearing.

• **Cause**: The heroes receive the Scroll of Mists.

Effect: They are now equipped with knowledge to face the dangers of the Swamp of Mists.

POETRY PACK ACTIVITY SHEET - BALLAD POEM

Poem Text:

Ballad Poem: The Ballad of the Wonder Hole

In the heart of darkness, where whispers hold,
Lies the fearsome cave of legends told,
The Wonder Hole, where secrets sleep,
Guarded by Grootslang, in shadows deep.
Our heroes brave, with hearts so bold,
Approached the cave where the wind blew cold,
With steps unsure, yet spirits high,
Underneath the cavern's watchful eye.

(... **Poem continues** — *see full version in Chapter 12!*)

@ STUDENT POETRY ACTIVITIES

ACTIVITY 1: HERO'S MOOD TRACKER

Color in the emotions the heroes feel through the poem!
(You can color more than once.)

- Brave
- Nervous
- Clever
- Excited
- Scared
- Confident

ACTIVITY 2: CREATE YOUR OWN RIDDLE

Grootslang asks a tricky riddle. Now **write your own riddle**!
Use the same style: something mysterious and hard to guess.
Example Starter:
"I have keys but no doors, I open no locks. What am I?"
Your Riddle:

ACTIVITY 3: CHARACTER SPOTLIGHT

Choose ONE hero (Scatter, Tusker, Ernie, or Henry).
Write 2–3 sentences describing how they help the group during
the adventure.
✎ **Hero's Name:** _____
How They Help:

ACTIVITY 4: RHYME TIME!

Ballads often use rhymes.
Find two sets of rhyming words from the poem:

• First Rhyming Pair: _____ & _____
• Second Rhyming Pair: _____ & _____
Then write **one new rhyming couplet** of your own!
Example Starter:
"Through the misty swamp they tread, / Dreams of hope inside their head."

※

✎ CER WRITING — ENRICHMENT

⬤ Mini CER Activity — **Wisdom vs. Force**

Question: Why was wisdom more powerful than force in the Wonder Hole?

📣 CLAIM

✎ *I believe wisdom was more powerful than force in this chapter because...*

📚 EVIDENCE

✎ *One example is when...*

✎ *Another part that shows this is...*

REASONING

✎ *This proves that...*

✎ *It means that...*

☞ TEACHER CER ANSWER KEY — WISDOM VS. FORCE

Question: *Why was wisdom more powerful than force in the Wonder Hole?*

☑ Sample CLAIM

I believe wisdom was more powerful than force in this chapter because it was clever thinking—not strength—that helped the heroes survive Grootslang's challenge.

✅ Sample EVIDENCE

One example is when Grootslang gives the group a riddle instead of attacking them.

Another part that shows this is when Scatter remembers the bottle and solves the riddle, which earns them safe passage.

✅ Sample REASONING

This proves that solving problems with your mind can be more effective than using physical power.

It means that wisdom, teamwork, and calm thinking helped the group succeed where force would have failed—and might have put them in danger.

⚜

TEACHER TIP (SMALL PRINT)

✅ Standards Alignment:
- Rhyme Identification
- Character Understanding
- Creative Writing (Riddles and Couplet Creation)

✅ Science of Reading Focus:
- Phonemic Awareness (Rhyming)
- Inference and Character Motivation

BONUS IDEA:

Role Play Challenge: Students act out the heroes facing Grootslang and delivering their riddle answers with *dramatic flair!*

✥ 13 ✥
THE SWAMP OF MISTS

▣ TEACHER'S ANNOTATED GUIDE

P**roverb**: "Show me your friends and I will show you your character."

CHAPTER OVERVIEW

The Swamp of Mists is both setting and symbol. The fog challenges the group emotionally and morally, revealing deep fears and fractured trust. The guardians' demand for truth or memory forces powerful sacrifices. This is a turning point for leadership, betrayal, and character transformation.

◎ LEARNING OBJECTIVES

• Analyze character decisions shaped by environment
  • Decode key vocabulary through morphology
  • Practice expressive tone during dramatic reading
  • Explore betrayal, sacrifice, and emotional growth
  • Make real-life connections to facing difficult truths

🔤 VOCABULARY FOCUS

Key Words: *murky, daunting, mistrust, eerie, character*
Strategies:
- Morphology breakdown of "daunting" and "mistrust"
- Use of emotion webs and "mood tracking" for each term

🐚 FLUENCY & PROSODY PROMPTS

- Read Swamp Guardian lines with eerie stillness
  - Ernie's confession: trembling, emotional
  - Scatter's response: layered anger and sadness
  Use echo reading and Reader's Theater for emotional pacing.

◆ CHAPTER 13 MINI-LESSON: "THE SWAMP OF MISTS"

Theme: *Facing Truth, Betrayal, and Emotional Growth*
🎯 Objective:
Students will explore the emotional journey of the heroes in the swamp. They'll analyze how fear, honesty, and trust are tested—and what it means to forgive or be forgiven.
🖼 Quick Teach: Emotional Truth & Symbolism
1. Proverb Anchor:
"Show me your friends and I will show you your character."
➤ *Discuss:* How does this proverb apply to Ernie, Scatter, and Henry?
2. Symbol Mapping Activity:
Match symbols to their deeper meanings:
Symbol
Meaning
Fog
Confusion / Illusion

MOONFLOWERS

Hope / Hidden guidance

THE GUARDIANS
Moral judgment / Memory vs. truth

ERNIE'S CONFESSION
Regret and redemption
3. Critical Thinking Question:
➤ *Why do you think the swamp forces the heroes to give something up—either a truth or a memory?*
4. Short Write Prompt:
✎ *If you had to choose between losing a memory or revealing a difficult truth, which would you choose—and why?*

🔍 COMPREHENSION STRATEGY GUIDE – CHAPTER 13

"The Swamp of Mists"
📖 Before Reading
• What do you think the swamp represents in the story? Why might the author place a major emotional challenge here?

• Look at the chapter title and poem. What do the words "whispers," "fog," and "truth" suggest about the kind of challenges the characters might face?

• Activate background knowledge: Have you read or seen stories with magical forests or swamps? What usually happens there?

Before Reading Question:

"The Scroll of Mists shows two paths—one safe and one dangerous. What do you think will happen if the heroes choose the wrong one? What kind of tricks or tests might the swamp use?"

📙 DURING READING

• Why do the Guardians ask the heroes to choose between *truth* and *memory*? What does this say about what the swamp values?

• Track how each hero responds to the swamp's challenges. What does their reaction reveal about their character?

• When Ernie confesses his past, what clues show how Scatter is feeling (both in words and actions)?

After Reading

• What lessons did the heroes learn in the swamp—about themselves and each other?

• Why does Scatter say the *right* path is the one that "doesn't feel safe"? What does this mean in real life?

• How has Henry grown as a character from the desert to the swamp?

COMPREHENSION FOCUS

• Inference: What drives each character's choices?
  • How do confession and forgiveness function in this scene?
  Activities:
  • Emotion Tracker
  • Motivation Map

SCHEMA CONNECTIONS

• Fog as a metaphor: confusion, uncertainty
  • Swamps in global folklore: Celtic, Yoruba
  • Emotional literacy: when truth is hard to face

LITERARY ANALYSIS FOCUS

• Symbolism: Fog = moral and emotional obscurity
  • Blue Orchid Moonflower = hope in darkness
  • Swamp Guardians = ethical gatekeepers
  • Foreshadowing: Grootslang's warning realized

Ⅲ ASSESSMENT IDEAS

Formative:
- Exit Ticket: "Truth or memory—which would you give up?"
- Inference Chart with quotes
- Vocabulary sort and sentence building

Summative:
- Short answer on theme of trust
- Creative diary entry from Scatter's POV

✿ DIFFERENTIATION STRATEGIES

- Visual: Moodboards + color-coded maps of emotion
    - Kinesthetic: Obstacle "fog walk" around the room
    - ELL: Simplified language supports and visual vocab
    - Advanced: Character arc tracking + literary essay

❧ FLUENCY & LITERARY FOCUS – CHAPTER 13

▶ Fluency Practice

Voice & Tone Roles:
- **Scatter:** mix of caution, inner strength, rising emotion (especially during confrontation with Ernie)
    - **Ernie:** regretful, hesitant, breathy tone when confessing
    - **Tusker:** grounded, protective, emotionally steady
    - **Swamp Guardians:** eerie, slow, whisper-like intonation; add echo if performing

Dramatic Pause Prompts:
- Pause before the Guardians speak their truth-or-memory ultimatum
- Use whispering tones to mirror the mist and tension in the setting
- Emphasize words like *"forgiveness," "truth,"* and *"borrowed"* with slowed pacing and emotional stress

Choral/Group Options:

• Group echo-read the repeated line: *"Nothing in the swamp is given. Everything is borrowed."*

• Assign one student as narrator, others as characters in Reader's Theater format

FLUENCY & PROSODY PROMPTS

• Read Swamp Guardian lines with eerie stillness
  • Ernie's confession: trembling, emotional
  • Scatter's response: layered anger and sadness
  Use echo reading and Reader's Theater for emotional pacing.

SUMMARY SHEET

Chapter Title: The Swamp of Mists

Main Setting: Fog-choked swamp filled with illusions, guardians, and emotional trials

Key Themes: Facing Fears, Truth vs. Illusion, Inner Strength, Forgiveness and Betrayal

Short Summary:

The heroes enter the eerie Swamp of Mists, a living maze of secrets and fear. Guided by the mysterious Scroll of Mists and glowing Blue Orchid Moonflowers, they face confusing illusions and haunting memories. The Swamp Guardians challenge their intent, demanding a "truth for passage." Henry confesses his feelings of not belonging. Later, the group is attacked by monstrous swamp creatures and a deadly Swamp Vulture. Help arrives from an unexpected ally—Harry the water mongoose. But the greatest blow comes when Ernie reveals he accidentally devoured Scatter's parents in a moment of predatory instinct. Devastated, Scatter rejects him, and the group's unity is shaken. The swamp tests not only their path —but their hearts.

Comprehension Focus:

- What does the swamp symbolize for each hero?
- Why is honesty essential in their journey?
- How does Scatter react to betrayal?

🦁 **Main Characters Introduced/Expanded**:

- **Scatter**: Emotionally tested, brave but broken by betrayal
- **Ernie**: Reveals a haunting truth about his past, seeking forgiveness
- **Henry**: Admits his insecurities, growing in emotional maturity
- **Swamp Guardians**: Mysterious beings who test intentions
- **Harry**: Water mongoose ally with impeccable timing and courage
- **Ugmo**: Vicious Swamp Vulture antagonist

🧩 **Key Vocabulary Words**:

- Illusion – A false appearance or idea
- Betrayal – Deep hurt from broken trust
- Redemption – Trying to make up for past wrongs
- Guardian – A being that protects sacred places or truths
- Vulnerability – Willingness to show deep feelings or fears

🪶 **Notable Quotes**:

- "We only seek passage." — Scatter
- "Leave behind a truth or lose a memory." — Swamp Guardian
- "You ate them?" — Scatter
- "The hardest battles… were the battles inside." — Narration

🔍 **Look For in Illustrations**:

- Mist-shrouded swamp glowing with blue flowers
- The Swamp Guardians cloaked in vines
- The Swamp Vulture lurking
- Ernie diving to tackle the attacking vulture

🪷

📖🖊 REFLECTION QUESTIONS

Theme: Truth, Forgiveness, and Facing Inner Demons

 "Show me your friends and I will show you your character."

Reflection Prompts:

1. The swamp tests each hero with illusions, fears, and hard truths. What truth would be hardest for *you* to face?

2. Ernie reveals a devastating secret. Do you think some mistakes can never be forgiven? Why or why not?

3. The Guardians of the Swamp say: "Nothing in the swamp is given. Everything is borrowed." What do you think this means?

4. Scatter says the real path doesn't feel safe. Why do you think the right choice is sometimes the scariest?

✐ SENTENCE STARTERS FOR REFLECTION QUESTIONS

1. The hardest truth I could face would be…

2. I think some mistakes can/can't be forgiven because…

3. "Nothing in the swamp is given" means to me that…

4. The right choice is sometimes scary because…

● TOKEN EARNED:

● Truthfulness and Emotional Strength

Write or draw a memory you would give up if you had to:

POETRY PACK ACTIVITY SHEET - NARRATIVE POEM

✎ Poem Text:

Narrative Poem: Whispers of the Swamp

In the heart of the forest, under moon's ghostly light,
Through twisted ironwood trees, past the edge of night,
Lies the Swamp of Mists, where secrets sleep tight,
And shadows dance with the fog's eerie sight.

(… **Poem continues** — *see full version in Chapter 13!*)

☀ STUDENT POETRY ACTIVITIES

ACTIVITY 1: Mood Map

The swamp has many moods! Match the lines below to the feeling they create:

Line from Poem
Feeling: Circle One

"Blue Orchid Moonflowers glow without a sound"
a) Hopeful b) Scary

"Shadows dance with the fog's eerie sight"
a) Excited b) Creepy

"Friends show their truth, and their character appears"
a) Brave b) Nervous

ACTIVITY 2: Sketch the Swamp

Use the description in the poem to **draw a quick sketch** of the Swamp of Mists:

What do you see?

What grows there?

What color is the light?

Sketch Area:

(*Leave a space for students to doodle or quick-draw!*)

ACTIVITY 3: Fog Words

The swamp is full of "whispers" and "fog."

Write 3 *foggy* words — soft, mysterious, or spooky-sounding words you think fit this place!

Example: misty, silent, cold

Your Words:

1.

2.

3.

. . .

ACTIVITY 4: STORY STARTER

Imagine you are standing in the Swamp of Mists.
Finish this story starter in **2–3 sentences**:
"Through the thick mist, I spotted a faint blue light..."

QUICK TEACHER TOOLS SNAPSHOT

Chapter 13: The Swamp of Mists

- **Essential Question:** What does it take to rebuild trust after betrayal?
- **Core Strategy:** Character motivation and emotional inference
- **Fluency Tip:** Read the Guardian dialogue with breathy stillness and measured timing
- **Focus Skill:** Vocabulary (daunting, betrayal), Symbolism (fog, blue flowers), Literary Mood
- **SEL Anchor:** Emotional self-awareness, conflict resolution
- **Flexible Extension:** Students write or perform a "fog trial" for a new hero—what would the swamp ask of *them*?

TEACHER TIP (SMALL PRINT)

Standards Alignment:
- Descriptive Language
- Mood and Setting Understanding
- Vocabulary Expansion

Science of Reading Focus:
- Text-to-Self Connections
- Visualization and Language Comprehension

BONUS IDEA:

Foggy Word Art: Students pick one fog word and design a spooky poster or mystery title using it!

❧ 14 ❧
TRAPPED AND TRICKED

🍎 TEACHER'S ANNOTATED GUIDE

Proverb: "No matter how many times you wash a goat, it will still smell like a goat."

CHAPTER OVERVIEW

In the Congo jungle, Gurr leads the Ugalla animals into danger, using strategy instead of brute strength. The group faces predators, river crossings, and moral challenges. Gurr reclaims Wakaduo through deception—but his methods cast doubt on whether he is truly worthy. Tau's shadow remains.

🎯 LEARNING OBJECTIVES

• Analyze motives, leadership, and ethical dilemmas
  • Decode multisyllabic vocabulary with morphology
  • Visualize setting and suspenseful tone
  • Explore symbolism in proverbs and natural elements
  • Predict next steps based on plot clues

📚 VOCABULARY + MORPHOLOGY FOCUS

Proverb Focus: "Even the clever can be fooled."

🔤 Key Vocabulary Words
- **Ambush** – (n.) a surprise attack
- **Deceive** – (v.) to make someone believe something that is not true
  - **Lure** – (v.) to tempt or attract someone to a trap
- **Instinct** – (n.) a natural or automatic way of behaving or reacting
  - **Escape** – (v.) to get away from danger or confinement

🧬 MORPHOLOGY TIE-IN

1. Deceive
- **Prefix:** *de-* (down, away from)
- **Root:** *-ceive* (from Latin *capere* = to take or seize)
- **Related Words:** deceive, perception, receive, accept

🔖 **Mini-lesson:** Have students build a web of words from the *-ceive/cap-* family and explore how their meanings relate to "taking."

2. Instinct
- **Prefix:** *in-* (in or into)
- **Root:** *stinct* (from Latin *stinguere* = to prick or goad)
- **Related Words:** instinctive, extinguish, distinct

🔖 **Discussion Prompt:** What does it mean for something to come from "within" or to be a natural reaction?

3. Ambush
- **Prefix:** *am-* (from *amb-* meaning around)
- **Root:** *-buschier* (Old French, "to hide in the bushes")
- **Related Words:** bush, shrubbery (surprise from hiding)

🔖 Have students draw a scene labeled "ambush," and use context clues from the chapter to describe what happens in one.

4. Lure
- Often used as both noun and verb
- Related to *lure* in fishing: bait or trap

☞ **Writing prompt:** Ask: How was Tricker lured into danger? How might someone avoid being lured?

5. Escape
- **Prefix:** *es-* (from Latin *ex-* = out)
- **Root:** *-capere* (to seize, take)

☞ **Connection Point:** Escape = to be "taken out of" danger. Relate to *deceive*, which shares the same Latin root.

✎ **VOCABULARY ACTIVITIES**

- **Root Word Puzzle:** Provide root pieces (*cap*, *ceive*, *in*, *de*, *per*) and have students build real words with definitions.

- **Flipbook of Traps:** Students draw each vocabulary word in a scene (e.g., *ambush*, *lure*), then write a short caption.

- **"True or Trick" Sorting Game:** Read scenarios aloud— students hold up "Truth" or "Trick" signs depending on whether deception is involved.

◆ CHAPTER 14 MINI-LESSON: "TRAPPED AND TRICKED"

Theme: *Sacrifice, Strategy, and Leadership in Crisis*

◎ **Objective:**

Students will evaluate Gurr's leadership decisions and the consequences of desperate choices. They'll examine cause and effect, character traits under pressure, and how trust and strategy shape outcomes.

▣ QUICK TEACH: STRATEGY & COURAGE UNDER PRESSURE

1. Proverb Anchor:

"No matter how many times you wash a goat, it still smells like a goat."

➤ *Ask:* What does this say about changing behavior—or not? Does Gurr change, or stay true to himself?

2. Cause & Effect Sorting Activity:

Match these:

◦ Cause: Gurr distracts the hunters → Effect: His band escapes on rafts

◦ Cause: River's raging current → Effect: Gurr nearly dies fighting Tiger Fish

◦ Cause: Tomba leads the group → Effect: They reach Wakaduo

➤ Students create their own 4th cause-effect pair from the chapter.

3. Debate Circle Prompt:

➤ *Was Gurr brave or reckless when he sacrificed himself to distract the hunters?*

Use evidence from the chapter to argue either side.

4. Quick Reflection Write:

✎ *Describe a moment in this chapter that showed what kind of leader Gurr is. Would you follow him?*

📖 COMPREHENSION STRATEGY GUIDE

🔍 Before Reading

• Preview the title: *Trapped and Tricked.* What do you predict the "trap" might be? Who might be "tricked"?

• Discuss the proverb: "No matter how many times you wash a goat…" — What might this mean about someone pretending to be something they're not?

• Activate prior knowledge: What do you know about jungle environments or animals that might live in places like the Congo?

Before Reading Question:

"Gurr's group is entering Wakaduo, but not honestly. What do you think might happen when the heroes return and discover he's taken over? Will there be a battle, or something else?"

📕 During Reading

• How does Gurr's leadership change when danger increases? What does that show about his character?

• What clues foreshadow that the takeover of Wakaduo might not be heroic?

• How do the animals' reactions during the river crossing show fear, loyalty, or courage?

▣ After Reading

• Gurr uses strategy instead of fighting. Was that the right choice? Why or why not?

• What do you think Tau will do when he hears Gurr took Wakaduo?

• Do you think Gurr deserves to be called king? Why or why not?

🐾 COMPREHENSION STRATEGY PROMPTS

• What are Gurr's deeper motivations?

• Predict how Tau will respond to the takeover

• Text-to-self prompt: "Have you ever trusted a leader you weren't sure about?"

🌐 SCHEMA CONNECTIONS

• Tropical jungle and river dangers

• Predatory behavior in the wild and in politics

• Proverb discussion: can people truly change?

📚 LITERARY ANALYSIS FOCUS

• Symbol: The river = transformation and survival

• Proverb = essence of character remains the same

• Foreshadowing: "What about Tau?" sets up next conflict

🐾 FLUENCY & LITERARY FOCUS – CHAPTER 14

🎭 Fluency Performance Focus

• **Gurr's Dialogue**: Practice two tones—(1) calm and calculated (leader), (2) intense and threatening (takeover scene).

- **Undarvu**: Worried and maternal; her lines can be read with soft urgency.
- **Raft scene**: Group echo reading of action lines like *"Get to the rafts!"* with crescendo pacing.

📚 Literary Devices in Focus

- **Foreshadowing**: "What about Tau?" subtly hints at future conflict.
- **Symbolism**:
  - **River** = transformation, risk, no return
  - **Boulder of Passage** = trust, gateway to change (or deception)
- **Irony**: Wakaduo's safety becomes its weakness when Gurr uses trickery to enter.

📌 Mini Activity:

Identify one line that uses foreshadowing. Rewrite it to make the clue even stronger.

🌍 FLUENCY PROMPTS

Scene: Gurr claims the throne

- Read Gurr's speech with calm confidence or with rising tension—two versions for comparison
- Contrast with Undarvu's anxious tone

Reader's Theater: Use contrasting tones to explore how voice shifts meaning.

📊 ASSESSMENT IDEAS

Formative:
- Vocabulary quiz
- Character comparison chart
- Multiple choice comprehension

Summative:
- Reflective writing: "Is Gurr a true leader?"
- Creative badge design: Gurr or Tau's leadership qualities

· · ·

DIFFERENTIATION STRATEGIES
- Visual: Mood sketching of Congo jungle
- Kinesthetic: Act out the river crossing or throne claim
- ELL: Idiom and figurative language breakdown
- Support Readers: Guided sentence stems for inference

SUMMARY SHEET

Main Setting: Congo jungle path, Ugalla River, and secret Boulder of Passage at Wakaduo

Key Themes: Strategy, Sacrifice, Deception, Leadership in Crisis

SHORT SUMMARY:

Gurr and the Ugalla predators take a shortcut through the perilous Congo, dodging human hunters and battling fierce river currents. Using vines and logs, they build rafts to cross the deadly Ugalla River. Gurr distracts hunters with a daring charge, sacrificing safety for his pack. After surviving a Tiger Fish ambush, the predators reach Wakaduo. Disguised and tricking the guardians, they use the Boulder of Passage to infiltrate the sacred land. Gurr declares himself king, trapping the villagers inside. As Scatter and her friends near Wakaduo, unaware of its fall, the shadow of a new ruler already grips their home.

Comprehension Focus:
- What risks does Gurr take for his group?
- How does the takeover reflect a theme of betrayal?
- Why is strategy more important than brute strength?

Main Characters Introduced/Expanded:
- **Gurr**: Cunning and charismatic leader, willing to risk all for his mission
- **Undarvu**: Fierce lioness concerned for the young
- **Tomba**: Wise elephant advisor, tactical and steady

- **Piny and Nasty**: Spies who help deceive Wakaduo's gate-keepers
  - **Wakaduo Villagers**: Unwittingly trapped under Gurr's rule
  - **Key Vocabulary Words**:
  - Deception – Misleading others for a goal
  - Gambit – A risky move to gain advantage
  - Infiltration – Entering secretly for control
  - Resistance – Fighting back against oppression
  - Usurper – One who takes power by force
  - **Notable Quotes**:
  - "Close it… or we attack your friends." — Gurr
  - "To Wakaduo we sail." — Gurr
  - "I am the new king." — Gurr
  - **Look For in Illustrations**:
  - Tiger Fish leaping out of the Ugalla River
  - Poachers on the hunt
  - Boulder of Passage rumbling open under deception

REFLECTION QUESTIONS

Theme: Power, Deception, and the Cost of Survival

"No matter how many times you wash a goat, it will still smell like a goat."

REFLECTION PROMPTS:

1. Gurr takes Wakaduo by surprise. Do you think he's a hero, a villain, or something in between? Why?

2. Tomba and Undarvu have to choose between safety and sacrifice. When have you seen someone make a brave choice for others?

3. Gurr says, "Together, we are strong." Do you agree with this? When has being part of a group helped you be brave?

4. The Boulder of Passage opens for a lie. What are the dangers of pretending to be someone you're not?

Token Earned:
Leadership Through Strategy
If you were in Wakaduo when Gurr arrived, what would you do?

***

✍ CER WRITING PROMPT – CHAPTER 14

Prompt:
Was Gurr right to take Wakaduo by deception? Or did he go too far?

Claim
✎ I think Gurr (was/was not) right to take Wakaduo because...

Evidence
✎ One part of the chapter that supports my thinking is:

THIS SHOWS THAT...

Reasoning
✎ This means Gurr's actions were (justified/unfair) because...
☑ Checklist:
✔ I stated a clear opinion
✔ I used at least one text quote
✔ I explained my reasoning

POETRY PACK - NARRATIVE POEM

✐ **Narrative Poem Text:**
Narrative Poem: The Old Path Through the Congo
Through the winding paths where wild vines creep,
Gurr's band pressed on, through jungle deep.

The trees stood watch, both friend and foe,
Where dangers lurked in the green below.

THE RIVER ROARED, A BEAST UNSEEN,
Its waters dark, its teeth so keen.
Quicksand whispered beneath the leaves,
A trap for those whom fate deceives.

SHADOWS SLITHERED, SILENT, FAST,
The jungle hummed of dangers past.
A hunter's snare, a stalker's gaze,
Through tangled green, the fireflies blazed.

YET GURR, WITH EYES BOTH SHARP AND WISE,
Saw through the jungle's clever guise.
"This path deceives, but we'll outplay,
Not by strength, but wits today."

THEY MOVED LIKE WHISPERS, SWIFT AND LOW,
Through river's breath and tangled woe.
To cross the tide, to test their fate,
With cunning hearts, they'd shift their state.

◎ Student Poetry Activities
ACTIVITY 1: Danger Detectives

The jungle is full of dangers!

Underline all the dangers mentioned in the poem:

• River's roar
• Friendly frogs
• Quicksand
• Fireflies
• Stalker's gaze

· · ·

ACTIVITY 2: SOUND EXPLORER

The jungle "hums" and "roars."

List **two sounds** you imagine hearing in this wild jungle:

Example: rushing water, whispering leaves, snapping branches

Your Sounds:

1.
2.

ACTIVITY 3: WHAT WOULD YOU DO?

Imagine you are part of Gurr's band, stuck in the jungle!

You see quicksand ahead.

What clever idea would you use to escape?

(Write 2–3 sentences describing your plan!)

TEACHER TIP (SMALL PRINT)

☑ Standards Alignment:

- Cause-and-Effect
- Sensory Language
- Creative Thinking

☑ Science of Reading Focus:

- Vocabulary Development
- Inference Making
- Reading Comprehension Strategies

☑ CASEL Focus:

- *Responsible Decision-Making* – Gurr's actions raise ethical dilemmas.
- *Social Awareness* – Undarvu and others show empathy and concern for group safety.

BONUS IDEA:

⏱ **Map It Out!** — Students draw a mini "danger map" of the jungle, showing the quicksand, roaring rivers, and safe paths!

15

LAKE EYASI

🍎 TEACHER'S ANNOTATED GUIDE

Proverb: "A beautiful thing is never perfect."

CHAPTER OVERVIEW

Lake Eyasi appears serene, but its beauty hides danger. Tusker and the others face crocodiles and quicksand, and it takes courage—and a hippo's help—to cross safely. Lebron, the Sacred Ibis, promises to carry a message back to Wakaduo. This chapter explores trust, appearances, and hidden strength.

🎯 LEARNING OBJECTIVES

• Analyze how setting reveals theme
  • Decode complex vocabulary with roots
  • Infer character growth through action
  • Explore the theme of appearance vs. reality
  • Practice expressive reading and visualization

▌ VOCABULARY + MORPHOLOGY FOCUS

Theme Connection: Strategy, resilience, environment, and internal conflict

Proverb Connection: *"Even the calmest lake hides its depths."*

▌Vocabulary (Context-Based Tier 2 Terms)

These words appear directly in the chapter and are central to student understanding:

- **Camouflage** – To blend in with the surroundings for protection or concealment
- **Navigation** – The process of finding or planning a route or direction
- **Tension** – A state of nervousness, stress, or unease in a situation
- **Reflection** – A mirrored image or serious thought
- **Instinct** – A natural, inborn way of acting or responding
- **Lurking** – Hiding while waiting to attack or watch unnoticed
- **Evasive** – Avoiding danger or questions cleverly
- **Stillness** – A complete lack of movement or sound
- **Rippling** – Moving in small waves or gentle motion

    Tip: Use image prompts (e.g., rippling water, camouflaged animals) to connect visual literacy to vocabulary.

▌ MORPHOLOGY TIE-IN

These **morphologically rich** words may not appear directly in the student glossary but can be introduced as part of decoding and meaning-building practice:

- **Navigate** – *nav* (ship) + *-gate* (to lead): to lead or guide through a path
- **Reflective** – *re-* (again) + *flect* (bend): bending light back, or thinking deeply again
- **Evasion** – *e-* (out) + *vad* (go) + *-sion* (noun): the act of avoiding
- **Suspicion** – *sus-* (under) + *spec* (look): the act of looking under the surface

• **Tension** – *tens* (stretch) + *-ion* (noun): the state of being stretched (mentally or emotionally)

Discussion Prompt: How does a word like **reflection** show both a physical and emotional meaning?

SoR-Based Teaching Suggestions:
Word Web Activity:

Choose *"reflective"* or *"tension"* and build a web with related words (reflect, deflect, inflection... or tense, tensile, intense). Discuss how the root affects the meaning.

Mini-Morph Lesson:

Introduce prefixes like *re-*, *e-*, and roots like *spec* and *flect*. Use them in a word-sorting center or interactive notebook foldables.

Context Clue Spotlight:

Highlight "camouflage" and "evasive" in the text. Ask: *What clues around this word helped you figure out what it means?*

◆ CHAPTER 15 MINI-LESSON: "LAKE EYASI"

Theme: *Resilience, Beauty and Danger, and Sending Hope Forward*

Objective:

Students will analyze how danger and beauty coexist in nature and emotion. They'll reflect on how setting deepens theme and how acts of courage carry forward into hope.

Quick Teach: Contrast & Reflection

1. Proverb Anchor:

"A beautiful thing is never perfect."

➤ *Prompt:* What does Lake Eyasi teach the characters about this idea?

2. Contrast Map Activity:

Fill in this chart:

Element
Beautiful
Dangerous

. . .

LAKE EYASI
Reflection, cranes, still water
Crocodiles, murky depths

HEROES' JOURNEY
Friendship, teamwork
Betrayal, physical danger
3. Quick Poetic Response:
✎ *Write 4–6 free-verse lines that show something beautiful AND dangerous.*
Example starter:
"The lake shines like silver / but monsters hide beneath."
4. Message of Hope Mini Write:
➤ *Write the message YOU would send with Lebron the Ibis back to Wakaduo. What do the villagers need to hear most right now?*

📖 COMPREHENSION STRATEGY GUIDE — CHAPTER 15

🔍 Before Reading
• Preview the chapter title and poem: What do you think "Whispers of Lake Eyasi" might refer to?
• Proverb Reflection: "A beautiful thing is never perfect."
→ What do you think that means? Can something be both wonderful *and* dangerous?
• Prediction Prompt (see below)
Prompt:
"The lake looks beautiful, but Tusker warns that it hides secrets. What kind of challenges do you think the group will face as they cross it?"
Optional Sentence Starter:
I think the heroes will have to face…

📙 DURING READING

• As the characters cross the lake, how does each one respond to fear or danger?

• How do the glowing mushrooms and mysterious lake elements contribute to mood?

• Track the tension: Where in the chapter does the tone shift from wonder to fear?

After Reading

• Why do you think the hippo helped Tusker? What does that say about unexpected allies?

• How did this experience change the way the characters think about beauty and danger?

• Why is Lebron's message so important for the future of Wakaduo?

Comprehension Strategy Prompts

• Infer meaning of: "A beautiful thing is never perfect."
• Visualize and sketch Lake Eyasi
• Predict impact of Lebron's message

FLUENCY & LITERARY FOCUS – CHAPTER 15

Fluency Practice:

• **Tusker (in danger):** Strong, slow tones that shift to sudden intensity.

• **Ernie (from the sky):** Sharp and urgent—simulate alarmed calls from above.

• **Lebron:** Calm and noble, with long pauses for emphasis. Encourage a "messenger" tone.

Activity Suggestion:

Choral Reading with Tone Shifts — Practice changing tone as the lake changes from peaceful to chaotic.

Literary Devices in Focus

• **Metaphor:** The lake is a mirror, reflecting not only the sky but the journey itself.

• **Symbolism:**

- ◦ **Lake Eyasi** = Beauty that contains hidden danger.
- ◦ **Glowcap Mushrooms** = Light in dark times.
- ◦ **Lebron** = Messenger of hope; symbol of rising above chaos.
- • **Tone Shift**: The calm, lyrical opening is replaced by a harrowing midsection, then returns to quiet strength.

🐚 FLUENCY FOCUS
Scene: Tusker's water struggle, Ernie's aerial alert
- • Deep, slow tones vs. fast, alarmed cries
- • Group reading of urgent dialogue with role-play props

⊕ SCHEMA CONNECTIONS
- • African lakes and ecosystems
- • Hippo vs. crocodile behaviors
- • Symbolism of mirrors and water in folklore

📚 LITERARY STRUCTURE
- • Lake = metaphor for unseen danger
- • Tone shift: calm → chaos → relief
- • Foreshadowing: "The water hides secrets…"

📊 ASSESSMENT IDEAS
Formative:
- • Vocabulary match
- • Scene sequencing
- • Journal entry on theme
Summative:
- • Literary essay: Lake Eyasi as metaphor
- • Creative fable: Inspired by the proverb

🧩 DIFFERENTIATION STRATEGIES

- Visual: Storyboard crossing scene
- Kinesthetic: Act out rope crossing
- ELL: Sentence frames with images
- Advanced: Poetic retelling from hippo's POV

SUMMARY SHEET

Main Setting: The mystical lake surrounded by glowing mushrooms and ancient trees

Key Themes: Beauty and Danger, Resilience, Trust, Message of Hope

Short Summary:

The heroes arrive at the stunning Lake Eyasi, unaware of Wakaduo's fall. Though serene, the lake harbors danger beneath its calm waters. As they cross on Tusker's back, a crocodile attacks—but a heroic hippo intervenes. The experience bonds the group even tighter. On the far shore, they meet Lebron the Sacred Ibis, who agrees to deliver a message of hope to Wakaduo. This moment of peace and promise is short-lived, as dangers continue to grow beyond the horizon.

Comprehension Focus:
- How is Lake Eyasi both beautiful and dangerous?
- What lessons do the heroes learn during the crossing?
- Why is Lebron's message important?

Main Characters Introduced/Expanded:
- **Tusker**: Brave and maternal, leads the lake crossing
- **Henry and Scatter**: Bonded through trust and memory
- **Lebron**: Sacred Ibis and wise messenger
- **Crocodile and Hippo**: Representing hidden danger and unlikely help

Key Vocabulary Words:
- Resilience – Ability to recover from hardship

- Messenger – One who carries a message
- Reflection – A mirrored image, or a moment of thought
- Harmony – Peaceful balance between things
- Serene – Calm and undisturbed

Additional Key Vocabulary:

- **Grace**

Definition: A quality of elegance, calm strength, or compassion in movement or behavior.

Application: Use when describing Tusker's crossing or Lebron's flight.

Literary Link: The lake is described with both danger and grace—offering a metaphor for hidden strength.

Instructional Idea: Have students list behaviors that show "grace under pressure" (e.g., how Tusker leads calmly while under attack).

NOTABLE QUOTES:

- "Stick together, and we'll be fine." — Tusker
- "Your courage must travel where you cannot." — Lebron
- "A beautiful thing is never perfect." — Tree of Life Wisdom

Look For in Illustrations:

- Tusker crossing the shimmering lake with Henry and Scatter
- A hippo attacking the crocodile underwater
- Lebron flying high with the heroes' message
- The glimmering waters of Lake Eyasi

REFLECTION QUESTIONS

Theme: Beauty, Fear, and Messages of Hope

 "A beautiful thing is never perfect."

REFLECTION PROMPTS:

1. Lake Eyasi is beautiful, but dangerous. How can something be both safe and risky at the same time?

2. Lebron agrees to carry the heroes' message. Who in your life helps *carry your message*—your hopes, dreams, or beliefs?

3. A hippo saves the group when Tusker is attacked. Have you ever been helped by someone unexpected?

4. Scatter says, "We go on, stronger because of the truths we've faced." What truth have *you* faced that made you stronger?

🌑 Token Earned:

🔴 Hope in Dark Places

If you had to send a message to your home, what would it say?

✍ CER WRITING — ENRICHMENT

Prompt:

How do Tusker and Lebron each show leadership in different ways? Which one do you think is the stronger leader in this chapter?

📣 Claim

☞ *Start your answer with a clear opinion:*

I believe that _____ is the stronger leader because...

📜 Evidence

☞ *Use a detail from the story to support your idea:*

In the chapter, _____ shows leadership when...

Another example is when...

Reasoning

☞ *Explain why your evidence proves your claim:*

This shows that _____ leads by...

It also proves that _____ helps others by...

. . .

THEIR LEADERSHIP MATTERS BECAUSE...
☑ Quick Checklist
• Did I clearly choose one leader?
• Did I give a strong example from the story?
• Did I explain *why* that makes them a strong leader?

▮ MINI CER — TEACHER ANSWER KEY
Prompt Recap:
How do Tusker and Lebron each show leadership in different ways? Which one is the stronger leader in this chapter?
☑ Sample CER Response (Advanced Example)
Claim:
I believe that **Tusker** is the stronger leader in this chapter because she leads with calm action during a moment of danger.

Evidence:
In the story, Tusker carries the group across the lake and stays strong even when a crocodile attacks. She tells the group to "stick together," which helps everyone stay focused and brave.

Reasoning:
This shows that Tusker leads by protecting others and staying calm even when things go wrong. While Lebron offers wisdom, Tusker risks herself to keep the group safe. Her courage and steady actions show strong, protective leadership.

HERE'S A **DIFFERENTIATED** CER WRITING VERSION OF THE PROMPT, tailored for **emerging writers** and **English Language Learners (ELLs)**. It includes **sentence starters** embedded in each section and a simplified vocabulary focus.

▬ MINI CER: COMPARING TUSKER AND LEBRON'S LEADERSHIP
Prompt: *Who is the stronger leader in Chapter 15—Tusker or Lebron? Use what you know from the story to explain.*

· · ·

✎ STUDENT-FRIENDLY CER WITH SENTENCE STARTERS

1. Claim

I think the stronger leader in this chapter is...

☞ I think the stronger leader is **Tusker / Lebron** because...

2. EVIDENCE

In the story, they...

☞ In the story, **Tusker / Lebron** showed leadership when they...

☞ ONE EXAMPLE IS WHEN...

3. REASONING

This shows they are a leader because...

☞ This shows they are a good leader because...

☞ THEY HELPED OTHERS BY...

☞ THEIR ACTIONS MADE THE GROUP FEEL...

EXAMPLE ANSWER USING SENTENCE STARTERS (MODEL)

Claim:

I think the stronger leader is **Tusker** because she helped the group during danger.

Evidence:

In the story, Tusker carried everyone across the lake and stayed calm when a crocodile attacked.

Reasoning:

This shows she is a leader because she was brave and helped her friends feel safe.

POETRY PACK

Poetry Activity Sheet — *Lyric Poem*
Poem Text:
Lyric Poem: Whispers of Lake Eyasi

In the early dawn's embrace,
Where whispers dress the morning's face,
Lake Eyasi reveals her grace,
Mirroring the sky's wide space.
(... **Poem continues** — *see full version in Chapter 15!*)

STUDENT POETRY ACTIVITIES
ACTIVITY 1: Hidden Dangers

The poem talks about beauty *and* danger at Lake Eyasi.
Circle the dangerous things mentioned:
• Crocodiles
• Fireflies
• Murky waters
• Glowing mushrooms
• Azure cranes
(*Students recognize details while practicing critical reading!*)

ACTIVITY 2: NATURE'S MIRROR

Lake Eyasi is called a "mirror."
In your own words, explain:
  What does the lake reflect besides the sky?
(*Write 1-2 sentences.*)

ACTIVITY 3: CREATE A "WHISPER" LINE

Imagine Lake Eyasi whispers a secret to you.

Write a short "whisper" line (one poetic sentence) from the lake!

Example:

"Trust the stars to guide your way."

Your Whisper:

ACTIVITY 4: Sketch It!

🖌️ **Draw a quick sketch** of what you imagine Lake Eyasi looks like —

Include one *beautiful* thing and one *dangerous* thing in your drawing! (*Use poetry as inspiration for visual creativity!*)

⚐ FINAL TEACHER NOTES

"Lake Eyasi reminds us that our students—like the lake—may carry calm on the surface but deep emotions underneath. Let them explore the balance of bravery and vulnerability as they reflect on this chapter."

Teacher Tip (Small Print)

☑ **Standards Alignment:**

- Identifying Themes and Details
- Metaphor & Symbolism
- Sensory Language Exploration

☑ **Science of Reading Focus:**

- Reading Comprehension
- Making Inferences
- Expressive Writing

Bonus Activity:

📖 **Compare and Contrast!** — Students make a mini Venn Diagram:

Beauty vs. **Danger** at Lake Eyasi based on poem clues.

❧ 16 ❧
PREDATOR'S BATTLE

🍎 TEACHER'S ANNOTATED GUIDE

P roverb Focus
"A being who uses force is afraid of reasoning."
"Knowledge without wisdom is like water in the sand."

⏱ CHAPTER OVERVIEW

This pivotal chapter explores leadership, alliance, and deception among the predators of Ruaha. Liona emerges as a diplomatic leader, urging peace among rival species. The fragile unity reveals deeper tensions and foreshadows betrayal. Dirty Donald's skepticism and the leopard's silence hint at dangers to come.

🎯 LEARNING OBJECTIVES
- Define and apply vocabulary in context
- Analyze character motivations and leadership styles
- Sequence and interpret key decisions and plot turns
- Identify themes of power, unity, wisdom, and betrayal

• Make predictions using text-based evidence

VOCABULARY + MORPHOLOGY FOCUS

Chapter 16: Predator's Battle
Theme Connection: Power, leadership, unity, strategy, distrust
Proverb Connection:
• *"A being who uses force is afraid of reasoning."*
• *"Knowledge without wisdom is like water in the sand."*

VOCABULARY (CONTEXT-BASED TIER 2 TERMS)
These key words are essential for comprehension and thematic understanding in this chapter:
• **Alliance** – A union or agreement made between parties for mutual benefit
• **Confrontation** – A direct face-off or clash, often between opposing sides
• **Dominance** – Power and influence over others
• **Cunning** – Cleverness or skill in achieving goals by deceit or strategy
• **Grudgingly** – Done unwillingly or with reluctance
• **Tension** – Mental strain, unease, or conflict between characters
• **Unite / United** – To come together for a common purpose
• **Scheme** – A secret plan, often dishonest or tricky
• **Strategic** – Related to careful planning or calculated moves
• **Authority** – The power or right to give orders and make decisions
  Discussion Tip: Use "grudgingly" to explore subtle emotional cues in dialogue.

MORPHOLOGY TIE-IN
Introduce these morphologically rich terms with breakdowns for deeper vocabulary understanding and retention:

- **Confrontation** = *con-* (with) + *front* (face) + *-ation* (action): a face-to-face encounter
- **Alliance** = *alli-* (bind together) + *-ance* (state): the state of being bound in agreement
- **Dominance** = *domin-* (master) + *-ance* (state of): the state of having control
- **Strategic** = *strat-* (army or plan) + *-ic* (relating to): relating to planning or tactics
- **Authority** = *auth-* (origin, creator) + *-ity* (state): the state of having original power or control
- **Grudgingly** = *grudge* (resentment) + *-ing* (doing) + *-ly* (how): done with resentment

✑ *Mini-Lesson Idea:* Compare *strategic*, *strategy*, and *strategist*. Discuss how suffixes shift word function (adjective, noun, person).

🧰 SOR-BASED TEACHING SUGGESTIONS:

Root Sorting Game
Prepare word cards with roots (e.g., *front, dom, auth*) and suffixes (*-ance, -ity, -tion*). Have students build real words and use them in leadership-themed sentences.

Context Clue Circle
Highlight "cunning" and "scheme" in context. Ask: *How does this word show the difference between cleverness and wisdom?*

Concept Anchor Activity
Use "authority" and "dominance" to compare leadership styles of Liona vs. Dirty Donald or Tau. Create a trait chart.

◆ CHAPTER 16 MINI-LESSON: "THE FALSE KING"

Theme: *Power, Deception, and Resistance*
◎ Objective:
Students will analyze how Gurr's takeover changes Wakaduo's dynamics and explore how power can be used to lead or control.
🗔 Quick Teach: Power & Resistance
1. Proverb Anchor:

"He who wears the crown must bear its weight."

➤ **Discuss:** Is Gurr acting like a true leader or a ruler of fear? What's the difference between leading with vision and leading through fear?

2. Character Role Reflection:

Have students fill in or discuss the following for each character:

Gurr

• *Wants:* Control of Wakaduo
• *Fears:* Losing power, being exposed
• *Strategy:* Manipulation and intimidation

Adira

• *Wants:* To protect her people
• *Fears:* Failing in her mission
• *Strategy:* Staying hidden and gathering allies

Villagers

• *Want:* Peace and justice
• *Fear:* Gurr's retaliation
• *Strategy:* Passive resistance or secret support of the heroes

3. QUICK WRITE PROMPT:

✎ *Should Adira have opened the Boulder of Passage? Why or why not?*

➤ Use evidence from the chapter.

4. Debate/Discussion Circle Prompt:

➤ *Is it ever okay to use fear to protect or lead others? What are the consequences?*

📖 COMPREHENSION STRATEGY GUIDE – CHAPTER 16: *PREDATOR'S BATTLE*

🔍 **Before Reading**

• Discuss the two proverbs:

"A being who uses force is afraid of reasoning."

"Knowledge without wisdom is like water in the sand."

→ What do you think these might mean for a group of predators?

• Prediction Prompt (see below)

Prompt:

Before reading: "A powerful lioness wants to stop the predators from fighting each other. What could go wrong with this plan?"

Optional sentence starter:

I think some predators will...

🗔 DURING READING

• What strategies does Liona use to stop the fight?

• Track the attitudes of each predator: Who supports Liona? Who doesn't?

• How does the author use sound and silence to build suspense?

🗔 After Reading

• How do the characters' choices reflect deeper values like pride, fear, or ambition?

• Who do you think will stay loyal to the alliance—and who might betray it?

• Do you think the alliance will last? Why or why not?

🔍 COMPREHENSION FOCUS

• Inference: What does Liona's approach reveal about her values?

• Prediction: What might Dirty Donald or the leopard do next?

• Cause & Effect: How does stopping the fight lead to uneasy alliance?

• Theme Tracking: When is wisdom more powerful than brute force?

Activity: Visual timeline called *"Whispers of Betrayal"*

🪶 FLUENCY & LITERARY FOCUS — CHAPTER 16

🎭 Fluency Scenes to Rehearse

• **Liona halts the battle:** Steady, forceful tone; her words calm chaos.

• **Dirty Donald's rebuttal:** Snarky, dismissive, layered with disbelief.

• **Narrator passages:** Tension-building pace, rising with suspense and scheming.

✏ Activity Ideas:

• *Leadership Voice Workshop:* Students choose how to "voice" leaders—calm vs. angry vs. cunning.

• *Reader's Theater:* Assign roles: Liona, Donald, Leopard, Narrator—explore tone and pacing.

🎤 FLUENCY & PROSODY FOCUS

Key Scenes for Practice:
• Liona halts the fight
• Dirty Donald's mocking rebuttal

Fluency Coaching:
• Liona – steady, reasoned, calm
• Donald – sarcastic, dismissive
• Narrator – tense, rhythmic pacing

Activity: Reader's Theater + "Leadership Voice Workshop"

🌐 SCHEMA CONNECTIONS

• Real-world predator behavior (lions, leopards, wild dogs)
• Ecological alliances vs. solitary hunters
• How social tension mirrors animal dynamics

📜 LITERARY STRUCTURE & SYMBOLISM

• Liona = moral clarity and wise leadership
• Dirty Donald = chaos and ego
• Jungle clearing = temporary truce zone
• Foreshadowing: "The leopard lingered in the shadows..."

📊 ASSESSMENTS

Formative:
- Exit Ticket: "Which predator do you trust least—and why?"
- Quick Write: "What kind of leader is Liona?"
- Think-Pair-Share on the alliance

Summative:
- Essay: Compare Liona vs. Dirty Donald as leaders
- Theme Reflection: What makes an alliance strong or fragile?

DIFFERENTIATION STRATEGIES
- Visual: Character webs and alliance charts
- Kinesthetic: Roleplay negotiations
- ELL: Vocabulary visuals and sentence stems
- Advanced: Debate: "Should predators use wisdom over force?"

SoR INTEGRATION
- Phonemic Awareness: Break apart confrontation, deceptive
- Fluency: Dramatic tone control and pacing shifts
- Comprehension: Cause and effect
- Text Structure: Build-up to uneasy group unity

ESSENTIAL QUESTION
Can reason overcome instinct—and can enemies become allies?

SUMMARY SHEET

Main Setting: Ruaha jungle clearing, under moonlight

Key Themes: Power Struggles, Unlikely Alliances, Strategy Over Force, Rising Leadership

SHORT SUMMARY:

In the jungle of Ruaha, rival predators gather to debate and battle over future power. Liona, a rare maned lioness, asserts herself as a leader and calls for unity against the heroes of Wakaduo. Despite fierce tension and near-violence, her commanding presence halts the chaos. While some predators remain suspicious, a temporary alliance is formed. The predators are now united in a shared purpose—to stop the heroes. As betrayal simmers under the surface, the final confrontation looms.

Comprehension Focus:
- How does Liona show leadership during conflict?
- Why is unity among predators dangerous for the heroes?
- What does the gathering reveal about predator politics?

Main Characters Introduced/Expanded:
- **Liona**: Charismatic lioness, wise and commanding
- **Dirty Donald**: Skeptical, sarcastic hyena with a sharp tongue
- **Leopard and Caracal**: Agile predators with secret motives
- **Lebron**: Observer and silent recorder of unfolding alliances

Key Vocabulary Words:
- Alliance – A union formed for mutual benefit
- Confrontation – A face-off or clash of wills
- Manipulation – Skillful control for personal gain
- Trust – Reliance on the honesty or ability of others
- Betrayal – The act of breaking trust for selfish reasons

Notable Quotes:
- "Stop. Enough." — Liona
- "We're wasting our strength fighting when there are bigger threats." — Liona
- "Together… they were united." — Narration

Look For in Illustrations:
- Liona halting the battle with her powerful stance
- Predators in tense formation beneath the moon
- Dirty Donald smirking behind bared teeth
- Lebron silently watching from above

REFLECTION QUESTIONS

Theme: Power Struggles, Uneasy Alliances, and Hidden Motives
"A being who uses force is afraid of reasoning."

REFLECTION PROMPTS:

1. Why do you think Liona was able to stop the fight when no one else could?

2. Dirty Donald and the leopard don't fully trust Liona—can people work together even when trust is missing?

3. What makes Liona a different kind of leader from Tau or Gurr?

4. "Together, we're strong like a storm; alone, we're weak like a breeze." — When have you seen this in real life?

Wisdom Stone Earned:

Unity in Conflict

Draw a symbol of what Liona's roar means to you (a thundercloud, crown, pawprint...):

⚜️

CER WRITING: COMPARING LEADERS

Prompt:

Who is the more effective leader in this chapter—**Liona** or **Dirty Donald**? Use evidence from the story to support your claim.

CER Sentence Frame (Student Version)

Claim:

I believe _____ is the more effective leader because _____.

EVIDENCE:

One moment that shows this is when _____.

. . .

REASONING:

This _____ shows _____ that
_____. It proves that
_____.

📖 TEACHER KEY (SAMPLE ANSWER)

Claim:

I believe Liona is the more effective leader because she stops the predators from fighting and brings temporary unity.

Evidence:

One moment that shows this is when she says, "We're wasting our strength fighting when there are bigger threats," and all the predators go silent.

Reasoning:

This shows that Liona uses wisdom and calm reasoning to lead instead of fear or force. It proves she can shift the mood and gain control without violence, which is why her leadership is respected— even by rivals like Dirty Donald.

✅ SKILLS FOCUS:

- RL.4.1: Supporting ideas with evidence
- RL.4.3: Analyzing character actions and traits
- W.4.1: Opinion writing structure
- SEL: Leadership and emotional intelligence

📜 POETRY PACK - FREE VERSE POEM - "WHISPER OF WAR"

🖋 Poem Text:

🪶 Free Verse Poem: Whisper of War

In the cool shadows of Ruaha,
where whispers weave through the leaves,
and the air shivers with the growls of the night,
the earth itself holds its breath...
The air hums—thick with unsaid threats,
alliances shifting like sand in a river,
where old grudges sharpen their claws,
and battle cries promise a dawn of dust and blood.

STUDENT POETRY ACTIVITIES
ACTIVITY 1: Find the Feelings
Underline words that show feelings of:
• Danger
• Fear
• Tension
(*Students practice detecting mood and tone!*)

ACTIVITY 2: IMAGERY EXPLOSION
The poet uses vivid imagery (descriptions that paint pictures).
Pick your favorite line that creates a strong image in your mind.
• **Favorite Line:**
"_____"
• **Sketch a quick picture** based on that line!

ACTIVITY 3: SOUND EFFECTS
The poem mentions **growls**, **whispers**, and **cries**.
Write 3 sound words (onomatopoeia) you might hear in this battle scene!
Examples:
• Roar
• Crackle
• Snap

Your Sound Words:
1.

2.

3.

ACTIVITY 4: Write a "Warning Whisper"

Pretend you are a tree in Ruaha hearing all these whispers.
What warning would you whisper to the heroes?
Example:
"Stay low... danger moves with the wind."
Your Whisper:
" _____ "

Teacher Tip (Small Print)
✅ **Standards Alignment:**
• Identifying Mood and Tone
• Sensory Language
• Expressive & Descriptive Writing
✅ **Science of Reading Focus:**
• Vocabulary Development
• Text Evidence
• Inference Skills

Bonus Challenge:

🎙 **Perform It!** — Students practice reading the poem aloud *dramatically*, using voices to match the emotions (fear, suspense, tension).

. . .

* Here are the Poetry activities found in the Student Workbook:
 🪨 **Student-Facing Poetry Pack Page: Chapter 16**
 To plug directly into the workbook

🪨 *Poetry Pack – Chapter 16: "Whisper of War"*
Poem Type: Free Verse
Proverb Focus:
• "A being who uses force is afraid of reasoning."
• "Knowledge without wisdom is like water in the sand."

✏ *Read the Poem Excerpt*
In the cool shadows of Ruaha,
where whispers weave through the leaves,
and the air shivers with the growls of the night,
the earth itself holds its breath…
The air hums—thick with unsaid threats,
alliances shifting like sand in a river,
where old grudges sharpen their claws,
and battle cries promise a dawn of dust and blood.

ACTIVITY 1: Mood & Tone Detectives
 ✒ Circle **2–3 words** from the poem that show:
• Danger
• Tension
• Fear
 ✏ *Words I circled:*

ACTIVITY 2: Vivid Images 🖼
Pick your favorite line that gives you a clear picture in your mind.
Favorite Line:

" _____ "

Now draw it! What do you imagine?

📍 *Quick Sketch Area:*

ACTIVITY 3: SOUND WORDS (ONOMATOPOEIA)

🐾 The jungle is alive with sound. Write 3 sounds you might hear in this scene.

Examples: *crack, growl, hush*

1

2

3

ACTIVITY 4: WARNING WHISPER (CREATIVE WRITING Prompt)

Imagine you are one of the trees, hearing the predator alliance begin.

Write one "warning whisper" to the heroes:

✎ *Whisper Line:*

☑ *POETRY PACK SKILL FOCUS:*
- Mood and tone
- Descriptive language and imagery
- Emotional expression
- Inference and symbolism
- Vocabulary in context

☑ *Standards Links:*
- RL.4.4 – Interpreting figurative language
- RL.4.1 – Using text evidence
- W.4.3 – Writing with descriptive detail

✎ **FINAL TEACHER NOTES**

"This chapter gives students a chance to reflect on what true leadership looks like. Invite them to compare Liona's calm wisdom with other characters across the book. What kind of leader would they be in a moment of chaos?"

❧ 17 ❧
TRAPPED

🍎 TEACHER'S ANNOTATED GUIDE

Proverb Focus
"To run is not necessarily to arrive."

⊘ CHAPTER OVERVIEW

Tricker, captured by predators, must choose between survival and loyalty. This emotionally charged chapter explores betrayal, guilt, and courage. Henry's actions rescue the group, summoning bees in a moment of instinct and bravery. The consequences of Tricker's decision unfold with powerful emotional weight.

🎯 LEARNING OBJECTIVES
- Define vocabulary: treachery, predicament, deceived
- Analyze character choices and moral consequences
- Infer motivation using text evidence
- Explore themes of betrayal and redemption
- Create alternative outcomes and predictions

■ VOCABULARY + MORPHOLOGY FOCUS

Chapter 17: Trapped

Theme Connection: Betrayal, guilt, redemption, instinct vs. loyalty

Proverb Connection:

- *"To run is not necessarily to arrive."*

■ VOCABULARY (CONTEXT-BASED TIER 2 TERMS)

These vocabulary words support comprehension and character development throughout the chapter:

- **Betrayal** – The act of breaking trust or turning against someone
- **Instinct** – A natural, automatic feeling or reaction
- **Treachery** – Dishonest or harmful behavior against someone who trusts you
- **Predicament** – A difficult or dangerous situation
- **Deceived** – Tricked or misled
- **Desperation** – A feeling of hopelessness leading to risky choices
- **Redemption** – Making up for past mistakes; a second chance
- **Consequences** – Results or outcomes of an action, often negative
- **Loyalty** – Faithfulness or devotion to someone or something
- **Intervention** – The act of stepping in to change what is happening

‣ *Class Prompt:* Ask students how "betrayal" and "redemption" are connected in this story.

■ MORPHOLOGY TIE-IN

Use the following word breakdowns to build meaning and increase word awareness:

- **Treachery** = *treach-* (to betray) + *-ery* (act of): the act of betrayal

• **Predicament** = *pre-* (before) + *dicare* (to say/state) + *-ment* (result): a declared difficult situation

• **Deceived** = *de-* (away/off) + *ceive* (to take) + *-ed* (past tense): taken in or tricked

• **Redemption** = *re-* (again) + *dem* (to buy or take) + *-tion* (act): the act of buying back or making right again

• **Instinct** = *in-* (within) + *stinct* (to prick, drive): the inner drive or urge

• **Consequences** = *con-* (with) + *sequ* (to follow) + *-ence* (state/result): what follows an action

✐ *Word Building Activity:* Give roots like *dem, ceive, sequ* and let students form words (e.g., deceive, perceive, sequence) and define them.

🧰 SOR-BASED TEACHING SUGGESTIONS:

Redemption Wall

Create a classroom anchor chart called "The Road to Redemption." Add character actions under categories like *Betrayal*, *Consequences*, and *Second Chances*. Update it through the unit.

Root + Suffix Sort

Provide students with color-coded cards of prefixes (*de-*, *pre-*, etc.), roots (*ceive, dict, dem*), and suffixes (*-tion, -ment*). Let them match to form real words and define them in context.

Character Lens: Emotion Words

Use "desperation," "loyalty," and "intervention" to discuss the emotional stakes. Have students write dialogue from Tricker's or Henry's POV using at least one focus word.

◆ CHAPTER 17 MINI-LESSON: "THE RECKONING BEGINS"

Theme: *Truth Revealed, Hope Ignited, and the Spark of Rebellion*

🎯 Objective:

Students will track how scattered truths and reunited friends can ignite change. They'll examine how courage and information become tools for action.

📖 Quick Teach: Truth as Power

1. Proverb Anchor:

"Even the smallest fire can light the darkest cave."

➤ *Prompt:* What small moment gives hope in this chapter?

2. Reunited Roles Activity:

➤ Choose two characters reunited in this chapter (Scatter/Adira, Tusker/villagers, etc.).

Complete:

Character 1

• **What they've learned:** (Example: "Scatter has learned he's stronger when connected to others.")

• **What they share:** A warning, a truth, or emotional strength

• **How it changes others:** Inspires action, creates trust, rekindles hope

Character 2

• **What they've learned:**

• WHAT THEY SHARE:

• HOW IT CHANGES OTHERS:

(REPEAT STRUCTURE AS NEEDED FOR STUDENT PAIRS.)

3. Quick Write Prompt:

✎ *Who is the true leader now: Gurr or Scatter? Why?*

4. CALL TO ACTION MINI POSTER:

➤ *Design a short chant that villagers could use to resist Gurr's rule.*
Example: "Wakaduo is not afraid!"

📖 COMPREHENSION STRATEGY GUIDE — *CHAPTER 17: TRAPPED*

🔍 Before Reading
• Review the proverb: "To run is not necessarily to arrive."
• Ask students: *Have you ever made a decision out of fear? What were the consequences?*

Prediction Prompt:
What might happen if one of the heroes is caught by the predators?

Prompt:
Imagine you are part of the Heroes' group. You don't yet know if Tricker betrayed you. What signs might help you figure it out?

Optional Writing Starter:
If I were Scatter, I would feel...

🗒 DURING READING
• Track Tricker's emotional responses: fear → hesitation → compromise → regret
• Listen for figurative language that builds tension (similes, foreshadowing)
• Identify turning points: when does Tricker make his biggest decision?

🗒 AFTER READING
• Why does Henry call on the bees? What does this moment reveal about him?
• What do you think the group should do now that Tricker is back?
• Explore: *Is survival a good enough reason to betray someone?*

🔍 COMPREHENSION STRATEGY FOCUS
• Inference: What drives Tricker to choose betrayal?

• Prediction: Will the group forgive him?
• Cause & Effect: How did Henry's instinct save the day?
Activity: *"What If?" Pathways* – Students map alternate decisions.

🐝 FLUENCY & LITERARY FOCUS

🎵 Fluency Scenes:
• **Tricker's surrender:** Soft, uncertain, manipulative
• **Tau's judgment:** Quiet, cold authority
• **Henry's call to the bees:** Urgent, rising in intensity

🎤 Performance Ideas:
• "Tone Circle": Students read one line ("I know where they are…") with 3 emotional tones: frightened, proud, ashamed
• "Simile Workshop": Build new similes inspired by the chapter (e.g., "like thunder before a storm")

✏️ Literary Focus:
• Symbolism: Bees = justice, natural intervention, moral consequence
• Parallel structure: Tricker's fear vs. Henry's loyalty
• Theme development: Survival vs. betrayal, redemption

🔨 FLUENCY & TONE PRACTICE
Key Scenes:
• Tricker's surrender
• Tau's threats
• Henry's bee-summoning
Tone Stations: Students read same dialogue with different emotional tones (desperate, brave, manipulative)

🗿 LITERARY ELEMENTS
• Foreshadowing: "Scatter was haunted by a dream…"
• Theme: Trust, survival, courage
• Symbolism: Bees = sudden justice or nature's judgment

. . .

📊 Assessments

Formative:
- Exit Ticket: "Could you forgive Tricker?"
- Character Motivation Chart
- Quote matching (who said it, what it means)

Summative:
- Rewrite: Diary Entry from Tricker
- Plot Diagram: Emotional beat map

💼 Differentiation Strategies

- Visual: Dual character drawing (Tricker before/after)
- Auditory: Record lines and reflect on tone
- ELL: Vocabulary cards + sentence frames
- Advanced: Debate—Can betrayal be justified?

📚 SoR Integration

- Phonemic: Break treachery, consequence, forgiveness
- Fluency: Dialogues with high emotion
- Comprehension: Alternate plot outcomes
- Vocabulary: Morphology mapping
- Text Structure: Parallel plotlines (betrayal vs. rescue)

💬 Essential Question

Can you undo betrayal—or only learn to live with it?

SUMMARY SHEET

Main Setting: Dark forest and Lake Eyasi

Key Themes: Betrayal, Forgiveness, Deception, Instinct vs. Loyalty

· · ·

📜 SHORT SUMMARY:

As the heroes move cautiously through the shadowy forest, Tricker the hare is captured by Charlese the cheetah and Willie the wild dog. To save himself, Tricker reluctantly agrees to lead them to the heroes' trail. Meanwhile, Scatter senses danger and urges the heroes to retreat across Lake Eyasi. The predators follow Tricker's lead only to find the heroes gone, triggering Tau's wrath. Just as punishment looms, Henry calls upon the killer bees of the Tree of Life, saving Tricker from execution. Tricker returns to camp with a heavy heart, unsure if forgiveness awaits. The chapter explores fear, survival, and the fragile bond of trust.

🧠 COMPREHENSION FOCUS:
- Why did Tricker betray the group?
- How does fear influence Tricker's choices?
- What do the bees represent in this chapter?

🐾 MAIN CHARACTERS INTRODUCED/EXPANDED:
- Tricker: Clever but fearful hare caught in a moral dilemma
- Charlese: Swift and cunning cheetah with a sharp tongue
- Willie: Fierce and calculating wild dog
- Tau: Commanding lion leader of Ruaha
- Henry: Loyal friend who initiates the rescue

🔍 VOCABULARY TO PRE-TEACH:
- Betrayal
- Instinct
- Treachery
- Consequences
- Redemption

📕 FIGURATIVE LANGUAGE OR LITERARY DEVICES:

• "Like warriors of the wind, they swarmed with purpose and fury." *(Simile)*

• "A slow exhale—deep and rumbling, like thunder before a storm." *(Foreshadowing, simile)*

📖 QUOTE OF THE CHAPTER:

"To run is not necessarily to arrive."

🌐 REAL-WORLD CONNECTION OR SEL TIE-IN:

This chapter explores what it means to make hard choices under pressure. Discuss the impact of fear on decision-making and how we rebuild trust after a mistake.

⚜️

📖 ✍ REFLECTION QUESTIONS

Theme: Betrayal, Survival, and Forgiveness

🌰 *"To run is not necessarily to arrive."*

REFLECTION PROMPTS:

1. Tricker betrayed his friends out of fear. Do you think he deserves forgiveness?

2. Would you have made the same choice in Tricker's place? Why or why not?

3. The predators were tricked, and they lashed out. What does this tell you about how fear and pride can work together?

4. Henry called the bees for help. What do the bees represent in this story?

🔵 Wisdom Stone Earned:

🐝 Truth Through Fear

✍ *Write a short apology Tricker might say that comes from the heart:*

༺৩৩༻

CER WRITING - CLAIM, EVIDENCE, REASONING

Use this structured writing prompt to support deeper thinking and text-based writing. The CER framework guides students to:
- Form a clear claim
- Support their thinking with specific textual evidence
- Explain how that evidence proves their point
- Practice academic writing sentence starters
- Build argumentative and persuasive thinking
  - *Ideal after discussion, close reading, or as a lead-in to a short response*

CER WORKSHEET
Title: Chapter 17 — *Trapped*
Prompt/Question:
Why was Tricker's choice so difficult when he was trapped?

1. CLAIM
(What do you believe?)
Starter: *I believe that...*

2. EVIDENCE
(Find a quote or describe something that happened.)
Starters:
- *In the story it says...*
- *One example is when...*
- *The author shows that...*

3. REASONING
(Explain why your evidence proves your claim)
Starters:

- *This shows that...*
- *This proves that...*
- *This means...*

⊙ QUICK CHECKLIST
☑ Clear answer?
☑ Strong evidence?
☑ Good explanation?

WHEN TO USE:
☑ After discussion or reading group
☑ Before writing paragraphs or journal reflections
☑ As a formative assessment
☑ For writing support or enrichment

📖 *PREDICTION TRACKER*

🔵 *Post-Reading Prediction Tracker: What Will Tricker Do Next?*

Tricker has made a difficult choice. Now it's time to predict what might happen next.

Think about his actions and how others might respond. Use the space to write your predictions.

1. WHAT TRICKER DID:
He led the predators toward the heroes — a betrayal.

HOW OTHERS MIGHT REACT:
Scatter might stay silent, pull away, or struggle with trust.

∙ ∙ ∙

WHAT TRICKER MIGHT DO NEXT:

🖊 I think Tricker might...

2. WHAT TRICKER DID:

He was rescued by Henry and the bees.

HOW OTHERS MIGHT REACT:

Henry might defend him and believe in second chances.

WHAT TRICKER MIGHT DO NEXT:

🖊 I think Tricker might...

✍ DISCUSSION STARTERS

- What would you do if you were Tricker?
- What's harder—earning forgiveness or forgiving someone?
- Do you think the group *should* forgive him? Why or why not?

✍ FINAL TEACHER NOTE

This chapter opens space for deep emotional reflection. Use Tricker's dilemma to talk about how we respond when we feel trapped—by fear, peer pressure, or guilt. Let students debate, write, or role-play how forgiveness works and how it feels.

❧ 18 ❧

A HERO'S WELCOME

■ TEACHER'S ANNOTATED GUIDE

◷ CHAPTER OVERVIEW

The heroes return to Wakaduo, but all is not well. Gurr's predators have taken control. The chapter explores how appearances deceive, how forgiveness is tested, and how leadership emerges under pressure. Tricker's confession and Scatter's wisdom move the story toward its emotional climax.

◎ **INSTRUCTIONAL GOALS**
- Identify mood shifts through setting
- Analyze redemption through character action
- Infer character motivations and foreshadowing
- Explore metaphor, tone, and rising conflict
- Apply vocabulary in meaningful ways

🝰 **KEY DISCUSSION PROMPTS**

• Is Scatter's forgiveness of Tricker strength or weakness?

• How does Gurr's arrival change the meaning of "A Hero's Welcome"?

• How do tone and language create suspense?

📖 VOCABULARY + MORPHOLOGY FOCUS

Chapter 18: A Hero's Welcome

Theme Connection: Homecoming, forgiveness, leadership under pressure

Proverb Link:

• *"We fix our bags and our friendships."*

▇ VOCABULARY (TIER 2 FOCUS FOR EMOTIONAL & LEADERSHIP THEMES)

These words help students explore the emotional tension and leadership choices in the chapter:

• **Forgiveness** – Letting go of anger toward someone who hurt you

• **Redemption** – Earning back trust after doing something wrong

• **Confrontation** – A direct meeting that may involve conflict

• **Alliance** – A group formed to support and protect each other

• **Leadership** – The ability to guide others with purpose

• **Trust** – Believing someone will do the right thing

• **Suspicion** – A feeling of doubt or mistrust

• **Homecoming** – Returning to one's home after a journey

• **Challenge** – A test of strength or ability

• **Reconciliation** – The act of making peace after conflict

💬 *Prompt for Class Discussion:* What makes "forgiveness" different from "reconciliation"? Can you have one without the other?

🖼 MORPHOLOGY TIE-IN

Let students unpack key words using root-based analysis to grow vocabulary awareness:

- **Forgiveness** = *for-* (completely) + *give* (to offer) + *-ness* (state of): the act of completely offering pardon
- **Redemption** = *re-* (again) + *dem* (to buy/take back) + *-tion* (act): the act of earning back or restoring
- **Confrontation** = *con-* (together) + *front* (face) + *-ation* (act of): the act of facing someone directly
- **Alliance** = *alli-* (to bind or join) + *-ance* (state of): the state of being joined or united
- **Suspicion** = *sub-* (under) + *spec* (to look/see) + *-ion* (act/state): the act of looking underneath — doubting
- **Reconciliation** = *re-* (again) + *concili* (to make friendly) + *-ation* (act of): the act of becoming friendly again

Activity Tip: Use color-coded prefix/root/suffix cards and let students mix and define new words (e.g., "sub" + "spec" = "suspect").

SOR-INFORMED LITERACY STRATEGIES:

Morphology Map: The Word 'Forgiveness'

Create a visual diagram showing how *give*, *forgive*, and *forgiveness* are related. Add emotional vocabulary around it like "mercy," "healing," and "honor."

Leadership Language Sort

Have students sort vocabulary into 3 columns:

1 Words that describe strong leadership (*challenge, alliance*)
2 Words that show emotion (*forgiveness, trust*)
3 Words that hint at danger or tension (*confrontation, suspicion*)

Rewrite Moment

Ask students to rewrite a moment of Gurr's confrontation using vocabulary words like *trust, confrontation*, or *redemption*. How does language change tone?

◆ CHAPTER 18 MINI-LESSON: "THE FINAL STORM BUILDS"

Theme: *Preparation, Loyalty, and Inner Strength Before Battle*

☞ **Objective:**

Students will explore the emotional build-up before the climax. They'll analyze how fear and unity shape heroes before a major turning point.

📖 **Quick Teach: Readiness & Reflection**

1. Proverb Anchor:

"The tree that bends in the storm survives the wind."

➤ *Ask:* What does this mean for Scatter, Ernie, and Henry?

2. Battle Prep Table:

➤ What does each hero bring to the battle—emotionally and physically?

Scatter
- **Strength:** Deep intuition and courage
- **Fear:** Losing friends
- **Role in the Fight:** Moral compass, visionary

Ernie
- **Strength:** Bravery, loyalty
- **Fear:** Failing to protect
- **Role in the Fight:** Frontline protector

Henry
- **Strength:** Intelligence and compassion
- **Fear:** Being overlooked or unheard
- **Role in the Fight:** Strategic thinker, healer

3. QUICK WRITE PROMPT:

✎ *What's more powerful in a battle—strength or belief? Why?*

4. Poetry Response (Mini):

➤ Using the storm metaphor, write a 2-line poem about facing fear.

Example: "The wind may howl, but I stand still— / my heart a stone against the chill."

🔍 COMPREHENSION GUIDE: CHAPTER 18 — A HERO'S WELCOME

Proverb Focus: "Clouds come floating into my life, no longer usher storm or carry destruction, but add color to my sunset sky."

⬤ BEFORE READING

Purpose: Prepare for tone shifts, emotional stakes, and layered themes of return and confrontation.

Discussion Starters:

• What do you think it feels like to return home after a long journey?

• Have you ever expected a warm welcome, only to find something had changed?

• Look at the chapter title and proverb—what do you predict the "clouds" might represent?

Prediction Prompt:

▶️ *What challenges do you think the heroes might face when they return to Wakaduo?*

✏️ "I think they might..."

✏️ "Maybe someone has changed..."

✏️ "The title makes me wonder if..."

⬤ DURING READING

Purpose: Track emotions, tone shifts, and literary contrasts.

Guided Reading Prompts:

• What clues show that something is not quite right in Wakaduo, even during celebration?

• What does Scatter's reaction to Tricker's apology reveal about her leadership?

• How does the author use *light and shadow* (literal and figurative) throughout the chapter?

Vocabulary-in-Context Prompts:

• What does it mean that the celebration "vanished like mist before a storm"?

• How does Gurr "orchestrate" a moment of dominance? What does that word suggest?

• How is the metaphor of "grain in a bag with a hole" a lesson in trust?

⬤ AFTER READING

Purpose: Reflect on transformation, conflict, and emotional truths.

Discussion & Writing Prompts:

1 What does this chapter teach us about what "home" really means?

2 How do the heroes handle the surprise of Gurr's takeover?

3 Do you think Tricker is truly forgiven? Why or why not?

4 What kind of hero is Scatter becoming? Use evidence from her speech or actions.

Activity Suggestion:

🐾 *Mood Map* — Create a visual of how the mood shifts from joy → unease → confrontation across three color zones (e.g., yellow → gray → deep red). Add keywords or symbols in each zone.

🐾 FLUENCY & LITERARY FOCUS: CHAPTER 18

📺 Scene-Based Fluency Practice

Key Scenes to Practice:

1 Tricker's Apology and Scatter's Response

◦ *Tone Focus:* Regret, vulnerability, gentle strength

◦ *Practice Tip:* Have students practice speaking Tricker's lines in a whisper or low voice, followed by Scatter's firm but soft forgiveness.

2 Gurr's Confrontation

◦ *Tone Focus:* Cold control, mocking dominance

◦ *Practice Tip:* Assign a student narrator to describe the scene's visuals while another voices Gurr with controlled, menacing rhythm.

3 Scatter's Stand

○ *Tone Focus:* Courage, rising resolve, subtle defiance

○ *Practice Tip:* Compare reading her speech calmly vs. with quiet fire. Invite students to stand when delivering it as a performance.

⟁ LITERARY STRUCTURE FOCUS

Highlighted Devices:
- **Juxtaposition:** Celebration vs. Confrontation
- **Simile & Personification:** Mist/storm + shadows that "bow" to Gurr
- **Metaphor:** "Grain in a bag with a hole" = broken trust
- **Symbolism:** The setting sun = end of innocence, beginning of reckoning

Student Literary Task:

➡ *Identify 2 examples of figurative language in the chapter. What mood or message do they help create?*

➡ Bonus: Write a figurative line of your own about **what it feels like when home no longer feels safe.**

🔍 LITERARY ANALYSIS
- Foreshadowing: "The elders whispered among themselves…"
- Juxtaposition: Celebration shifts to confrontation
- Metaphor: "Grain in a bag with a hole" = lost trust
- Symbolism: Sunset = end of peace

📊 ASSESSMENTS
Formative:
- Explain the grain metaphor in your own words
- Map the mood change in the chapter using colors or images
- Exit Ticket: "What would YOU do in Scatter's place?"

Summative:
- Character letter: Tricker to Wakaduo
- Creative Rewrite: Scatter's speech to the villagers

· · ·

💼 DIFFERENTIATION STRATEGIES
- Emerging Readers: Chunk text into visual panels
- ELL: Use sentence stems and translation support
- Advanced: Rewrite Gurr's speech as a persuasive argument
- Kinesthetic: Freeze-frame scenes for tone

📚 SoR INTEGRATION
- Fluency: Gurr's cold tone vs. Scatter's calm
- Vocabulary: morpheme analysis
- Comprehension: Compare character arcs
- Literary Structure: Climax and tone shift

💬 ESSENTIAL QUESTION
What does it mean to come home changed—and what happens when home has changed, too?

SUMMARY SHEET

Main Setting: Wakaduo village

Key Themes: Homecoming, Redemption, Celebration vs. Conflict, Standing Up for What's Right

📋 SHORT SUMMARY:
The heroes return to Wakaduo, greeted with laughter, decorations, and a sense of pride. While most animals rejoice, Tricker is haunted by guilt over his betrayal. In a tender moment, Scatter forgives him, affirming their bond and offering a path toward healing. But the joy of homecoming quickly turns to dread when Gurr, now leading a group of predators, confronts them. Gurr declares dominance over Wakaduo, turning celebration into confrontation. The heroes must now defend their homeland from within, realizing

that true heroism means facing threats even in the places they love most.

⟡ Comprehension Focus:
• What does Tricker's apology and Scatter's response teach us about forgiveness?
• How does Gurr's takeover shift the tone of the chapter?
• Why is it important for the heroes to stand together now?

⟡ Main Characters Introduced/Expanded:
• Tricker: Vulnerable but sincere, seeking redemption
• Scatter: A compassionate leader who values loyalty and growth
• Gurr: Dominant predator who seeks to control Wakaduo
• Village Elders: Symbol of tradition and rising concern

⟡ Vocabulary to Preteach:
• Forgiveness
• Confrontation
• Redemption
• Alliance

⟡ Figurative Language or Literary Devices:
• "The shadows lengthened as if bowing to his rule." *(Personification)*
• "The warmth of homecoming vanished like mist before a storm." *(Simile)*

⟡ Quote of the Chapter:
"This isn't the welcome we hoped for, but it's the challenge we have to face."

. . .

🌐 REAL-WORLD CONNECTION OR SEL TIE-IN:

This chapter explores the power of forgiveness and standing up for your values. Discuss moments when students had to make hard choices in friendships or confront unfairness in their communities.

📖 ✍ REFLECTION QUESTIONS

Theme: Homecoming, Betrayal, and Rising Leadership

💬 *"We fix our bags and our friendships."*

REFLECTION PROMPTS:

1. Scatter says, "We thought we'd come home to friends." How does that line hit you?

2. What makes a place "home" when it's no longer safe?

3. Tricker says he's bad at keeping secrets. What does Scatter's forgiveness teach us about second chances?

4. Would you fight to protect your home if it changed while you were gone?

🌑 Wisdom Stone Earned:

🖼 Courage Under Twilight

🪨 *Draw what Wakaduo used to look like—and what it looks like now:*

✍ CER WRITING (CLAIM–EVIDENCE–REASONING)

Use this structured writing prompt to support deeper thinking and text-based writing. The CER framework guides students to:

• Form a clear claim
• Support their thinking with specific textual evidence
• Explain how that evidence proves their point
• Practice academic writing sentence starters
• Build argumentative and persuasive thinking

Ideal after discussion, close reading, or as a lead-in to a short response

CER Worksheet

Title: Chapter 18 — *A Hero's Welcome*

Prompt/Question:

Why was forgiveness important for Tricker and the heroes?

1. CLAIM

(What do you believe?)

Starter: *I believe that...*

2. EVIDENCE

(Find a quote or describe something that happened.)

Starters:

• *In the story it says...*

• *One example is when...*

• *The author shows that...*

3. REASONING

(Explain why your evidence proves your claim)

Starters:

• *This shows that...*

• *This proves that...*

• *This means...*

QUICK CHECKLIST

☑ Clear answer?

☑ Strong evidence?

☑ Good explanation?

. . .

WHEN TO USE:

- ✅ After discussion or reading group
- ✅ Before writing paragraphs or journal reflections
- ✅ As a formative assessment
- ✅ For writing support or enrichment

BONUS (OPTIONAL):

Draw a picture of Scatter forgiving Tricker.

CER PEER REVIEW CHECKLIST: WARM FEEDBACK FOR Chapter 18

Trade CER responses with a partner. Use this checklist to help each other revise and grow!

✅ **Check Each One:**

✅

Review Questions

Does the response have a **clear claim** about forgiveness?

Does it include **specific text evidence** from the chapter?

Does it have a strong **explanation** showing why the evidence matters?

Does it stay focused on the question: *Why was forgiveness important?*

💬 **Give One Kind Comment:**

"You did a great job explaining…"

GIVE ONE HELPFUL SUGGESTION:

"Next time, maybe add more about…"

BONUS (OPTIONAL):

Draw a quick symbol for *forgiveness* (a bridge, a hand, a sunrise…)

POETRY PACK ACTIVITY SHEET - SONNET

✏ Poem Text:
Sonnet: The Welcome of Shadows and Light

Upon our return to fields once so bright,
The shadows stretch out, taking the light.
Our hearts full with tales of lands far and wide,
Find home transformed, with dusk where dawn once lied.
Marula whispers, children's laughter sings,
Yet beneath this joy, tension tightly clings.
Faces of old, with worry lines marked deep,
Stirring doubts that creep in, disrupting our sleep.
Yet here we stand, where roots and dreams entwine,
Wakaduo's soil, with destiny's design.
Gurr stands, his challenge dark against the sky,
Our welcome warm now a cold battle cry.
But heroes we are, through trials forged and tried,
Together we stand, with truth as our guide.

☉ STUDENT POETRY ACTIVITIES
ACTIVITY 1: Find the Contrast

This poem contrasts **light and dark** and **hope and fear**.
☑ **Underline** words related to:
• **Light / Hope**
• **Darkness / Fear**
(Encourages students to detect themes and imagery!)

ACTIVITY 2: WHAT CHANGED?
Answer in 2-3 sentences:

How is Wakaduo different now compared to how the heroes left it?

" _____

_____."

ACTIVITY 3: Sound and Rhythm ♫

Sonnets have a musical rhythm called **iambic pentameter** (soft-LOUD pattern, five beats per line).

☑ **Clap out the beats** in one of these lines:
• "Upon our return to fields once so bright."
☑ Then **write your own 5-beat line** about Wakaduo:

" _____."

(*Strengthens phonological awareness and fluency!*)

ACTIVITY 4: Write Your Own "Welcome" Line

Imagine YOU returning home after a long, hard journey.

Write a line showing your feelings (happy, nervous, hopeful?).

" _____."

Teacher Tip (Small Print)
☑ **Standards Alignment:**
• Identify Theme and Tone
• Analyze Word Choice and Meaning
• Practice Rhythm and Fluency
☑ **Science of Reading Focus:**
• Prosody (Expression)
• Vocabulary Expansion
• Reading Comprehension

❦

Here is the Student Workbook Prediction Tracker:

PREDICTION TRACKER

Prediction Tracker: What Will They Do Next?

After reading Chapter 18, think about what each character is feeling — and what choices they might make going forward. Write a few sentences for each character below.

TRICKER

- What is Tricker feeling right now?
- What might he do next?
- Why do you think that?
- Your Response:

SCATTER

- How is Scatter handling everything?
- What might she do next as a leader?
- Why?
- Your Response:

GURR

- What is Gurr's attitude at the end of the chapter?
- What do you think he'll try next?
- What clues from the story support your idea?
- Your Response:

BONUS CHALLENGE:

Drama Time! — Students can perform the sonnet dramatically, assigning emotions to each part (joy, sadness, hope, tension).

INTERLUDE — WHISPERS
BEFORE THE STORM

TEACHER'S ANNOTATED GUIDE

CHAPTER OVERVIEW

This Interlude brings the journey of *Unleashing Greatness: The kingdom of Shadows* into reflection. It introduces three final chapters that enrich the world of Wakaduo and Ruaha, deepen the reader's understanding of leadership, identity, and courage, and connect the fictional quest to the real-life journeys of readers themselves. These chapters—on Adira and Tau, the Predators' Plot, and Alice and the Stone Bracelet—serve as bridges between past and future, action and insight.

The interlude is a space for synthesizing meaning. It calls readers to pause, question, and recognize the legacy the heroes carry forward—and the greatness that lives in all of us when we lead with courage, compassion, and purpose.

INSTRUCTIONAL FOCUS

- Deepen comprehension of character development and leadership themes
- Apply context clues to infer motivation and meaning
- Analyze symbolism and the structure of the epilogue
- Reflect on personal connections to the heroes' journey
- Synthesize themes of unity, resilience, and growth

READING SKILLS SECTION

1. VOCABULARY DEVELOPMENT

Key Terms: *Synergistic, nefarious, epilogue*

- Discuss meaning using student-friendly definitions.
- Explore how these words relate to relationships, choices, and structure in the story.
- Example Prompt: *What does it mean when leaders are "synergistic"? How do Adira and Tau demonstrate or fail at this?*

◆ CHAPTER 19 MINI-LESSON:

Theme: Reflection, Legacy, and the Calm Before Chaos
◎ Objective:
Students will explore how reflection and storytelling connect past actions to future challenges. They'll identify key questions posed by the interlude and synthesize how history informs leadership and legacy.

🔍 QUICK TEACH: REFLECTION AS PREPARATION
1. Proverb Anchor:
"Not every battle is fought with swords. Some begin in silence."
💬 *Discuss:* Why might silence—or storytelling—be powerful before a big decision?

2. Timeline Sketch Activity:

Draw a 3-box timeline:

- ◦ 📦 Box 1: *What happened before the storm?*
- ◦ 🛡 Box 2: *What fears or questions are rising now?*
- ◦ 🔔 Box 3: *What might the future hold for the heroes?*

3. Mini-Reflection Write:

✎ *What is one quiet lesson the characters (or you) learn from silence before a storm?*

"Sometimes we need to slow down to understand…"

4. Discussion Prompt:

➤ Which of the three upcoming chapters are you most curious about—Adira and Tau, the predator plot, or the Stone Bracelet? Why?

2. COMPREHENSION THROUGH CONTEXT CLUES

a. Inferring Character Traits from Actions

Text Example: *"Adira, her expression bearing an unusual gravity, gestured for the heroes to enter."*

Inference: Her silence and serious demeanor suggest wisdom and protective intent.

b. Visualizing Scene and Mood from Setting

Text Example: *"The ground trembled beneath them, rocks tumbling as the giant boulder slowly gave way."*

Activity: Ask students to draw or describe what they imagine. What emotions are evoked?

3. READING FOR DETAILS

- Examine the past relationship between Adira and Tau.
- Identify what held Wakaduo and Ruaha together before the conflict.
- Ask: *What clues show that this peace was once strong but fragile?*

4. UNDERSTANDING CAUSE AND EFFECT

- Trace the predators' plan to undermine Wakaduo.
- Analyze how fear and misinformation nearly succeeded.
- Reflect on the heroes' actions in restoring unity.

5. SEQUENCING

Have students list the three chapters of the epilogue in order:

1. Adira, the Tortoise, and Tau, the Lion
2. The Predator's Plot
3. Alice and the Stone Bracelet
4. Then, ask how each builds on the last and prepares the reader for the story's conclusion.

6. CHARACTER ANALYSIS

Focus: **Alice**

- What does her discovery of the Stone Bracelet symbolize?
- How does her story connect past, present, and future?
- Ask: *How has Alice changed? How does she carry forward the heroes' legacy?*

7. SUMMARIZING AND SYNTHESIZING

- Summarize each epilogue chapter.
- Synthesize: *What big ideas do they all share? What message do they leave readers with?*

8. DRAWING CONCLUSIONS

Compare Tau and Adira's leadership:

- Tau leads through strength; Adira through reflection.
- Their synergy—when it happens—shows how diverse leadership styles can coexist.
- Discussion Prompt: *What kind of leader would you be?*

THEME AND LITERARY STRUCTURE

Central Themes:

- Leadership as evolving and responsive
- Unity as both strength and responsibility
- Legacy as something passed through action and memory
- The journey as ongoing, even after a "final" victory

Structure Focus:

The interlude follows the *"Return with the Elixir"* stage of the Hero's Journey.

Ask students: *What "elixirs" (gifts, lessons, powers) do the heroes bring back?*

🜚 FLUENCY & LITERARY FOCUS: CHAPTER 18

🜚 Key Scenes for Fluency Practice:

1 Tricker's Apology and Scatter's Response

° *Tone Focus:* Regret, vulnerability, gentle strength

° *Practice Tip:* Have students practice speaking Tricker's lines in a whisper or low voice, followed by Scatter's firm but soft forgiveness.

2 Gurr's Confrontation

° *Tone Focus:* Cold control, mocking dominance

° *Practice Tip:* Assign a student narrator to describe the scene's visuals, another voices Gurr with menacing rhythm.

3 Scatter's Stand

○ *Tone Focus:* Courage, rising resolve, subtle defiance
○ *Practice Tip:* Compare reading her speech calmly vs. with quiet fire. Invite students to stand and perform delivery.

FLUENCY & PROSODY PRACTICE

Choose short reflective passages from the Interlude for dramatic reading:

- Tone: Thoughtful, hopeful, reflective
- Encourage pauses to emphasize big ideas

Discussion Prompts

1. What questions does the epilogue help you answer?
2. Why do you think the author chose to include three additional chapters?
3. How is the story of Scatter and her friends like real-world leadership journeys?
4. What kind of legacy do you think the heroes will leave behind? What legacy do you want to leave?

WRITING PROMPTS

- Reflect: *What lesson did you learn from one of the heroes?*
- Narrative: *Write a new chapter of your life where you discover your "inner greatness."*
- Creative: *If you found the Stone Bracelet, what would it show you?*
- Informative: *Explain how misinformation affected Wakaduo— and how communities can resist it.*

ASSESSMENT IDEAS

Exit Slip Questions:

- What is one big idea you took from the interlude?
- Which character do you want to learn more about?
- What new question do you have after reading these chapters?

Formative Options:

- Interlude Timeline
- Character Reflection Journals
- Partner Discussion Circles

Summative Ideas:

- Short essay: *Compare Tau's and Adira's leadership styles*
- Presentation: *What does "Unleashing Greatness" mean? to you?*
- Project: *Design a symbol that represents your legacy as a young leader*

✐ LITERARY STRUCTURE FOCUS

Highlighted Devices:

- **Juxtaposition:** Celebration vs. Confrontation
- **Simile & Personification:** Mist/storm + shadows that "bow" to Gurr
- **Metaphor:** "Grain in a bag with a hole" = broken trust
- **Symbolism:** The setting sun = end of innocence, beginning of reckoning

Student Literary Task:

➡ *Identify 2 examples of figurative language in the chapter. What mood or message do they help create?*

➡ Bonus: Write a figurative line of your own about **what it feels like when home no longer feels safe.**

DIFFERENTIATION STRATEGIES

Visual Learners – Interlude story map; Create a mood collage.

Auditory Learners – Partner reading of epilogue with musical underscore

   Kinesthetic Learners – Create symbolic "bracelets" or "tooth tokens" from clay or paper

   Struggling Readers – Use guided reading cards with sentence stems and simplified summaries

   Advanced Readers – Write their own interlude chapter from another character's point of view

Cross-Curricular Extensions

Social Studies: Study how leaders from history used wisdom or power to lead their communities.

   Art: Illustrate one of the three interlude chapters or design a "Legacy Banner."

   Science: Explore how misinformation spreads (social psychology or biology metaphor).

   SEL (Social Emotional Learning): Reflect on personal journeys, mistakes, and transformations.

Final Reflection Prompt

"Through the adventures of Scatter and her friends, this story asks you to think about your own journey. What is your greatness—and how will you unleash it?"

Have students write their own short "Interlude Reflection" on what they've learned about leadership, unity, courage, or community from this novel—and how they'll carry those lessons forward.

SUMMARY SHEET - WHISPERS BEFORE THE STORM

Main Setting: Narrative reflection between Wakaduo and Ruaha
    Key Themes: Reflection, History, Hidden Lessons, Prelude to Conflict, Community Wisdom

📄 SHORT SUMMARY:

This special interlude offers readers a moment of reflection before the final climax. It poses deep questions: What held Wakaduo and Ruaha together before the conflict? What role did predators' misinformation play in nearly tearing the land apart? What is the meaning behind the mysterious Stone Bracelet? The interlude sets the stage for three powerful chapters—each unpacking critical history, hidden motivations, and the tension between power and peace. The chapter invites readers to consider how the past influences the present and how unity can arise from shared understanding, even amid difference.

🧠 COMPREHENSION FOCUS:

• Why is it important to reflect before a major event?
• What questions does the interlude ask the reader to think about?
• How does this section prepare you for what's to come?

💀 MAIN CHARACTERS INTRODUCED/EXPANDED:

• Adira: The wise tortoise who understands history and balance
• Tau: Proud lion leader whose choices define the path ahead
• Alice: An explorer whose discovery links generations
• The Community of Wakaduo: Collective memory and hope

🔍 VOCABULARY TO PRETEACH:

Interlude, Unity, Misinformation, Reflection, Legacy

. . .

🪡 FIGURATIVE LANGUAGE OR LITERARY DEVICES:

- "Not every battle is fought with swords. Some begin in silence." *(Metaphor)*
- "The heroes stand as testament to the enduring power of unity." *(Symbolism)*

📖 QUOTE OF THE CHAPTER:

"Not every battle is fought with swords. Some begin in silence."

🌐 REAL-WORLD CONNECTION OR SEL TIE-IN:

This chapter encourages self-reflection. Ask students to consider: What lessons from your past shape who you are? How can knowing history help us make better choices for the future?

☙❧

📖 ✎ REFLECTION QUESTIONS

Theme: Reflection, Backstory, and Foreshadowing

 "Not every battle is fought with swords. Some begin in silence."

Reflection Prompts:

1. Why do you think the author included this interlude before the final battle?

2. Of the three bonus chapters mentioned, which one are you most interested in and why?

3. How do quiet moments—like this pause—help us understand the bigger story better?

4. Do you think stories need to slow down sometimes in order to move forward?

🌑 Wisdom Stone Earned:

The Silence Before the Storm

✎ *Design a "whisper symbol"—a mark of quiet strength:*

❧ 20 ❧

ADIRA, THE TORTOISE AND TAU, THE LION

🍎 TEACHER'S ANNOTATED GUIDE

P roverb:
    "When the music changes, so does the dance."

🔍 CHAPTER OVERVIEW

This chapter centers on a high-stakes diplomatic meeting between **Adira**, the wise tortoise of Wakaduo, and **Tau**, the lion king of Ruaha. As dark storm clouds loom over both lands, Adira proposes opening a long-sealed passage between the prey and predator realms to foster unity and prepare for shared threats. Tau, torn between his instincts, legacy, and leadership responsibilities, ultimately rejects the proposal, asserting the ancient divide between predator and prey. The literal boulder that separates their worlds remains unmoved—mirroring the ideological divide between tradition and change. The chapter explores **leadership, diplomacy, fear of change**, and the cost of missed opportunity.

. . .

THEMES:

Leadership, change vs. tradition, diplomacy, survival, unity, fear, and the weight of decision-making.

🪨 LEARNING OBJECTIVES
- Analyze contrasting leadership styles (Adira vs. Tau)
- Identify symbolic meaning in setting (storm, boulder)
- Explore figurative language (proverb, metaphor)
- Reflect on change and unity using text evidence
- Apply cause-and-effect reasoning and make predictions

📖 VOCABULARY & MORPHOLOGY TIE-IN — CHAPTER 20

Proverb: *"When the music changes, so does the dance."*

Themes: Leadership, diplomacy, tradition vs. change

🧩 Key Vocabulary Words

1 Refuge
- Root: Latin *fugere* ("to flee")
- Meaning: A place of safety or shelter
- Context: "Wakaduo was a refuge where prey ruled."

2 Diplomacy
- Root: *diploma* (Greek, "folded paper" → agreement/treaty)
- Suffix: -cy (makes it a noun, "state or quality of")
- Meaning: The art of negotiation and peacemaking
- Context: "Adira's words carried the weight of diplomacy."

3 Instinct
- As seen in Ch. 22, also appears here in Tau's internal conflict
- "Can peace truly reign when one's nature is to devour the other?"

4 Tradition
- Prefix: *tra-* (Latin *trans*, "across")
- Root: *dit* (from *dare*, "to give")
- Meaning: Something passed down
- Context: "Tau heard the voices of his ancestors…"

. . .

🔤 MORPHOLOGY ACTIVITIES
- **Word Webs**: Create clusters around *refuge, tradition*, and *instinct*
- **Compare & Contrast**: Define *diplomacy* vs. *dominance* using real-world examples
- **Proverb Analysis**: How does "When the music changes…" relate to vocabulary about change and habit?

📖 APPLICATION PROMPT
➡ Choose one vocabulary word and explain how it shapes Tau's or Adira's decision-making.

◆ CHAPTER 20 MINI-LESSON:

Theme: Leadership, Tradition vs. Change, and Missed Opportunity

🎯 Objective:
Students will compare Tau and Adira's leadership philosophies and evaluate the impact of fear, tradition, and pride on decision-making.

📖 QUICK TEACH: DIPLOMACY VS. DOMINANCE
1. Proverb Anchor:
"When the music changes, so does the dance."

🎵 *Prompt*: What is the "music" in this story? How are the characters being asked to change their "dance"?

2. T-CHART ACTIVITY: COMPARE LEADERSHIP STYLES

Adira (Tortoise)	Tau (Lion)
Patient, wise	Strong, traditional
Wants unity	Fears disorder

➤ *Add one quote or behavior for each leader.*

3. Short Write Prompt:

✎ *If you were Tau, would you open the boulder? Why or why not?*
Use the line: "I believe Tau should/should not…"

4. Discussion Circle:

➤ "What does it take for two very different groups to work together? Can peace exist without trust?"

📖 KEY TEACHING NOTES & ANNOTATIONS

Opening Line:

"The land of Wakaduo was a safe haven…"
Prompt: What makes Wakaduo feel peaceful? What does "haven" suggest?

Adira's Arrival:

"She sought a meeting with Tau…"
Why does Adira want to negotiate? What does this reveal about her leadership?

Tau's Resistance:

"We are predators. You are prey. That will never change."
Compare Tau's traditionalism with Adira's progressivism. Which is more effective?

Symbolic Setting:

"Dark storm clouds loomed…"
The storm symbolizes rising conflict—ask students to track visual metaphors throughout the scene.

Proverb Connection:

"When the music changes, so does the dance."
Ask: What does this imply about flexibility in leadership?

🔍 COMPREHENSION GUIDE – CHAPTER 20: ADIRA THE TORTOISE AND TAU THE LION

Proverb Focus: *"When the music changes, so does the dance."*

⬤ BEFORE READING

Purpose: Introduce contrasting leadership styles and prepare students to think symbolically about settings and tone.

Discussion Starters:

• What do you expect will happen when two very different leaders meet to solve a problem?

• Based on the title, how do you think Tau and Adira might view the world differently?

• Read the proverb aloud. What might it mean for leaders or for change?

Prediction Prompt:

➡️ *What could the "music" be in this chapter, and how might the "dance" change?*

✎ "Maybe the music is the storm or a new threat..."

✎ "I think Tau and Adira will…"

⬤ DURING READING

Purpose: Guide comprehension around character conflict, symbolism, and leadership philosophy.

Guided Reading Prompts:

• How does the author describe Wakaduo vs. Ruaha? What words or images stand out?

• What does Adira want from Tau? Why is it important?

• What does Tau fear most about opening the boulder?

• How does the storm reflect what's happening between the characters?

Vocabulary-in-Context Prompts:

• What does "refuge" mean in the context of Wakaduo?

• When Tau says "We are predators. And you are prey," what does he mean?

• What is "diplomacy," and how is it shown here?

● AFTER READING

Purpose: Reflect on symbolism, foreshadowing, and the unresolved tension between peace and power.

Reflection & Discussion Prompts:

1 Why do you think Tau really says no—even though he respects Adira?

2 What does the storm represent? How does it show both danger and urgency?

3 Was the meeting a failure or a success? Why?

4 What might happen next if neither kingdom unites?

Activity Suggestion:

● *Boulder Metaphor Map* — Students draw the boulder and label it with quotes, emotions, and what it symbolizes (division, safety, fear, missed opportunity, etc.).

GUIDED READING PROMPTS:

• Before: What happens when predator and prey try to negotiate?

• During: How do Tau's words and body language reveal internal struggle?

• After: Why does Adira remain hopeful despite rejection?

● DIFFERENTIATED INSTRUCTION

• Visual: Storyboard the meeting using storm imagery and character positioning

• Auditory: Dramatic reading of dialogue between Adira and Tau

• Kinesthetic: Roleplay the negotiation with students assigned varied character perspectives

• ELL: Vocabulary glossary and sentence stems

✿ FLUENCY & LITERARY FOCUS

Key Passages for Performance:

1 Adira's Plea

- *Tone Practice:* Warm, wise, hopeful
- *Line:* "Change our dance… together strong, let's forge ahead."
- *Practice Tip:* Read it gently, like a guiding elder.

2 Tau's Conflict

- *Tone Practice:* Commanding → reflective → torn
- *Line:* "Can peace truly reign when one's nature is to devour the other?"
- *Practice Tip:* Practice the shift in emotion—read first like a ruler, then like someone doubting their own belief.

3 Final Declaration

- *Tone Practice:* Firm, sorrowful
- *Line:* "We are Predators. And you are Prey. That will never change."
- *Practice Tip:* Read this line slowly, with emphasis on finality and internal struggle.

Group Fluency Challenge:

▶ Divide students into "Adira voices" and "Tau voices." Each side reads a selected passage in chorus with expressive tone, adjusting speed and emphasis.

LITERARY DEVICES FOCUS – CHAPTER 20

1. Symbolism

- **The Boulder** represents the barrier between predator and prey—both literal and ideological. Though it is a physical object, it also symbolizes generational resistance to change.
- **The Storm Clouds** stand for rising tensions and the threat of external forces (like nature, conflict, or time) that could overwhelm both kingdoms if unity is not achieved.

2. Proverb as Theme Device

"When the music changes, so does the dance."

This guiding proverb reinforces the theme of adaptability in leadership. It challenges characters (and readers) to consider how old ways may not suit new challenges.

3. Metaphor

"The boulder that separated our lands can also connect us."

Adira reframes the obstacle as a potential bridge, offering a metaphor for shifting perspectives and the power of shared purpose.

4. Personification

"The storm rumbled above, mirroring the battle within him."

The weather reflects Tau's internal conflict. This personification connects the external setting to his emotional and psychological state.

5. Juxtaposition

The peaceful wisdom of Adira is directly contrasted with the proud caution of Tau. Their dialogue reveals two different philosophies—cooperation versus control—setting the ideological conflict in motion.

6. Dialogue as Characterization

Tau's lines are heavy with pride, tradition, and suppressed doubt. Adira's speech is calm, layered with logic and empathy. Their exchanges deepen the reader's understanding of their leadership styles and values.

7. Foreshadowing

Tau's refusal and the mention of unrest within Ruaha hint that his grip on control may falter. This sets the stage for future conflict and the eventual challenge to his authority.

8. Allusion to Natural Law

Tau references the predator/prey relationship as unchangeable: *"We are predators. And you are prey."* This evokes a larger philosophical debate about nature, choice, and the possibility (or impossibility) of peace through change.

STUDENT WRITING PROMPT:

▶ *Choose a literary device used in this chapter. What does it help you understand about the characters or their choices?*

Optional Extension:

◡ Write your own mini-scene between two leaders who must decide whether to unite or stay divided. Use at least one metaphor or symbol.

STANDARDS ALIGNMENT
- RL.4.1 – Text evidence
- RL.4.3 – Describe characters and events
- RL.4.4 – Word meaning in context
- RL.4.6 – Compare viewpoints
- W.4.1 – Opinion writing

✒ ASSESSMENTS

• Formative: Exit slip – "Was Tau's decision wise?"

• Summative: Write a letter from Adira explaining the failed negotiation

• Creative Extension: Rewrite the chapter with Tau saying yes

📚 CROSS-CURRICULAR CONNECTIONS
- Science: Predator-prey relationships, natural migration
- Social Studies: Peace negotiations, diplomacy
- SEL: Ethical decision-making and emotional complexity in leadership

💬 REFLECTION QUESTIONS

1. Why couldn't Tau say yes—even if he wanted to?
2. What does the proverb reveal about change?
3. Can different communities live in peace? What would it take?

Closure Activity:

"Storm Forecast" sticky note exit slip: "What do the clouds represent? What happens if Wakaduo and Ruaha remain divided?"

SUMMARY SHEET

Main Setting: Border of Wakaduo and Ruaha (near the Boulder Passage)

Key Themes: Leadership, Wisdom vs. Power, Negotiation, Tradition vs. Change

SHORT SUMMARY:

Adira, the ancient and wise tortoise, seeks a peaceful alliance with Tau, ruler of Ruaha. The two leaders meet at the great boulder that separates their realms to discuss the growing storm and a potential pathway between their kingdoms. Adira urges unity, but Tau hesitates, bound by the beliefs and hunger of his predator kind. Though he respects Adira's wisdom, Tau ultimately refuses to open the path, declaring that prey and predator cannot truly coexist. Their meeting ends with the boulder unmoved—both literally and metaphorically. The chapter showcases a deep struggle between diplomacy and dominance, revealing how old beliefs may block the path to progress.

COMPREHENSION FOCUS:

• What do Adira and Tau each represent in this chapter?
• Why does Tau refuse to open the path between Ruaha and Wakaduo?
• How does nature serve as a symbol in this scene?

MAIN CHARACTERS INTRODUCED / EXPANDED:

• Adira: Peace-seeking tortoise who values unity and foresight

• Tau: Noble yet proud lion leader, torn between legacy and change
• Skylar: The eagle scout who alerts Tau to the coming storm
• Wakaduo and Ruaha: Representing opposing but interdependent societies

⚲ Vocabulary to Preteach:

• Refuge, Authority, Coexist, Diplomacy, Instinct

▉ Figurative Language or Literary Devices:

• "The same boulder that has separated our lands can also connect us." *(Symbolism)*
• "The storm rumbled above, mirroring the battle within him." *(Personification)*

▥ Quote of the Chapter:

"We are Predators. And you are Prey. That will never change."

◉ Real-World Connection or SEL Tie-In:

This chapter explores conflict resolution and the challenges of bridging cultural divides. Discuss with students how leaders can use wisdom instead of power to bring people together.

࿂

▦ ✐ REFLECTION QUESTIONS / PROMPTS

Theme: Leadership, Fear of Change, and Missed Opportunity

 "When the music changes, so does the dance."

Reflection Prompts:

1. What is Tau afraid of when Adira asks to open the boulder?

2. If you were in Tau's place, would you have opened the passage? Why or why not?

3. What does Adira represent in the story—and why does her role matter so much?

4. What do you think will happen now that the passage remains closed?

Wisdom Stone Earned:

The Stone of Wisdom & Regret

Write a letter that Adira might send to Tau after the meeting:

✒ OPTIONAL CER WRITING

Use this structured writing prompt to support deeper thinking and text-based writing. The CER framework guides students to:

- Form a clear claim
- Support their thinking with specific textual evidence
- Explain how that evidence proves their point
- Practice academic writing sentence starters
- Build argumentative and persuasive thinking

  Ideal after discussion, close reading, or as a lead-in to a short response

CER Worksheet

Prompt/Question:

What lesson about leadership did Adira try to teach Tau?

1. CLAIM

(What do you believe?)

Starter: *I believe that...*

2. EVIDENCE

(Find a quote or describe something that happened.)

✎ Starters:

• *In the story it says...*
• *One example is when...*
• *The author shows that...*

3. ⸱ REASONING

(Explain why your evidence proves your claim)

✎ Starters:

• *This shows that...*
• *This proves that...*
• *This means...*

◎ QUICK CHECKLIST

☑ Clear answer?

☑ Strong evidence?

☑ Good explanation?

⸱ WHEN TO USE:

☑ After discussion or reading group

☑ Before writing paragraphs or journal reflections

☑ As a formative assessment

☑ For writing support or enrichment

⸱ BONUS (OPTIONAL):

Draw a picture of Adira and Tau meeting at the giant boulder.

POETRY ACTIVITY PACK - BALLAD

✏ Poem Text:

The Ballad of Two Realms

In lands apart yet bound by fate,
Two leaders stood at destiny's gate.
Adira wise, with shell so old,
Guarded secrets and tales untold.
Beside the boulder, vast and wide,
Tau, the lion, with regal stride,
Ruled his realm with might and roar,
Where weaker beasts did him adore.
Together met where borders bind,
To discuss the fears that plagued their mind.
The storm clouds brewed a darkened brew,
Foretelling troubles, old and new.
"Change our dance," the tortoise pled,
"Together strong, let's forge ahead."
But Tau, with pride, his mane unfurled,
Spoke of nature's rule in their world.
The boulder stood, no passage gave,
Each returned to the lands they save.
The storm still looms with threatening sway,
As leaders ponder another day.

☉ STUDENT POETRY ACTIVITIES

ACTIVITY 1: MAIN CHARACTERS

✅ **Circle** the names of the two leaders in the poem.
✅ Then **write one describing word** about each:

• **Adira**: _____
• **Tau**: _____

(Focuses on comprehension and character traits!)

· · ·

ACTIVITY 2: PREDICT THE FUTURE!

The poem ends with the leaders separated and the storm coming.

In 2-3 sentences, predict what might happen next!

"_____

_____."

ACTIVITY 3: RHYME HUNT ♫

☑ Ballads often use **rhyme** to make the story feel musical.

☑ **Highlight** 3 pairs of rhyming words from the poem.

Example: fate/gate

ACTIVITY 4: WRITE A "TWO LEADERS" POEM

Imagine two very different leaders (maybe a hawk and a turtle?)

Write 2-4 lines about how they would work together — or disagree!

"_____

_____."

TEACHER TIP (SMALL PRINT)

☑ **Standards Alignment:**

• Identify Characters and Relationships
• Analyze Plot and Conflict
• Recognize and Create Rhyme

☑ **Science of Reading Focus:**

• Vocabulary Development
• Comprehension and Inference
• Phonological Awareness (through rhyme)

BONUS CHALLENGE:

🗣 **Readers' Theater!** — Split the class into two groups (Adira's side and Tau's side) and **act out** their meeting at the boulder!

❧ 21 ❧

THE PREDATORS' PLOT

🐾 TEACHER'S ANNOTATED GUIDE

P roverb:
"Do not look where you fell, but where you slipped."

🔍 CHAPTER OVERVIEW

In the shadows of Ruaha, predators gather under the leadership of Hugger the Rock Python to devise a deceitful plan: use **fear** instead of force to drive Wakaduo's prey from their homeland. Despite Tau's command to leave Wakaduo in peace, predators like Dirty Donald, Leona, and even the young Kael conspire to hoist **Crusher the crocodile** into a secret cave. There, his **booming roar**—the so-called "Voice of Doom"—sends terror sweeping through Wakaduo. The prey animals flee in panic, seemingly paving the way for the predators' takeover. However, just as the predators celebrate, **Skylar the eagle** delivers grave news: **Mount Tanganyika is erupting**, threatening both kingdoms. This chapter weaves themes of **deception, fear tactics, ambition,**

and natural consequences, setting the stage for coming confrontations and awakenings.

THEMES:
Deception, jealousy, consequence, loyalty, fear, and groupthink

☀ LEARNING OBJECTIVES
- Analyze predator motives and shifting alliances
- Evaluate fear as a leadership tactic
- Identify cause-effect relationships
- Interpret the proverb in light of actions
- Track foreshadowing and suspense

🍃 VOCABULARY & MORPHOLOGY TIE-IN — CHAPTER 21

Chapter Title: *The Predators' Plot*
Proverb: *"Do not look where you fell, but where you slipped."*
Themes: Deception, jealousy, manipulation

🧩 KEY VOCABULARY WORDS
1 Deception
- Prefix: de- ("off, down")
- Root: *cept* ("to take")
- Suffix: -ion (noun, "act of")
- Meaning: The act of misleading or tricking
- Context: "Their scheme relied on sound—an echo of deception."

2 Concoct
- Root: Latin *concoquere* ("to cook together")
- Meaning: To invent or devise, especially with trickery
- Context: "Hugger the Python concocts a plan…"

3 Treachery

- ° Root: Old French *trechier*, "to cheat"
- ° Suffix: -ery (turns it into a noun)
- ° Meaning: Betrayal of trust
- ° Context: "Kael hesitated at the edge of treachery."

4 Authority
- ° Root: Latin *auctoritas*, "influence, command"
- ° Meaning: The power to give orders or make decisions
- ° Context: "Tau's authority was being tested from afar."

MORPHOLOGY ACTIVITIES

• **Word Sorts**: Group vocabulary by emotional tone (e.g., negative: treachery, deception)

• **Root Tracking**: Explore *cept*, *con*, and *thor/tor* for cross-content relevance

• **Cause/Effect Vocabulary Map**: How do *concoct* and *authority* connect in the predator alliance?

APPLICATION PROMPT

➡ Choose one vocabulary word and explain how it represents **Hugger's leadership style**.

◆ CHAPTER 21 MINI-LESSON: "THE PREDATORS' PLOT"

Theme: Deception, Fear, and Consequences

Objective:
Students will evaluate how fear can be used as a tool of manipulation, and reflect on the morality of Hugger's strategy.

QUICK TEACH: FEAR VS. FORCE
1. Proverb Anchor:
"Do not look where you fell, but where you slipped."

🎩 *Prompt*: Where did the predators go wrong? Was it the plan—or the reason behind it?

2. Cause & Effect Activity:

Match the predator actions with outcomes:

Action	Effect
Lifted Crusher to cave	Made prey panic
Kael questioned plan	Showed internal conflict
Skylar warned of eruption	Real danger now threatens both kingdoms

3. Quick Write Prompt:

🖋 *Was Hugger a good leader or a dangerous one? Defend your answer using one example from the chapter.*

4. PARTNER DISCUSSION:

➤ "Can leadership built on fear ever succeed long-term? Why or why not?"

📖 TEACHING NOTES

Opening Line:

"The predators of Ruaha had long envied the peace of Wakaduo..."

What emotions drive their jealousy? What's the difference in values?

Secret Meeting under the Baobab:

Use symbolism. Baobab = wisdom or betrayal? Mood = ominous.

Crusher's Roar:

Model dramatic reading. Use tone and volume to build suspense.

Skylar's Return:

Ask: How do natural events challenge their plan?

Proverb Connection:

"Where did they slip?" = jealousy, deception, insecurity

🔍 COMPREHENSION GUIDE — CHAPTER 21: *THE PREDATORS' PLOT*

Proverb Focus:

"Do not look where you fell, but where you slipped."

🔵 BEFORE READING

Purpose: Activate background knowledge on jealousy, peer pressure, and fear-based leadership.

Discussion Starters:

• Have you ever seen someone use fear to get what they want?

• Why might someone choose to scare others instead of talking things out?

• The title mentions a "plot"—what do you think is going to happen?

Prediction Prompt:

✎ "I think the predators will try to scare the prey animals out of Wakaduo because..."

⚪ DURING READING

Purpose: Track key cause-effect events and internal character conflicts (especially Kael).

Guided Reading Prompts:

• Why does Hugger believe fear will work better than a fight?

• What is the "Voice of Doom"? How does it trick the prey animals?

• How do Kael's questions help us see a different side of the group?

• What do the characters say (or not say) about Tau's leadership?

Vocabulary-in-Context Prompts:

• What does "concoct" mean in the line "Hugger concocts a plan"? What word clues help?

• Why is this plan called "deception"? What's the root word?

· · ·

◉ AFTER READING

Purpose: Reflect on manipulation, group dynamics, and what the proverb teaches about missteps.

Discussion & Reflection Prompts:

1 Why did the predators slip, not just fall? What went wrong in their values or choices?

2 Did they work together successfully? Why might that be dangerous in this case?

3 What would you have done if you were Kael? Would you have spoken up more—or gone along?

4 What does Skylar's news (about the volcano) suggest might happen next?

Optional Visual Response:

🖊 *Draw a three-panel comic:*
- Panel 1: The meeting under the Baobab tree
- Panel 2: Crusher roaring into the cave
- Panel 3: The panic spreading through Wakaduo

◉ CORE COMPREHENSION ACTIVITIES

- Vocabulary: *concoct, amplify, treachery, sinister, deceive*
- Word map and synonym hunt
- Guided questions:

    - Why does Kael hesitate?
    - Is Hugger a leader or a manipulator?

◉ DIFFERENTIATION OPTIONS

- Visual: Comic strip of predator plan
- Auditory: Roleplay predator meeting
- Kinesthetic: Freeze-frame the roar
- ELL: Vocabulary visuals + sentence starters
- Advanced: Write monologue from Kael's POV

🦎 FLUENCY & LITERARY FOCUS — CHAPTER 21: *THE PREDATORS' PLOT*

Key Passages for Performance:
 1 Hugger's Whispering Manipulation
 - *Tone Practice:* Slow, persuasive, slithering
 - *Line:* "Fear won't feed you. But if Tau were to fall… wouldn't Ruaha need a new ruler?"
 - *Practice Tip:* Speak in a low, measured voice with sly pauses.

 2 Crusher's Roar
 - *Tone Practice:* Deep, echoing, terrifying
 - *Line:* "Leave now! Run for your lives before disaster strikes!"
 - *Practice Tip:* Project the line from deep in the chest—then repeat it with a "cave echo" style to mirror the scene.

 3 Kael's Doubt
 - *Tone Practice:* Quiet, hesitant, questioning
 - *Line:* "But what about Tau? He told us not to bother Wakaduo…"
 - *Practice Tip:* Use volume and pacing to show conflict—speed up for nervousness, slow down for hesitation.

 Fluency Mini-Workshop: "Whisper vs. Roar"
 ➡️ Practice contrast between soft, conspiratorial tones (Hugger and Kael) and loud, alarming ones (Crusher and the prey animals reacting).

📐 LITERARY DEVICES FOCUS

1. Personification

"Fear moved like shadows through the bushes."

Fear is given a lifelike, creeping presence, enhancing the sense of dread sweeping through Wakaduo. This device helps readers visualize fear as a physical force rather than an abstract feeling.

2. Irony

"The predators stood, panting—stunned at how close they had come to being crushed by their own scheme."

This moment is a darkly humorous twist. The very plan

designed to scare others nearly ends in disaster for the predators themselves, highlighting the dangers of overconfidence and flawed teamwork.

3. Symbolism

• **The Cave of Doom** represents both deception and the power of illusion. It echoes the theme that fear can be created with sound alone—words and volume, not violence.

• **Crusher** symbolizes brute force being manipulated by more cunning minds (like Hugger's), representing how fear often requires a "face" to become real.

4. Foreshadowing

Skylar's urgent return with news of the volcanic eruption signals that nature itself may soon unravel the predators' illusion. The eruption foreshadows chaos that will surpass any plan the predators have devised.

5. Alliteration

"Voices rise, a storm's brew / In Ruaha, dark plans stew..."

This repetition of consonant sounds in the poem creates rhythm and tension, drawing attention to the gathering threat and making the scene more memorable.

6. Repetition (for emphasis)

"Run for your lives... Run!"

The repeated command intensifies panic in Wakaduo and demonstrates how fear spreads through repetition and mob reaction —essential to the predators' strategy.

7. Dramatic Irony

The audience knows the "Voice of Doom" is a trick, while the prey animals do not. This device increases tension, as we watch innocent characters fall for a deception readers can see through.

 EXTENSION CHALLENGE (ADVANCED READERS)

 Write a paragraph comparing two predators: Hugger and Kael.

How are they different in motivation and morality? Use text evidence.

Design a propaganda poster from Hugger's point of view encouraging other predators to join her plot, using persuasive phrases like:

"Fear feeds the bold!" or *"Wakaduo is yours—if you dare to roar!"*

ASSESSMENTS

• Formative: Exit Ticket – "What fear tactic did Hugger use?"
  • Summative:

  • Essay: Was their plan justified?
  • Creative: Diary entry from Kael

CROSS-CURRICULAR LINKS
  • Science: Real-world predator behavior
  • SEL: Ethical decisions & fear manipulation
  • Music: Create soundscape for Crusher's roar

DISCUSSION PROMPTS

  1. What drives Hugger to act alone?
  2. Can fear unite—or only destroy?
  3. What happens when leaders break trust?

SUMMARY SHEET

Main Setting: Ruaha's secret gathering near the Baobab Tree & the Cave of Doom

Key Themes: Jealousy, Deception, Groupthink, Disobedience, Strategic Fear

· · ·

▮ Short Summary:

In the cover of night, Hugger the Rock Python gathers Ruaha's predators beneath the ancient Baobab tree to hatch a plan: scare the animals of Wakaduo into fleeing, so the predators can take over. Despite Tau's past warnings, Hugger proposes using the deep voice of Crusher the crocodile inside a sound-enhancing cave to create a terrifying illusion—the "Voice of Doom." Dirty Donald, Kael, Leona, and others help lift the giant crocodile into the cave. The plan works: his booming roars send waves of panic through Wakaduo. While the prey animals scramble in fear, Skylar the eagle brings grim news—Mount Tanganyika is erupting, threatening both kingdoms. The predators' false victory is short-lived, and the story foreshadows the storm to come.

◔ Comprehension Focus:

• What motivates Hugger and the predators to plot against Wakaduo?

• How does the "Voice of Doom" work, and why is it effective?

• What warnings or consequences are hinted at by the end of the chapter?

◉ Main Characters Introduced/Expanded:

• Hugger: Persuasive and power-hungry python
• Crusher: Gigantic crocodile whose roar triggers chaos
• Dirty Donald: Mocking, impulsive hyena
• Kael & Leona: Younger predators caught between fear and ambition
• Skylar: Messenger eagle who brings warning of real danger

◔ Vocabulary to Preteach:

Deception, Authority, Consequences, Illusion, Scheme

▮ Figurative Language or Literary Devices:

• "The predators stood, panting—stunned at how close they had come to being crushed by their own scheme." *(Irony)*

• "Fear moved like shadows through the bushes." *(Personification)*

QUOTE OF THE CHAPTER:

"Fear won't feed you. But if Tau were to fall… wouldn't Ruaha need a new ruler?"

● REAL-WORLD CONNECTION OR SEL TIE-IN:

This chapter dives into peer pressure, fear tactics, and how leaders influence followers—for better or worse. Discuss how rumors and groupthink can cause panic or mislead others in real life.

▮ ▲ REFLECTION QUESTIONS

Theme: *Deception and Fear as Tools of Control*

REFLECTION PROMPTS:

1. Why do the predators want to scare the animals away instead of fighting them directly?

2. Do you think Kael was right to question the plan? What would you have done?

3. What does this plan say about leadership when it's based on fear?

4. Can something built on deception last?

🐾 *Art Prompt:* Design a symbol for the "Voice of Doom" cave. What emotions would it project?

✍ OPTIONAL CER WRITING

Use this structured writing prompt to support deeper thinking and text-based writing. The CER framework guides students to:
- Form a clear claim
- Support their thinking with specific textual evidence
- Explain how that evidence proves their point
- Practice academic writing sentence starters
- Build argumentative and persuasive thinking
  - *Ideal after discussion, close reading, or as a lead-in to a short response*

 CER Worksheet
Title: Chapter 21 — *The Predators' Plot*
Prompt/Question:
Why did the predators choose fear instead of fighting in their plan against Wakaduo?

1. 📢 CLAIM
(What do you believe?)
✎ Starter: *I believe that...*

2. 📚 EVIDENCE
(Find a quote or describe something that happened.)
✎ Starters:
- *In the story it says...*
- *One example is when...*
- *The author shows that...*

3. ⚖ REASONING
(Explain why your evidence proves your claim)
✎ Starters:
- *This shows that...*

- *This proves that...*
- *This means...*

ⓔ QUICK CHECKLIST
- ✅ Clear answer?
- ✅ Strong evidence?
- ✅ Good explanation?

WHEN TO USE:
- ✅ After discussion or reading group
- ✅ Before writing paragraphs or journal reflections
- ✅ As a formative assessment
- ✅ For writing support or enrichment

BONUS (OPTIONAL):
🐚 Draw It!
Draw a small symbol or scene that shows the predators' sneaky plan (like Crusher roaring into the cave!).

⚜

POETRY PACK - NARRATIVE POEM (RHYMED STANZAS)

✏ Poem Text:
Whispers Under the Baobab Tree
Under the moon, by the Baobab's knee,
Predators plot with glee,
Hugger the Python, with her scale so sly,
Concocts a plan, "They will run or they'll die."
The night is still, the air is tight,
Dirty Donald laughs at their plight,
"Imagine the feast, oh, the glorious sight,

When the prey flees in the dead of the night."
But Kael, young and unsure,
Whispers, "Is this plan pure?
Tau has said, 'Let them be,'
Should we ignore him, set our greed free?"
Voices rise, a storm's brew,
In Ruaha, dark plans stew,
They speak of a cave, a voice of doom,
To chase the prey and seal their tomb.
Together they haul, with ropes they strive,
Crusher the croc, brought to life,
His roar so deep, through the cave it rings,
A false alarm of terrible things.
"Run for your lives," the echo lies,
In Wakaduo, fear multiplies,
As predators watch with hidden eyes,
Their hearts alight with the prize.

STUDENT POETRY ACTIVITIES

ACTIVITY 1: Mood Detective

✅ How does the mood of the poem feel?
(**Circle** one):
• Happy
• Excited
• Dark and Secretive
• Sad

✅ In one sentence, **explain** your choice:
_"The poem feels _____ because _____."

ACTIVITY 2: Character Check-In

✅ **List the characters** you meet in the poem:
•

•

. . .

•

☑ Who do you think has the biggest doubts about the plan? (Think about feelings, not just actions!)

ACTIVITY 3: RHYME CATCHER ♪♪
☑ **Find and highlight** 2 sets of rhyming words.
Example: knee / glee
☑ Bonus: **Make your own rhyming sentence** about a snake or a crocodile:

ACTIVITY 4: WRITE A SHORT "SECRET MEETING" POEM!
Imagine animals meeting at night in secret (but for a good reason, like saving their home!)
Write 2–4 lines:

TEACHER TIP (SMALL PRINT)
☑ **Standards Alignment:**
• Analyze Mood and Tone
• Identify Character Emotions
• Recognize and Produce Rhyme
☑ **Science of Reading Focus:**
• Oral Language Development
• Comprehension Strategies
• Phonemic Awareness (rhyme and rhythm)

BONUS CHALLENGE:
🐾 **Voice Play!** — Choose a predator and read their lines aloud, acting out how they might sound whispering or plotting in the dark! 🐱🐯

22

ALICE AND THE STONE BRACELET

🦪 TEACHER'S ANNOTATED GUIDE

P roverb:
"To get lost is to learn the way."

☑ CHAPTER OVERVIEW — CHAPTER 22: *ALICE AND THE STONE BRACELET*

Main Focus:

This chapter explores the tension of navigating unfamiliar paths, the layered meanings of trust, and how small acts of bravery can change the course of events.

Key Setting:

Rangu Forest – A dense, enchanted jungle teeming with hidden creatures, unpredictable guides, and unspoken secrets. The thick canopy, whispering trees, and hidden watchers contribute to a setting that feels alive and mysterious.

Plot Summary:

Lost in the depths of the Rangu Forest, the heroes meet Chimper, a charismatic but untrustworthy chimpanzee. Though he offers help, his motives are unclear. Meanwhile, Beyboy, a brave young Mangabey, overhears Chimper's secret plan and risks his life to warn the heroes—only to be captured by Alice, a legendary leopard. Beyboy bargains with a treasured bracelet to save himself. The bracelet becomes a symbol of survival, passing from monkey to Scatter, and finally to Chimper, as a test of trust. As the heroes rest, the dangers of Rangu remain hidden in the shadows. Alice awakens, and revenge is in her heart.

Key Themes:
- Trust and deception
- Bravery in small gestures
- Symbolic power of objects
- Navigating unfamiliar territory
- Redemption and suspicion

◎ Learning Objectives:
- Analyze multiple character motives (Chimper, Beyboy, Scatter, Alice)
  - Explore setting as a narrative force
  - Understand the bracelet as a metaphor for trust and survival
  - Compare truth and trickery in action
  - Practice fluency in dialogue

Essential Question:
Can a single gesture change someone's heart—or expose their true nature?

Themes:
Trust, identity, deception, survival, and change

📚 VOCABULARY & MORPHOLOGY TIE-IN — CHAPTER 22

Chapter Title: *Alice and the Stone Bracelet*

Theme Link: Trust, perception, deception, and transformation

Proverb Connection: *"To get lost is to learn the way."*

🧩 KEY VOCABULARY WORDS

1 Deception
- *Prefix*: de- ("away" or "down")
- *Root*: cept (from Latin *capere*, "to take")
- *Meaning*: The act of hiding the truth or misleading someone
- *Context Use*: "Chimper's voice was smooth, too smooth." → Subtle deception

2 Instinct
- *Prefix*: in- ("in" or "within")
- *Root*: stinct (from Latin *stinguere*, "to prick or incite")
- *Meaning*: A natural drive or inner impulse
- *Context Use*: "Henry's ears twitched. 'Something's here,' he said…"

3 Symbolic
- *Root*: symbol (Greek *symbolon*, "mark or token")
- *Suffix*: -ic (makes it an adjective: "relating to")
- *Meaning*: Representing something beyond the literal
- *Context Use*: "The bracelet became more than a trinket—it was a test."

4 Trinket
- *Definition*: A small decorative object, often with sentimental value
- *Use in Characterization*: Alice sees it as worthless; Beyboy sees it as everything.

5 Gesture
- *Root*: from Latin *gestus*, meaning "to carry" or "to bear"

◦ *Meaning*: A movement or action done to express a feeling or intention

◦ *Context Use*: Scatter's act of giving the bracelet is both a gesture and a signal.

🔤 MORPHOLOGY ACTIVITIES

• **Break It Down**: Students segment compound/multisyllabic vocabulary into prefix + root + suffix.

• **Word Tree Creation**: Build related word families (e.g., *deceive, deceiver, deception, deceptive*).

• **Context Clue Journals**: Highlight one sentence per vocabulary word. Students use clues from the sentence to define the term in their own words.

◆ CHAPTER 22 MINI-LESSON: "ALICE AND THE STONE BRACELET"

Theme: *Trust, Trickery, and Courage in Small Gestures*

◎ **Objective:**

Students will explore how trust and deception shape the heroes' path. They will analyze the symbolic meaning of the bracelet and how a single action can shift power.

📖 **Quick Teach: Symbolism & Motive**

1. Proverb Anchor:

"To get lost is to learn the way."

➤ *Ask:* How does getting lost help the heroes learn who to trust?

2. Symbol Match Activity:

Match each object or action to what it represents:

Item	Symbolic Meaning
The stone bracelet	Trust, survival, test of intention
Alice's attack	Jungle justice, power shift
Chimper's smile	Deception masked as kindness
Beyboy's offer	Bravery, sacrifice

3. Critical Thinking Question:

➤ Was Scatter truly showing trust when she gave Chimper the bracelet—or testing him?

4. Short Write Prompt:

✎ *Describe a time someone earned (or lost) your trust. What happened?*

📖 APPLICATION PROMPT

➡ "Choose one of today's words and explain how it connects to *more than one character* in the chapter."

Examples:

• How is **deception** used by both *Chimper* and *Scatter*?

• How does **instinct** help *Beyboy* survive and *Scatter* decide what to do?

🐚 FULL COMPREHENSION GUIDE – CHAPTER 22: *ALICE AND THE STONE BRACELET*

BEFORE Reading

• 🐾 *What do you think it means to trade something small to save something big?*

• 🐕 *What kinds of characters do you expect when the setting is a mysterious forest?*

• *Have you ever had to decide whether or not to trust someone you weren't sure about?*

DURING Reading

• 🐿 *How does Chimper try to win the heroes' trust? What makes Henry and Scatter suspicious?*

• 🐅 *How does Alice's character affect the story's tension? What does she represent in the forest?*

• 🎁 *What does the bracelet come to symbolize as it changes hands between Beyboy, Scatter, and Chimper?*

• 🌳 *What are some clues that show Chimper's motives aren't fully trustworthy?*

· · ·

AFTER Reading

- 🧠 *Was it wise of Scatter to give Chimper the bracelet? Why or why not?*
- 💬 *How did Beyboy's bravery change the outcome of the story?*
- ⚫ *What role does trust play in survival during this chapter? How do the characters test or earn it?*
- 🎯 *How does this chapter deepen the meaning of the proverb: "To get lost is to learn the way"?*

📖 Key Teaching Points

Sensory Setting:
"The air was damp and smelled of fruit..."
Visualization practice and mood-setting

Character Study – Chimper vs. Beyboy
- Use a Venn diagram to compare honesty, action, and change

Turning Point – Alice's Capture
- Cause-effect chain: Chimper's plan → Beyboy's warning → Alice's response

Final Gesture – The Bracelet
Ask: Is Scatter really trusting Chimper—or testing him?

🧩 Core Activities

- Roleplay: Chimper's reveal vs. Alice's confrontation
- Symbol Tracking: What does the bracelet represent to each character?
- Guided Reading: Close reading of key emotional moments

📈 Formative Assessments

- Quick-write: What does the bracelet symbolize?
- Character journal: Write as Chimper after the gift
- Group discussion: Is trust a tool—or a truth?

📚 Cross-Curricular Extensions

- Art: Design your own symbolic bracelet
- Science: Study animal stealth and camouflage
- SEL: Explore emotional intelligence and trust as survival tools

💬 REFLECTION PROMPT

Can people change—even after a betrayal?

SUMMARY SHEET

Main Setting: Rangu Forest, a dense and mysterious jungle full of ancient trees

Key Themes: Trust and Mistrust, Hidden Dangers, Cleverness Over Strength, Symbolic Objects, Courage in the Face of Fear

🪨 SHORT SUMMARY:

In the shadowy Rangu Forest, the heroes find themselves lost and cautious as they encounter Chimper, a clever chimpanzee who offers to guide them. Though seemingly helpful, Chimper secretly plots with Tau. A young monkey named Beyboy risks his life to warn the heroes but is caught by Alice, a stealthy leopard. Beyboy offers his only possession—a handcrafted stone bracelet—to spare his life. The bracelet becomes a symbol of trust and cleverness, eventually passed from Beyboy to Scatter and then gifted to Chimper to test his loyalty. As Chimper sleeps, unaware of the deeper meanings, Alice wakes with vengeance on her mind. The bracelet has now tied all their fates together in the shadows of Rangu.

🐚 Comprehension Focus:

- Why does Scatter trust Beyboy's bracelet as a symbol of safety?
- How do different characters use deception for both good and bad?
- What does the forest setting add to the tension in the story?

Main Characters Introduced/Expanded:

• **Chimper:** Trickster chimpanzee torn between mischief and redemption

• **Beyboy:** Brave young monkey with a heart full of loyalty

• **Alice:** Silent and fearsome leopard known as the "Ghost of Rangu"

Key Vocabulary Words:

• **Deception** – The act of hiding the truth or misleading someone

• **Instinct** – A natural ability or feeling that helps someone decide what to do

• **Trinket** – A small decorative object that may hold sentimental value

• **Symbolic** – Something that stands for or represents something else

✍ REFLECTION QUESTIONS

Ch. 22 – Alice and the Stone Bracelet

Theme: *Trust, Trickery, and Redemption*

REFLECTION PROMPTS:

1. Why do you think Scatter gave the bracelet to Chimper, even knowing he might be a trickster?

2. What do the bracelet and the Lion's Tooth represent in this chapter?

3. How do Beyboy and the Mangabeys show courage?

4. What does Alice's character add to the story?

Creative Prompt: Write a short scene showing Alice remembering a time she *was* the prey.

✍ OPTIONAL CER WRITING

Use this structured writing prompt to support deeper thinking and text-based writing. The CER framework guides students to:
- Form a clear claim
- Support their thinking with specific textual evidence
- Explain how that evidence proves their point
- Practice academic writing sentence starters
- Build argumentative and persuasive thinking
  - *Ideal after discussion, close reading, or as a lead-in to a short response*

📝 CER WORKSHEET

Title: Chapter 22 — *Alice and the Stone Bracelet*

Prompt/Question:

How did Scatter's kindness with the bracelet change what happened in Rangu Forest?

1. 🐾 CLAIM

(What do you believe?)

✎ Starter: *I believe that...*

2. 🍃 EVIDENCE

(Find a quote or describe something that happened.)

✎ Starters:
- *In the story it says...*
- *One example is when...*
- *The author shows that...*

3. 📝 REASONING

(Explain why your evidence proves your claim)

✎ Starters:
- *This shows that...*

- *This proves that...*
- *This means...*

☙ QUICK CHECKLIST
✅ Clear answer?
✅ Strong evidence?
✅ Good explanation?

WHEN TO USE:
✅ After discussion or reading group
✅ Before writing paragraphs or journal reflections
✅ As a formative assessment
✅ For writing support or enrichment

BONUS (OPTIONAL):
🐚 Draw It!
Draw Scatter giving Chimper the bracelet or Chimper's surprised face!

POETRY ACTIVITY PACK - *NARRATIVE POEM*

(Exploration and Suspense)

✏ POEM TEXT:
🐾 To Get Lost Is to Learn the Way
In Rangu's depths where shadows play,
The heroes walk the hidden way.
Lost beneath the towering trees,
Whispered secrets ride the breeze.
Henry leads with cautious pace,

Unknown perils they must face.
Ancient trees with stories grand,
Time's thick veil they understand.
The forest air, both wild and sweet,
Clings to skin with earthy peat.
Scatter touches mossy bark,
Wishing for a light in dark.
Chimper's voice, both bright and clear,
Promises to guide them near.
Yet in his eyes, a trickster's gleam,
Warns that things aren't as they seem.

STUDENT POETRY ACTIVITIES

ACTIVITY 1: SETTING DETECTIVE

☑ **Describe the setting** in one sentence:
_"The forest feels _____ because _____."

☑ **Circle** the words from the poem that describe the forest:

• towering trees
• whispering breeze
• shiny rivers
• earthy peat
• blazing fires

(☑ Bonus: Add one of your own!)

ACTIVITY 2: CHARACTER CLUES 🕵️

☑ Who seems most trustworthy? _____
☑ Who seems suspicious? _____

Explain:
_"I think _____ is suspicious because _____."

ACTIVITY 3: MOOD METERS

☑ **What is the main mood of the poem?**

(**Circle** one):
- Adventurous
- Mysterious
- Happy
- Scary

☑ Draw a quick emoji face that matches the poem's mood here:

🙂😨😮🌳

ACTIVITY 4: FOREST SOUND POEM 🌳🎵

Imagine you are lost in Rangu Forest. What sounds would you hear?

Write 2–3 lines describing the sounds around you:

"_____

_____."

TEACHER TIP (SMALL PRINT)

☑ **Standards Alignment:**
- Describe Setting
- Make Inferences About Characters
- Identify Mood and Atmosphere

☑ **Science of Reading Focus:**
- Text-Based Evidence
- Vocabulary in Context
- Oral Language Expansion

BONUS CHALLENGE:

✏ **Performance Practice!** — Read aloud the second stanza (Henry leading) but change your voice to match "cautious pace" and "unknown perils."

(Whisper, slow down, add suspense!)

❧ 23 ❧
"NEXT DAY"

📚 TEACHER'S ANNOTATED GUIDE

📖 CHAPTER OVERVIEW

Chapter 23: Next Day
Main Setting: The heart of Rangu Forest, morning after the bracelet exchange

Key Themes: Strategy over strength, deception and trust, jungle justice, leadership under pressure

Overview:

In this tension-filled chapter, the heroes awaken to signs that Chimper may be working against them. With Beybey's help and the bracelet plan in motion, Scatter leads the group through the forest while pretending to trust their trickster guide. Meanwhile, Alice stalks Chimper, angry over her stolen prey. When she attacks, justice is swift, and the bracelet—and the Lion's Tooth—are passed to Scatter. This chapter explores how clever planning, teamwork, and quiet bravery can outmaneuver even the deadliest enemies. Students will analyze cause-effect chains, symbolism, and the emotional weight of leadership.

. . .

Focus:
Strategic thinking, betrayal, trust, and redemption

⊚ **Instructional Goals**
- Use context to define layered vocabulary
- Track cause-effect through strategic actions
- Compare characters based on motivation
- Analyze symbolism and subtext
- Use dramatic reading to build fluency and tone awareness

📖 **VOCABULARY + MORPHOLOGY TIE-IN**

Target Vocabulary Words:
- **Treachery** – the act of betrayal or deception
- **Strategy** – a well-thought-out plan to reach a goal
- **Token** – a small object that represents a larger idea
- **Ambush** – a surprise attack from hiding
- **Symbol** – something that stands for something else

Morphology Breakdowns (Vellum-Friendly Format):
- **Treachery**

Root: *treach-* (related to deceive or trick)

Suffix: *-ery* (the act of)

➤ *Treachery = the act of deceiving someone*
- **Strategy**

Root: *strateg-* (Greek *strategos*, meaning military general or plan)

Suffix: *-y* (forms a noun)

➤ *Strategy = a plan or method used to achieve a goal*
- **Token**

Old English origin: *tacen* (sign, symbol, proof)

➤ *Token = a sign or symbol of something larger, like trust or promise*
- **Ambush**

Prefix: *am-* (from Latin *amb-* meaning "around")

Root: *-bush* (related to "hide" or "bush")

➤ *Ambush = a hiding attack from around or nearby*

• **Symbol**

Root: *sym-* (together) + *bol* (from Greek *ballein*, "to throw")

➤ *Symbol = something thrown together with meaning; an object with deeper meaning*

🐚 *Teacher Tip:* Ask students to turn one vocabulary word into a "story sketch" — a doodle or short sentence showing how the word comes to life in this chapter (e.g., Scatter using "strategy" to trick Chimper).

• Activity: Create character emotions via facial drawings or expression sketches

◆ CHAPTER 23 MINI-LESSON: "NEXT DAY"

Theme: *Strategy, Leadership, and the Power of Caution*

⊙ **Objective:**

Students will explore how the heroes use teamwork and strategy to survive deception. They will examine character growth through trust, clever planning, and hidden strength.

▌ QUICK TEACH: CAUSE & STRATEGY

1. Proverb Anchor:

"A good friend is like a four-leaf clover: hard to find and lucky to have."

➤ *Prompt:* Who proves to be a true friend in this chapter? How?

2. CAUSE & EFFECT CHAIN ACTIVITY:

Cause	Effect
Beybey warns the heroes	They become suspicious of Chimper
Scatter gives Chimper the bracelet	Chimper lowers his guard
Elephants trumpet loudly	Heroes move without being seen

| Alice confronts Chimper | He loses the Lion's Tooth |
➤ Students add a final cause-effect step that changes the story.

3. ROLEPLAY OR PARTNER DISCUSSION:

➤ One student plays Scatter, one plays Chimper. Reenact the bracelet exchange—but *Scatter knows something Chimper doesn't*. What subtext is being communicated?

4. QUICK REFLECTION WRITE:

✎ *Was it kind or clever for Scatter to give Chimper the bracelet? Can it be both?*

🐢 FULL COMPREHENSION GUIDE – CHAPTER 23: *NEXT DAY*

BEFORE Reading

• 🦁 *What do you think will happen now that the heroes are traveling with Chimper?*

• 🐵 *What do you remember about Alice from earlier chapters? What might she do next?*

• 🎁 *Can a gift also be a trap? What would make someone pretend to trust another person?*

DURING Reading

• 🔍 *What clues show that Chimper is hiding something? How do the heroes respond to these clues?*

• 🧿 *What role does the bracelet play in Scatter's secret plan?*

• 🐘 *How do the forest elephants help the heroes escape danger?*

• 🐆 *What does Alice's confrontation with Chimper reveal about justice in the jungle?*

AFTER Reading

- 🌙 *Why does Beybey give the Lion's Tooth to Scatter? What does that moment mean for her leadership?*
- 🌿 *How does the forest itself seem to react to what's happening? What moods or tones are created by the setting?*
- 😶 *Was Chimper's punishment fair? Why or why not?*
- 🎯 *What does this chapter teach about using strategy and kindness to outsmart an enemy?*

🔍 LITERARY DEVICES FOCUS

1. Dramatic Irony:

The reader knows Scatter is pretending to trust Chimper before he or Alice realize it.

➤ Ask: "How does it feel to know more than the characters?"

2. Symbolism:

- *Bracelet* = initially a gift of trust, becomes a tool of strategy
- *Lion's Tooth* = redemption and rightful leadership
- *Elephant trumpeting* = a coded signal for escape and community help

3. Personification:

- "The jungle seemed to shrink around her."
- "The sun painting the ground golden…"

4. Foreshadowing:

- The early whisper of betrayal from Beybey sets the tone.
- The bracelet's importance builds throughout the chapter.

🎭 FLUENCY & EXPRESSION FOCUS

• Read-Aloud Suggestion:

Perform the scene where Alice confronts Chimper. Assign readers for Alice, Chimper, and a narrator. Focus on tone (calm menace vs. panic), volume shifts, and pacing. Model how fear and power change vocal rhythm.

• Prosody Prompt:

"Try reading Alice's line: *'You stole from me.'*

Read it once as angry. Now try it quiet, but dangerous. Which one feels more powerful?"

⬤ SEL / Real-World Tie-In

Ask students:

"Have you ever pretended to trust someone while still being cautious?"

"How can kindness sometimes be used wisely in difficult situations?"

This chapter offers a great chance to discuss **strategic compassion** — how leaders can remain empathetic without becoming naïve.

⬤ Close Reading Highlight

"Scatter... had already thought ahead."

Dramatic irony – students know what Chimper doesn't

Is strategy also a form of kindness?

⬤ Cause and Effect Visual

- Beyboy warns → heroes suspect Chimper
- Bracelet "gift" → triggers Alice's attack
- Elephant distraction → escape
- Bracelet = trap or trust?

⬤ Character Contrast Table

- Chimper: sly → vulnerable
- Scatter: calm → strategist
- Alice: fierce → just
- Beyboy: loyal → wise

Debate: Was Scatter's deception justified?

. . .

✏ Symbol Timeline
- Bracelet = Trust, then Trap
- Trumpet = Escape
- Lion's Tooth = Redemption

Activity: Label symbols and their shifting meanings

🐾 Dramatic Reading Passages
- Alice's confrontation
- Scatter's inner thoughts

Fluency Focus: Tone, pacing, punctuation

💼 Differentiation Options
- Graphic organizers for betrayal chain
- ELL visuals and symbolic vocabulary
- Advanced: Compare Chimper to tricksters in myth
- Artistic: "Map of Trust" – alliances visualized

Mini-Project:

🐾 *Create a Symbol Chain:*

Have students draw a "symbol timeline" showing how the bracelet, elephant call, and Lion's Tooth shift in meaning across Chapters 22–23.

SUMMARY SHEET

Main Setting: Rangu Forest (continued), during a tense morning of shifting alliances

Key Themes: Deception and Strategy, Teamwork, Vigilance, Inner Strength, Trust and Betrayal

. . .

📄 SHORT SUMMARY:

As dawn breaks in Rangu, the heroes awaken with renewed hope but lingering doubts about Chimper's loyalty. Beybey shares overheard hints of a betrayal involving Tau. While pretending to trust Chimper, Scatter reveals a secret plan involving the bracelet she gifted him. The heroes strategize with their monkey allies and the forest elephants to create distractions, buying time to escape the potential trap. Meanwhile, Alice, furious over the stolen bracelet, stalks the jungle. She ambushes Chimper, exposing his betrayal. Chimper is dragged off, and the bracelet is recovered and passed to Scatter, who receives the Lion's Tooth as a symbol of true leadership. The forest celebrates the heroes' cleverness and bravery as they continue forward, stronger than before.

💭 Comprehension Focus:

• What does the bracelet symbolize throughout this chapter?

• How does Scatter use clever planning to stay ahead of danger?

• Why is Alice's confrontation with Chimper important to the plot?

🦁 Main Characters Introduced/Expanded:

• **Beybey:** Leader of the White Collard Monkeys, strategic and loyal

• **Chimper:** Exposed for his deception and faced consequences

• **Alice:** Becomes a symbol of natural justice and power

🧩 Key Vocabulary Words:

• **Ambush** – A surprise attack by someone lying in wait

• **Strategy** – A careful plan for achieving a goal, especially under pressure

• **Symbol** – An object that stands for a deeper meaning or idea

• **Deceit** – The act of tricking or misleading someone

📖 ✍ REFLECTION QUESTIONS

Theme: *Planning, Patience, and the Weight of Strategy*
Reflection Prompts:

1. What's Scatter's strategy for keeping the group safe?

2. What risks do the heroes take by continuing to follow Chimper?

3. What makes Henry suspicious, and why is his role important?

4. How do the elephants help create a turning point?

 Visual Task: Draw a "map of movement" — showing the group's journey from Chimper's path to the elephant meeting point.

৩৯৬

✍ CER WRITING (CLAIM–EVIDENCE–REASONING)

Use this structured writing prompt to support deeper thinking and text-based writing. The CER framework guides students to:
- Form a clear claim
- Support their thinking with specific textual evidence
- Explain how that evidence proves their point
- Practice academic writing sentence starters
- Build argumentative and persuasive thinking

  Ideal after discussion, close reading, or as a lead-in to a short response

CER Worksheet
Title: Chapter 23 — *Next Day*
Prompt/Question:
Why was trust so important for the heroes' survival in Rangu Forest?

1. CLAIM (What do you believe?)
  Starter: *I believe that...*

2. EVIDENCE (Find a quote or describe something)
  Starters:
  - *In the story it says...*

- *One example is when...*
- *The author shows that...*

3. REASONING (EXPLAIN WHY YOUR EVIDENCE PROVES YOUR claim)

Starters:
- *This shows that...*
- *This proves that...*
- *This means...*

QUICK CHECKLIST
☑ Clear answer?
☑ Strong evidence?
☑ Good explanation?

WHEN TO USE:
☑ After discussion or reading group
☑ Before writing paragraphs or journal reflections
☑ As a formative assessment
☑ For writing support or enrichment

BONUS (Optional):
Draw It!

Draw a picture of Scatter keeping a close watch on Chimper, or the monkeys helping each other.

✦✦✦

STANDARDS ALIGNMENT – GRADE 4
- RL.4.1 – Evidence for character motivation
- RL.4.3 – Compare character choices
- RL.4.4 – Vocabulary in context
- RL.4.5 – Sequence and structure
- RL.4.6 – POV analysis

Final Reflections

• Can leaders manipulate without becoming villains?
• What role does deception play in survival?

⚜

POETRY ACTIVITY PACK - NARRATIVE POEM

(Adventure and Courage)

Poem Text:

Journey of the Brave

In the heart of the Rangu's embrace,
Our heroes tread a hidden trace.
Forests thick with secrets deep,
Paths that twist and turns that leap.
Henry, with a cautious voice,
Reminds his friends they have a choice:
To find new ways through lands unknown,
And by these trials, they have grown.
Beybey waits with news to share,
Of treachery lurking in the air.
Chimper's plots weave dark and wide,
In shadows where dangers bide.
The heroes must, with cunning stride,
Navigate the forest's tide.
A journey not just of the feet,
But of the heart, their fears to meet.

STUDENT POETRY ACTIVITIES

ACTIVITY 1: Adventure Map Drawing

☑ Draw a simple map showing the heroes' forest journey
☑ Mark places like:
• "Hidden Secrets"
• "Twisting Paths"
• "Danger Zones"

(Use arrows, little trees, maybe even shadowy figures!)

ACTIVITY 2: CHARACTER DECISION TREE 🌳

☑ Henry says they must **choose their path**. Create a quick Choice Tree:
- If they go **Left**, they might find _____.
- If they go **Right**, they might face _____.

☑ **Bonus:** What choice would **YOU** make?

ACTIVITY 3: WORD BUILDER

☑ **Pick 3 power words** from the poem (examples: *cunning, treachery, brave*).

☑ For each word:
- Write a new sentence using the word.
- Draw a tiny symbol or doodle to represent it!

ACTIVITY 4: Courage Quote

☑ Write a 1-line **inspirational quote** a hero might say while facing the dangers of the Rangu Forest.

TEACHER TIP (SMALL PRINT)

☑ **Standards Alignment:**
- Summarizing Text Visually
- Decision-Making & Prediction
- Vocabulary Enrichment
- Quote Writing and Main Idea Expansion

☑ **Science of Reading Focus:**
- Comprehension & Story Mapping
- Word Relationships
- Oral and Written Expression

🎵 **Bonus Challenge: Perform the Poem!**

☑ Read aloud with a **brave explorer's voice**.

☑ Make your voice sound **bolder and stronger** as the poem nears the final stanza!

❧ 24 ❧

TESTED BY FIRE

📖 TEACHER'S ANNOTATED GUIDE

P roverb:
 "In the moment of crisis, the wise build bridges and the foolish build dams."

📘 CHAPTER OVERVIEW

Chapter Title: *Tested by Fire*

Main Setting: Mount Tanganyika, savanna paths, and the approach to Wakaduo

Key Themes: Trial by adversity, rising leadership, natural symbolism, courage and unity

Overview:

As the heroes approach Mount Tanganyika, nature itself becomes the final trial before they can reach home. With molten rock, toxic air, and the fear of ambush, they face both physical and emotional fire. Scatter emerges as a true leader, balancing fear with bold action. Ernie scouts danger, Tusker provides grounding strength, and even Tau's looming threat cannot extinguish their resolve. Through teamwork and internal growth, the heroes prove that fire can forge as well as destroy.

INSTRUCTIONAL FOCUS
- Building resilience under pressure
- Exploring natural symbolism (volcano = internal and external trial)
- Comparing leadership models (wisdom vs. force)
- Tracking emotional and strategic growth

CLOSE READING FOCUS
Text Quote:
"This journey isn't just about getting home. It's about proving we are strong enough to protect it." – Scatter
Discussion Prompt:
- What does this line reveal about Scatter's transformation?
- How does the meaning of "home" evolve in the story?

📖 VOCABULARY + MORPHOLOGY FOCUS

Target Vocabulary Words:
- **Daunting** – intimidating or difficult to face
- **Treacherous** – full of hidden dangers
- **Embers** – small glowing pieces of fire
- **Resolve** – strong determination
- **Volcano** – a mountain that can erupt with lava

Morphology Breakdown:

• Daunting

Root: *daunt* (from Latin *domitare*, to tame or subdue)

Suffix: *-ing* (adjective form)

➤ *Daunting = something that tames or intimidates you*

• Treacherous

Root: *treach-* (from "betrayal" or "danger")

Suffix: *-erous* (full of)

➤ *Treacherous = full of danger or deception*

• **Embers**

Root: *ember* (Old English *æmerge*, meaning "burning coal")

➤ *Embers = glowing remains of a fire*

• **Resolve**

Prefix: *re-* (again)

Root: *solve* (to loosen or settle)

➤ *Resolve = to settle again with firm intent; strong determination*

• **Volcano**

From Latin *Vulcanus* (Roman god of fire)

➤ *Volcano = a mountain that bursts with fire and molten rock*

🐚 *Extension Idea:* **Have students match each vocabulary word to a moment in the chapter where that word comes to life (e.g., "Resolve" when Scatter chooses to lead through danger).**

◆ CHAPTER 24 MINI-LESSON: "TESTED BY FIRE"

Theme: *Facing Fear, Becoming a Leader, Surviving Together*

◎ **Objective:**

Students will analyze how characters overcome emotional and physical trials. They will use evidence to discuss courage and how challenges shape leadership.

🔖 QUICK TEACH: FIRE AS METAPHOR

1. Proverb Anchor:

"In the moment of crisis, the wise build bridges and the foolish build dams."

➤ *Ask:* Who builds "bridges" in this chapter? Who tries to block progress?

2. FIRE METAPHOR MAP ACTIVITY:

Match challenge to what it represents:

Challenge......................**Emotional Meaning**

Volcano...........................Fear, transformation, pressure

Lava fields.........................Danger, urgency
Tau's trap........................Final confrontation with fear/past
Lion's Tooth.....................Worthy leadership, earned power

3. Quote Analysis & Voice Practice:

➤ Read aloud: *"We won't stop. We are the children of Wakaduo."*

✎ *Write what that line means to you.*

➤ Try reading it aloud in three tones: brave, scared-but-strong, victorious.

4. Short Write Prompt:

✎ *When was a time you had to be brave even when afraid? What helped you press on?*

🌑 FULL COMPREHENSION GUIDE – CHAPTER 24: *TESTED BY FIRE*

BEFORE Reading

Help students activate prior knowledge and anticipate key challenges:

• 🔺 *What do you already know about volcanoes? How might they affect animals or people trying to cross them?*

• ◌ *What does it mean to be "tested by fire"? Can you think of a time you faced a really difficult challenge?*

• 🦁 *Tau is still trying to stop the heroes. What might he do next? Predict what challenges the group will face in this chapter.*

DURING Reading

Encourage active thinking and tracking major shifts:

• 🔥 *How do the heroes respond to the heat, danger, and fear? Who stays calm? Who struggles?*

• 👁 *What do Scatter's words and actions show about her leadership?*

• 🐘 *Why is Tusker's line—"We can be just as wild, can't we?"—important? What does it mean?*

• 🦅 *What role does Ernie play in helping the group survive? Why is his timing so important?*

AFTER Reading

Support reflection, synthesis, and real-life connection:

• 🪨 *Why does the author place Tau at the boulder? What does this setting symbolize in the larger story?*

• *How has Scatter changed since the beginning of the novel? Use text evidence to support your answer.*

• 🌍 *What do you think the volcano represents emotionally for the group? How does overcoming it change them?*

• *If fire can destroy and shape at the same time, how does that idea connect to the heroes' journey?*

🔍 LITERARY DEVICES FOCUS

1. Symbolism

• *The volcano* = emotional intensity, transformation, danger
• *The embers* = endurance, the inner fire that survives challenges
• *The Lion's Tooth* = leadership earned through hardship

2. Foreshadowing

• Tau's ambush and his growing frustration predict an explosive final conflict.
• The volcano's increasing rumble mirrors the coming storm.

3. Imagery

• "Scorching ground," "toxic air," and "molten paths" create strong **sensory imagery**—ideal for visualization and fluency practice.

4. Repetition & Parallelism

• Scatter's rallying cry: *"We are the children of Wakaduo."*

➤ Builds rhythm and group identity, ideal for choral reading.

⟪ FLUENCY & PROSODY FOCUS

• **Performance Reading Prompt:**

Invite students to read Scatter's final speech aloud with increasing strength and pride in their voice.

➤ "Let us not be daunted by the fire…"

• **Prosody Cue:**

Practice **tone shifts** as the volcano erupts.

➤ Start with quiet tension, grow into louder urgency as the heat and stakes rise.

ACTIVITY SUGGESTIONS:

• Create "Trial Words" Wall Art using lava, ash, and symbolic imagery

• Break vocabulary into parts (e.g., **treacherous = treach + -erous**) and discuss meanings

CHARACTER MOTIVATIONS & INFERENCE

Scatter

• Leads group across molten terrain

• Shows maturity and rising courage

Tusker

• Describes fire as wild but alive

• Represents wisdom and mentorship

Ernie

• Scouts from above

• Displays loyalty and protector instincts

Tau

• Waits in ambush

• Reveals ruthlessness and strategy

Discussion Prompt:

Who shows more power—Scatter or Tau? What defines real power in this chapter?

. . .

THEMATIC FOCUS: TRIAL BY FIRE

Bridge Builders:

- Scatter
- Tusker
- Values: Unity, Courage, Adaptation

Dam Builders:

- Tau
- Predators
- Values: Fear, Control, Obstruction

Discussion Prompt:

What does it mean to build a bridge in a time of crisis?

SYMBOLISM BREAKDOWN

- **Volcano** – Adversity, transformation, rising pressure
- **Boulder** – Barrier between danger and safety
- **Embers** – Inner fire, courage, fear

Prompt:

If fire is both dangerous and beautiful, how does that reflect the choices the heroes face?

SEQUENCING REVIEW

1. Arrival at Mount Tanganyika>>>2. Volcano begins to erupt

3.Ernie scouts ahead and warns>>>4. Heroes cross molten terrain

5. Tau prepares his ambush

Mini-Project:

Create a "Hero's Path Timeline" with chapter flags or visuals.

CRITICAL THINKING PROMPTS

1 How does Scatter's leadership contrast with Tau's?

2 Why use a volcano here—what does it symbolize?

3 Did the heroes succeed even before the fight? Consider emotional victories.

. . .

DIFFERENTIATION STRATEGIES

Visual Learners:
- Draw a map of the lava crossing with character positions

Auditory Learners:
- Record or perform Scatter's speech

Struggling Readers:
- Use paragraph strips to summarize and sort the chapter

Advanced Learners:
- Write a journal entry from Tau's point of view while waiting

ASSESSMENT IDEAS

Quick-Write Prompt:
How does the volcano change how the group sees themselves?

Exit Slip Options:
- One word that describes the chapter's tone
- One prediction for the next confrontation
- One leadership lesson from Scatter

ELA COMMON CORE ALIGNMENT (GRADE 4)

- **RL.4.1** – Cite evidence for motivations and decisions
- **RL.4.3** – Describe characters' actions and what they reveal
- **RL.4.4** – Define content vocabulary in context
- **RL.4.5** – Analyze structure (this is a climax moment)
- **RL.4.7** – Visualize setting through illustrations or maps

TEACHER REFLECTION QUESTIONS

- How can we connect the volcano metaphor to real-life moments of pressure?
- What emotional milestones do the heroes pass in this chapter?

SUMMARY SHEET

Main Setting: Mount Tanganyika and surrounding savanna

Key Themes: Bravery, Determination, Teamwork, Natural Disasters, Overcoming Inner Doubt

🏛 SHORT SUMMARY:

With the volcano Mount Tanganyika looming ahead, the heroes face their most dangerous challenge yet. Lava flows, poisonous smoke, and unstable paths test their endurance. As Scatter leads the group through the heat and chaos, Ernie scouts ahead to report on predator positions. Tau, growing impatient, positions his forces at the boulder blocking Wakaduo's entrance. Meanwhile, the heroes brave the burning landscape, fueled by Scatter's resolve and Tusker's strength. As the mountain begins to erupt, they realize that time is running out. Every step forward demands courage and teamwork. They are not only tested by the volcano's fire—but also by the fire of leadership, trust, and hope burning within.

🧠 Comprehension Focus:

• What physical and emotional challenges do the heroes face?

• How do the heroes' strengths complement one another during this journey?

• What role does the volcano setting play in advancing the story?

💀 Main Characters Introduced/Expanded:

• **Tau:** Now in direct pursuit and laying his final trap

• **Scatter:** Demonstrates leadership under extreme pressure

• **Ernie:** Plays a crucial role in recon and warning

🧩 Key Vocabulary Words:

• **Eruption** – A sudden outburst, especially from a volcano

• **Resolve** – Firm determination to do something

• **Lava** – Molten rock expelled by a volcano

• **Savanna** – A grassy plain in tropical regions with few trees

📖 ✍ REFLECTION QUESTIONS / PROMPTS

Theme: *Resilience Through Adversity*

REFLECTION PROMPTS:

1. What makes Scatter's leadership stand out in this chapter?
2. How does fire test each character differently?
3. Why does Tau decide to go directly to the boulder instead of chasing them?
4. What do you think "being tested by fire" means in real life?

✍ *Writing Prompt:* Finish this sentence: "The fire could not defeat us, because…"

✍ CER WRITING (CLAIM–EVIDENCE–REASONING)

Use this structured writing prompt to support deeper thinking and text-based writing. The CER framework guides students to:

- Form a clear claim
- Support their thinking with specific textual evidence
- Explain how that evidence proves their point
- Practice academic writing sentence starters
- Build argumentative and persuasive thinking

Ideal after discussion, close reading, or as a lead-in to a short response

✍ **CER Worksheet**

Title: Chapter 24 — *Tested by Fire*

Prompt/Question:

How did Scatter and the heroes show true bravery when facing Mount Tanganyika?

1. 🔭 CLAIM

(What do you believe?)

✎ Starter: *I believe that...*

2. 📋 EVIDENCE

(Find a quote or describe something that happened.)

✎ Starters:

- *In the story it says...*

- *One example is when...*
- *The author shows that...*

3. REASONING

(Explain why your evidence proves your claim)

Starters:

- *This shows that...*
- *This proves that...*
- *This means...*

✪ QUICK CHECKLIST

☑ Clear answer?
☑ Strong evidence?
☑ Good explanation?

WHEN TO USE:

☑ After discussion or reading group
☑ Before writing paragraphs or journal reflections
☑ As a formative assessment
☑ For writing support or enrichment

BONUS (OPTIONAL):
Draw It!

Draw the heroes racing across the volcano or facing the erupting mountain!

POETRY ACTIVITY PACK - NARRATIVE POEM

(Perseverance and Unity)

POEM TEXT:
Tested by Fire

Before the mighty Tanganyika's fire,

Heroes stand, their spirits soaring higher.
Golden dawn breaks, skies alight with flame,
Each step they take, they pronounce their name.
Earth trembles beneath their weary feet,
Volcano's breath, sulfur's bitter greet.
Mountains of challenge, vast savannas wide,
Where shadows of fierce predators may hide.
"Press on!" cries Scatter, with fervor so bold,
"Not mountains nor foes our spirits will hold.
We're children of Wakaduo, brave and true,
Together, there's nothing we cannot do."
Ernie soars high, eyes sharp as the day,
Scouting the dangers that may block their way.
"The path is clear," he calls to his band,
"We must be swift to cross this heated land."
With courage that rivals the fire's fierce glow,
Through smoking ash and ember's flow,
They face each trial on this treacherous road,
United as one, bearing destiny's load.
Tusker, wise giant, feels the land's raw power,
"Our hearts must be strong in this fiery hour.
As beasts of the wild, we'll claim our fate,
Beyond this trial, Wakaduo's gate."

◎ Student Poetry Activities

ACTIVITY 1: Fire and Courage Comic Strip 🐾🦁

✅ Create a **4-panel comic strip** showing Scatter and friends crossing the fiery lands.

✅ Include speech bubbles for words of **encouragement**, **courage**, or **teamwork**.

(Example: Panel 1 - "Press on, brave ones!" Panel 2 - "The path clears!" etc.)

ACTIVITY 2: Sensory Imagery Builder 🌋🦁🕊

✅ In the poem, the **volcano's breath** and **earth trembling** create strong sensory images.

☑ List **2 things you would**:

- See
- Hear
- Smell
- Feel

If you were standing by Mount Tanganyika! *(Ex: Smell = sulfur)*

ACTIVITY 3: Build a Team Chant 🖊🏆

☑ The heroes encourage each other with powerful words.

☑ Write a **short team chant** (2–4 lines) that they might shout while crossing the lava fields!

"We march through fire, we rise with might!
Together as one, we claim our light!"

ACTIVITY 4: Theme Reflection

☑ What lesson about **perseverance** or **teamwork** does the poem teach?

☑ Write 2–3 sentences explaining what it means to be **"Tested by Fire."**

TEACHER TIP (SMALL PRINT)

☑ **Standards Alignment:**

- Visual Story Sequencing
- Sensory Language Practice
- Theme Identification
- Group/Individual Creative Writing

☑ **Science of Reading Focus:**

- Comprehension Expansion
- Visualization Skills
- Expressive Language Development

BONUS CHALLENGE: PERFORM THE POEM!

☑ Perform the poem aloud, **reading louder and more powerfully** during Scatter and Tusker's parts!

☑ Imagine your voice getting **stronger** like a hero facing the volcano!

❦ 25 ❦

THE CIRCLE OF UNITY

▰ TEACHER'S ANNOTATED GUIDE

Proverb:
   "You cannot ever leave Africa. It is always with you, there, inside your head."

Themes:
Leadership, Unity, Identity, Redemption, Wisdom over force

⏲ CHAPTER OVERVIEW

This chapter is the emotional and symbolic peak of the novel. The characters face their final trial not just through strength but through wisdom, unity, and shared leadership. Gurr and Tau's rivalry comes to a surprising end, and Scatter emerges not as a ruler, but as a unifier. Through cleverness, compassion, and courage, she shows that true greatness lies in community.

This chapter marks the "Return with the Elixir" stage of the Hero's Journey — a thematic resolution underscoring leadership, shared power, and lasting transformation.

📚 VOCABULARY + MORPHOLOGY TIE-IN

1. Proxy
Prefix: *pro-* (for, on behalf of)
Root: *agency* (Latin: *procure*, "to care for")
Definition: A person who acts on behalf of another.
➤ "Scatter claimed the Right of Proxy to finish the challenge for Tau."

2. Unity
Root: *unus* (Latin: "one")
Suffix: *-ity* (forms nouns indicating state or condition)
Definition: The state of being joined together for a common cause.
➤ "Unity among animals broke old cycles of conflict."

3. Challenge
Root: *calere* (Latin: "to arouse or incite")
➤ A task or situation that tests courage or ability.
➤ "Scatter faced each challenge not with size, but spirit."

4. Respect
Prefix: *re-* (again)
Root: *specere* (Latin: "to look at")
➤ To look at again — with admiration or recognition.
➤ "Tau's respect for Scatter changed the kingdom."

◆ CHAPTER 25 MINI-LESSON: "THE CIRCLE OF UNITY"

Theme: *Leadership, Shared Power, and Redemption*

☞ Objective:
Students will explore how leadership is defined through actions, choices, and values. They'll examine Scatter's claim of "Right of Proxy" and the final decision to rule *together* instead of alone.

📓 QUICK TEACH: POWER SHARED, NOT SEIZED
1. Proverb Anchor:

"You cannot ever leave Africa. It is always with you, there, inside your head."

➤ *Discuss:* What does this mean in the context of identity, history, and leadership?

2. Leadership Decision Map:

Fill in this chart with student responses:

Character............**Choice**.................**What It Shows**

Scatter......Claims Right of Proxy......Courage & responsibility

Gurr..........Fights by force.................Power through fear

Tau............Accepts shared rule...........Growth and humility

3. Quick Write Prompt:

✎ *Why did Scatter say "no" to ruling alone—even after she won? What kind of leader does that make her?*

4. Symbol Hunt (Whole Class Quick Match):

➤ Match the symbols with their meaning:

○ Volcano = Pressure and choices under heat

○ River = Challenge that requires balance

○ Wind at the end = Nature's acceptance of peace

5. Think-Pair-Share Prompt:

➤ *Is it harder to lead with others or alone? Why?*

Prompt: *How did Scatter show that true leadership means helping others?* Use this mini CER frame:

• **Claim**: I believe that...

• **Evidence**: In the story it says...

. . .

• **REASONING**: THIS SHOWS THAT...

FULL COMPREHENSION GUIDE

Before Reading
Preview Question:
• What does it mean to "lead together" instead of ruling alone?

• WHAT DO YOU EXPECT FROM A "FINAL TRIAL" IN A HERO'S journey?

VOCABULARY WARM-UP:
Review: *proxy, unity, challenge, respect*
Define each with visual or kinesthetic associations.

DURING READING
Close Reading Prompts:
• Why does Tau's fall matter so much to the story's theme?
• What does it show when Scatter uses wit instead of force?
• How do the volcano and pit symbolize inner growth?
Focus Quote:
"There is no prey. There is only the Circle of Unity."
➤ Ask: What do you think this means? Why is it powerful?

AFTER READING
Discussion Questions:
1 Why does Scatter share power at the end?
2 In what ways did Gurr lose before the final fall?
3 Why was the "Right of Proxy" an important tradition?
4 How does this chapter connect back to earlier themes?

Exit Slip Options:
• "One word that describes the ending"
• "One way I would lead if I were in Scatter's shoes"

KEY LITERARY FOCUS AREAS

Proverb Interpretation:
• What does it mean to carry a place inside you?

Symbolism Highlights:
• **River** = Strength and survival
• **Volcano** = Strategy and adaptability
• **Pit** = Wisdom and humility
• **Wind at the end** = Harmony and peace

Foreshadowing Connection:
• Scatter's cleverness from earlier chapters becomes key here

Conflict Types Explored:
• Man vs. Self
• Man vs. Nature
• Man vs. Power

Narrative Structure:
• Final phase of the Hero's Journey: Return with the elixir

COMMON CORE ALIGNMENT (GRADE 4–5)
• **RL.4.1 / RL.5.1** – Use quotes and draw inferences
• **RL.4.2 / RL.5.2** – Determine theme and summarize
• **RL.4.3 / RL.5.3** – Analyze character development
• **RL.4.4 / RL.5.4** – Figurative language and symbolism
• **RL.4.5 / RL.5.5** – Understand structure and resolution

COMPREHENSION Q&A (WITH SAMPLE INSIGHTS)
Why does Scatter step in as proxy?
• Because she believes leadership is about responsibility, not ego

What do the trials represent?
• River = Strength

• Volcano = Strategy
• Pit = Wisdom

Why is Gurr defeated?

• He relies on brute force, not community or growth

What does the wind symbolize?

• Nature's approval of peace and balance

LITERARY INFERENCE PROMPTS

"Tau bowed and said, 'You are the true King.'"

• Inference: Tau has embraced humility and shared leadership

"Scatter leapt across crocodile backs."

• Inference: She is resourceful and brave under pressure

MINI-LESSON IDEAS

Lesson 1: The Power of Proxy

• Discuss acting on behalf of others
• Real-world connections: student leaders, advocacy, representation

Lesson 2: Proverb Workshop

• Students choose a new proverb and rewrite the ending
• Prompt: "What if the story's theme was forgiveness instead of unity?"

WRITING & REFLECTION PROMPTS

• Write a journal entry from Scatter's point of view after the final trial
• Reflect on a time you led others with wisdom
• Write a letter of apology from Gurr to Scatter
• Design your own "Trial of Leadership" for the next generation

ASSESSMENT OPTIONS

Formative:
- Class discussion on symbolism of wind and the lion trials

Summative:
- Final unit quiz
- "Leadership Manifesto" project from Scatter's perspective

CROSS-CURRICULAR EXTENSIONS

Social Studies:
- Compare Scatter and Tau's shared leadership to real leaders like Mandela and de Klerk

Art:
- Create a Unity Banner for Wakaduo, Ruaha, and Ugalla

Science:
- Explore lion pride structures and roles in the savanna ecosystem

Music:
- Write and perform a Unity Chant for your classroom

SUMMARY SHEET

Main Setting: Entrance to Wakaduo, Mount Tanganyika, and the Cave of the Bottomless Pit

Key Themes: Unity, Leadership, Redemption, Community vs. Conflict, Power Shared not Seized

SHORT SUMMARY:

At the threshold of Wakaduo, the heroes confront their final test. Gurr and Tau, rival lions, prepare to battle for supremacy. When Tau is injured, Scatter claims the Right of Proxy and completes the ancient trials in his place. Cleverness, agility, and heart help her overcome Gurr's brute force across rivers, volcanoes, and cliffs. After a dramatic fall, Tau ascends and joins Scatter at the cave's edge. Rather than accept the title of king, Scatter proposes shared leadership. Together, they declare the formation of a united kingdom—Wakaduo, Ruaha, and Ugalla—ruled not by domination, but by cooperation and shared power.

🌑 Comprehension Focus:

• What does Scatter's victory teach us about leadership?

• How does this chapter show that strength is more than physical power?

• Why is unity the most important lesson at the end of this chapter?

💀 Main Characters Introduced/Expanded:

• **Gurr:** A rival lion filled with pride, ultimately defeated

• **Scatter:** Emerges as a unifying leader through courage and strategy

• **Adira:** Wise tortoise who enforces fairness and peace

🌸 Key Vocabulary Words:

• **Proxy** – A person authorized to act on behalf of another

• **Unity** – The state of being joined together for a common purpose

• **Challenge** – A task or situation that tests someone's ability or determination

• **Respect** – A feeling of deep admiration for someone due to their qualities or actions

📖 ✍ REFLECTION QUESTIONS

Theme: *Shared Leadership and Changing Hearts*

REFLECTION PROMPTS:

1. Why does Scatter refuse to rule alone after defeating Gurr?

2. How do the Rituals of the Lions test more than just strength?

3. What does Tau's surrender say about his growth?

4. "There is no prey. There is only the Circle of Unity." — What does that mean to you?

🐾 *Art Task:* Create a family crest or tribal mark that represents Wakaduo + Ruaha + Ugalla united.

✍ CER WRITING (CLAIM–EVIDENCE–REASONING)

Use this structured writing prompt to support deeper thinking and text-based writing. The CER framework guides students to:

• Form a clear claim
• Support their thinking with specific textual evidence
• Explain how that evidence proves their point
• Practice academic writing sentence starters
• Build argumentative and persuasive thinking

   Ideal after discussion, close reading, or as a lead-in to a short response

   CER Worksheet

Title: Chapter 25 — *The Circle of Unity*

Prompt/Question:

How did Scatter prove that true leadership is about unity, not power?

1. 📢 CLAIM

(What do you believe?)

✎ Starter: *I believe that...*

2. 📖 EVIDENCE

(Find a quote or describe something that happened.)

✎ Starters:

• *In the story it says...*
• *One example is when...*
• *The author shows that...*

. . .

3. REASONING

(Explain why your evidence proves your claim)

Starters:

- *This shows that...*
- *This proves that...*
- *This means...*

⊚ QUICK CHECKLIST

☑ Clear answer?

☑ Strong evidence?

☑ Good explanation?

WHEN TO USE:

☑ After discussion or reading group

☑ Before writing paragraphs or journal reflections

☑ As a formative assessment

☑ For writing support or enrichment

BONUS (OPTIONAL):
Draw It!

Draw the heroes racing across the volcano or facing the erupting mountain!

POETRY ACTIVITY PACK - LYRICAL POEM

(Unity, Wisdom, and Courage)

✐ POEM TEXT:
The Circle of Unity

In the heart of Africa, where the sun kisses the earth,

Lies a tale of valor, of untold worth.
Under skies wide and a horizon deep,
The heroes of Wakaduo their vigil keep.
Across the savanna, under Mount Tanganyika's gaze,
Through trials by fire, through the smoke and haze,
They've walked paths where lesser spirits would falter,
By strength and by wisdom, they refuse to alter.
"Unity," whispers the wind through the grass,
"A bond forged in trials, none can surpass."
The lions roar, the elephants trumpet call,
In unity, they stand, in unity, they fall.
Gurr and Tau, the lions, their might contested,
In the challenge of wills, their spirits tested.
Yet, when the earth shook and the fires did rage,
Together they turned, a new page.
For the wise build bridges, the foolish, dams,
In the circle of unity, the true power stands.
As Scatter and Tau, side by side,
Prove that together, wide is their stride.
In the Circle of Unity, under Africa's sun,
The journey of heroes, never truly done.
For each step on this land, each challenge met,
Is a beat of the heart, a further path set.
In every whisper of the wind, in every challenge they face,
Is the spirit of Africa, their enduring grace.
For you never leave Africa, nor does it you,
In the circle of unity, forever true.

STUDENT POETRY ACTIVITIES
ACTIVITY 1: Unity Symbols

Draw or design a **symbol** that shows *Unity* among animals (or people).

Examples:
a circle of paw prints,
a tree with many different animals around it,

Interlocking hands or tails
(1 small drawing = 1 BIG idea!)

ACTIVITY 2: POETRY PAIR LINES ✂️✏️

☑️ Pick **2 lines** from the poem that you think **go together** the best.

☑️ WRITE THEM DOWN AND EXPLAIN:
  • Why do these two lines belong together?
  • What message do they share?
  (Focus on Unity, Courage, or Hope!)

ACTIVITY 3: CREATE A "UNITY CHANT" 📣

☑️ Imagine Scatter and Tau leading the animals.
☑️ Write a **2–4 line chant** the heroes might shout to inspire everyone to work together.
Example Starter:
"One heart, one land, side by side we stand!"

ACTIVITY 4: CIRCLE OF LIFE REFLECTION 🌳

☑️ The poem says, "You never leave Africa, nor does it you."
☑️ Write a short reflection:
What places or people will YOU always carry in your heart, no matter where you go?

SEL JOURNAL ENTRY: "WHAT DOES IT MEAN TO CARRY A PLACE IN your heart?

ACTIVITY 5 – POETRY ILLUSTRATION PROJECT:

🖌️ Create a visual "Circle of Unity" using lines from the poem.

Students choose 4–6 lines and create an illustrated circle, banner, or scroll to reflect unity.

Bonus Challenge: Group Performance!

In a small group, each person reads one line from the final stanza:

In every whisper of the wind, in every challenge they face,
Is the spirit of Africa, their enduring grace.
For you never leave Africa, nor does it you,
In the circle of unity, forever true.

Tip: Read with pride and rhythm. Let each voice carry the spirit of the story!

Final Thought

Scatter's final act wasn't just courage—it was a **choice to share power**.

Unity isn't easy. It takes bravery, trust, and heart.

But when we build bridges—instead of walls—we rise together.

You are part of that circle now.

Keep writing. Keep leading.

You are not alone.

ॐ

Final Message

Scatter's final act—to **share power**—isn't just the end of a journey. It's a life lesson in leadership, collaboration, and identity.

❦ 26 ❧

FROM SHADOWS TO LIGHT

P**roverb:**
  "Wisdom does not come overnight."

THEMES
- Transformation
- Courage
- Community leadership
- Redemption
- Wisdom in action

CHAPTER OVERVIEW

The mythic journey now impacts the real world. In the face of an eclipse—a symbol of fear and broken unity—the children rise as community leaders. The power of their earned virtues, embodied in magical tokens, restores peace, clarity, and connection.

📖 VOCABULARY & MORPHOLOGY TIE-IN – CHAPTER 26: *FROM SHADOWS TO LIGHT*

This format supports decoding, vocabulary expansion, and morphology connections:

KEY VOCABULARY WORDS WITH MORPHOLOGY BREAKDOWN

Eclipse

Root: *eclipt-* (Greek *ekleipsis*, meaning "abandonment" or "failure to appear")

Definition: When one celestial body blocks another, creating darkness.

Use: The solar eclipse symbolized the growing fear and disconnection in the story.

TRANSFORMATION

Prefix: *trans-* (across, beyond)

Root: *form* (shape)

Suffix: *-ation* (the act or process of)

Definition: A complete change in form or nature.

Use: The children's transformation into animal forms reflects their inner growth.

UNITY

Root: *uni-* (one)

Suffix: *-ty* (state of being)

Definition: The state of being joined as a whole.

Use: Unity is the value that ultimately defeats the darkness.

EMPOWERMENT

Prefix: *em-* (put into)

Root: *power* (ability to act)

Suffix: *-ment* (the state of)

Definition: The process of becoming stronger and more confident.

Use: The children use the tokens to empower their community.

RESILIENCE

Root: *resil-* (Latin *resilire*, to spring back)

Suffix: *-ience* (state or quality of)

Definition: The capacity to recover quickly from difficulties.

Use: The heroes show resilience when the darkness nearly overcomes them.

● CHAPTER 26 MINI-LESSON: "FROM SHADOWS TO LIGHT"

Theme: *Transformation, Community Action, and the Light of Unity*

◎ Objective:

Students will connect mythic storytelling to real-life leadership and change. They'll analyze how the heroes use their Wakaduo experiences to guide and inspire their own community.

▣ QUICK TEACH: REAL-WORLD CHANGE STARTS SMALL

1. Proverb Anchor:

"Wisdom does not come overnight."

➤ *Ask:* How do we see this in the kids' transformation?

2. Token & Action Match Game:

◎ *Objective:* Help students reflect on how symbolic actions in the story translate to real-world leadership and community care.

INSTRUCTIONS:

Each hero earns a magical token throughout the story. Now that their journey is complete, match each token to the **real-world action** the hero takes to spark lasting change.

Use clues from the chapter and student memory of each character's personality and growth. Let them discuss, guess, or write their answers.

Tokens to Match:
- Tree of Life
- Lion's Tooth
- Swamp Scroll
- Unity Light

Heroes & Actions (Scrambled):
- **Malik** leads safe walking routes and paints murals in underpasses.
- **Zara** starts a book club that helps young readers find their voices.
- **Maya** restores the community park and tutors kids in math under the trees.
- **Jalen** runs basketball clinics and peace talks for neighborhood youth.

Match-Up Reflection Prompt (Optional Extension):
Ask students:
- Which action inspires you the most?
- What "token" would you want to earn in your life — and what action would go with it?

3. Critical Thinking Question:
➤ *Why does the eclipse only fade when the community joins in? What does that say about the power of unity?*

. . .

4. CREATIVE REFLECTION PROMPT:

✎ *If you had your own Token of Change, what would it look like? What would it help you change in your world?*

5. QUICK CLASS CHANT ACTIVITY:

➤ As a class, create a 2–4 line unity chant using Wakaduo themes.

Example starter: "Courage strong, our voices bright, / We rise together, we light the night!"

◢ BONUS OPTIONAL QUICK CER :

Prompt: *How did the Wakaduo kids show that true leadership means helping others?*

Use this mini CER frame:

• **Claim**: I believe that…

• **EVIDENCE**: IN THE STORY IT SAYS…

• **REASONING**: THIS SHOWS THAT…

⚲ FULL COMPREHENSION GUIDE – CHAPTER 26: *FROM SHADOWS TO LIGHT*

⟳ Before Reading

• **Discussion Prompt:** What is a *solar eclipse*? What feelings might it bring?

• **Prediction Prompt:** Based on the chapter title and artwork, what kind of "light" do you think the characters will discover?

• **Quick Review:** Remind students of the *Tokens of Tariq* and what they represent (courage, wisdom, compassion, unity).

. . .

📖 During Reading

Ask these questions at key moments to encourage active thinking:

- **Why do the children return to their animal forms?**
- **What does each token do, and where is it placed?**
- **How does the chant affect the eclipse?**
- **What moment shows Cedric starting to change?**
- **Which characters lead with action, and which with words?**

Encourage students to highlight phrases or dialogue that show:

- Leadership
- Turning points (like Cedric's hesitation)
- Community responses (e.g., the crowd joining the chant)

✅ After Reading

Reflection Questions:

1 What was the eclipse *literally*, and what did it *symbolize*?

2 Why do the tokens lose power until the community joins the chant?

3 What does Cedric's change of heart reveal about leadership and redemption?

4 Which real-world problems are hinted at in the story's resolution?

5 How do Maya, Jalen, Malik, and Zara each carry Wakaduo's lessons into their lives?

Creative Extension:

Write a short scene showing **you** using a Token of Change to improve your school, park, or neighborhood. What token do you choose and why?

KEY LITERARY DEVICES AND FOCUS

Symbolism:

- **Eclipse** = Fear, disconnection, confusion

- **Oak Tree** = Legacy, rooted wisdom
- **Tokens** = Inner virtues realized

Foreshadowing:
- Cedric's redemption is hinted at throughout the story

Narrative Structure:
- The final "Return with the Elixir" phase of the Hero's Journey
- Real-world impact of mythical learning

STANDARDS ALIGNMENT (GRADE 4–5)
- **RL.4.1 / RL.5.1** – Inference with text support
- **RL.4.2 / RL.5.2** – Theme identification
- **RL.4.3 / RL.5.3** – Track character arc
- **RL.4.4 / RL.5.4** – Vocabulary in figurative context
- **RL.4.5 / RL.5.5** – Analyze resolution
- **W.4.3 / W.5.3** – Reflective narrative writing

GUIDED DEEP THINKING QUESTIONS

1 What does the eclipse represent in both the literal and symbolic sense?

2 Why are the tokens powerful? What does each represent?

3 How and why does Cedric change?

4 Why is the word "Together" the most powerful in this chapter?

CAUSE AND EFFECT ANCHOR POINTS
- **Cause:** Children chant in unity
- **Effect:** The eclipse breaks
- **Cause:** Cedric sees the light from the tokens
- **Effect:** He chooses peace
- **Cause:** Tokens are placed at the oak
- **Effect:** Community heals

· · ·

SEQUENCING REVIEW

1 Eclipse darkens the park
2 Tokens are placed at the oak
3 Cedric and his gang confront the group
4 The children chant
5 Light breaks the eclipse
6 Cedric has a change of heart
7 Children return to human form
8 Maya plants the potion
9 Jalen speaks to the gang
10 Zara leads a book club

CHARACTER GROWTH REFLECTIONS

Maya:
• From unsure to community leader
Jalen:
• From competitive to peacekeeper
Malik:
• From shy artist to healing mentor
Zara:
• From bookish to inspirational storyteller
Cedric:
• From angry leader to redeemed ally

WRITING PROMPTS

• What does the proverb "Wisdom does not come overnight" mean to you?
• What would your Token of Change do for your community?
• Compare Maya to a leader in your life
• Create your own class Wakaduo chant

ASSESSMENT OPTIONS

Formative:
- Short reflections, vocabulary in use, sequencing events

Summative:
- Personal narrative: "How I used my token"
- Essay: "What leadership looks like"
- Reading comprehension quiz

FINAL REFLECTION

Quote:

"They had not only saved their world from the Eternal Darkness, but also ignited change in their community."

Classroom Prompt:

What will you do to be a light in your world?

Have students respond through art, writing, or performance.

SUMMARY SHEET

Main Setting: Inner city park during a solar eclipse

Key Themes: Transformation, Community Empowerment, Unity Across Worlds, Courage in Adversity, Healing and Leadership

SHORT SUMMARY:

As a solar eclipse casts darkness over the inner-city park, Zara, Jalen, Maya, and Malik transform into their Wakaduo animal forms and place the Tokens of Tariq around the ancient oak tree. Each token—representing courage, wisdom, compassion, and unity—glows as the community watches. As darkness deepens, their chant of Wakaduo stirs the park, awakening memories and drawing unity from fear. The gang's attempt to seize control fails as the tokens' light repels the eclipse. Through this experience, the young heroes not only save their world but ignite real change in their neighborhood. Their transformation inspires their community to reclaim peace and hope. Each hero returns to their role—whether through art, education, sports, or storytelling—helping to rebuild a stronger, united future.

Comprehension Focus:

• How does the real-world setting reflect the lessons learned in Wakaduo?

• What role does each hero's animal transformation play in stopping the darkness?

• Why is the park scene important to the story's final message?

🐾 Main Characters Introduced/Expanded:

• **Maya, Jalen, Malik, Zara:** Transformed back into leaders in their real lives

• **Cedric:** A former gang member who begins to change after witnessing true courage

🧩 Key Vocabulary Words:

• **Eclipse** – An event when one celestial body blocks another

• **Transformation** – A complete change in form or character

• **Unity** – Working together for a common goal

• **Empowerment** – Gaining strength and confidence to take control of your life

৩১৫৩

📖 ✍ REFLECTION QUESTIONS

Theme: *Real-World Transformation through Heroism*

REFLECTION PROMPTS:

1. What do the Tokens of Tariq represent in the human world?

2. How do Maya, Jalen, Malik, and Zara use their experiences to help others?

3. Cedric has a chance to change. What gives him that chance?

4. How can we use our own "Wakaduo lessons" to change our schools or communities?

Creative Task: Write your own "Chant of Wakaduo" using your core values.

❦

✍ CER WRITING (CLAIM–EVIDENCE–REASONING)

Use this structured writing prompt to support deeper thinking and text-based writing. The CER framework guides students to:
- Form a clear claim
- Support their thinking with specific textual evidence
- Explain how that evidence proves their point
- Practice academic writing sentence starters
- Build argumentative and persuasive thinking
  - *Ideal after discussion, close reading, or as a lead-in to a short response*

CER Worksheet

Title: Chapter 26 — *From Shadows to Light*

Prompt/Question:

How did the heroes bring real change to their community after returning home?

1. ➤ CLAIM

(What do you believe?)

✎ Starter: *I believe that...*

2. ✐ EVIDENCE

(Find a quote or describe something that happened.)

✎ Starters:
- *In the story it says...*
- *One example is when...*
- *The author shows that...*

3. ✐ REASONING

(Explain why your evidence proves your claim)

✎ Starters:
- *This shows that...*
- *This proves that...*

- *This means...*
☞ **Quick Checklist**
☑ Clear answer?
☑ Strong evidence?
☑ Good explanation?
  When to use:
☑ After discussion or reading group
☑ Before writing paragraphs or journal reflections
☑ As a formative assessment
☑ For writing support or enrichment
  BONUS (Optional):
🖌 **Draw It!**

Draw Maya healing the park or Jalen standing bravely on the basketball court!

POETRY ACTIVITY PACK - SONNET

(Reflection and Growth)

✏ PoEM TEXT:
  Legacy of Unity

In lands of myth, our spirits danced and grew,
Each trial faced, with hearts both brave and true.
From Wakaduo's fields to playgrounds near,
We carried forth our quest, devoid of fear.
Through games and stories, leadership took root,
In every act, our values absolute.
With courage gleaned from lands both fierce and grand,
We stand as one, a hopeful, steadfast band.
Our journey's not confined to tales of yore,
In every challenge faced, we open doors.
For wisdom's not a gift of fleeting night,
But morning's glow, a slow but spreading light.
So here beneath the stars, we pledge anew,
To live the lessons learned, and dreams pursue.

. . .

☺ STUDENT POETRY ACTIVITIES

ACTIVITY 1: "Legacy Footprints" Art 👣

☑ Draw **footprints** leading from Wakaduo to a school playground.

☑ Inside each footprint, write a **value or lesson** the heroes (or YOU!) carry forward.

Examples: Courage, Friendship, Wisdom, Leadership

ACTIVITY 2: Sonnet Star Words ☆

☑ Pick **2 "star words"** from the sonnet (examples: legacy, journey, courage, wisdom).

☑ For each word:

• Write its meaning in your own words.

• Use it in a new sentence about your own life.

ACTIVITY 3: Complete the Thought 💬

☑ Finish this reflection sentence:

_"Our journey's not confined to tales of yore, because _____."

☑ Explain how adventures and lessons continue in everyday life.

ACTIVITY 4: Dream Pledge 🎴

☑ At the end of the poem, the heroes **pledge** something under the stars.

☑ Write your **own pledge** for how you will use your dreams and lessons in real life!

Example Starter:

"I pledge to... (lead, dream, help, inspire)"

Teacher Tip (Small Print)

☑ **Standards Alignment:**

• Poetry Comprehension and Visualization

• Personal Connection to Text

• Vocabulary Expansion and Interpretation

☑ **Science of Reading Focus:**

• Story Extension and Real-World Connection

• Expressive Oral and Written Language

🐴 **Bonus Challenge: Legacy Chain**

✅ Form a circle with classmates.

✅ Each student says *one value* they want to carry into the future — no repeats!

✅ Make a "chain" of unity around the room!

To download lesson plans, templates, and the full teacher support suite, scan the QR code or visit: unleashinggreatnessedu.org

⣿ READING PROFICIENCY ASSESSMENT TOOLKIT

⣿ Reading Proficiency Assessment Toolkit

📖 PURPOSE

This toolkit helps teachers **measure growth in vocabulary, fluency, and comprehension** as students journey through *Unleashing Greatness: The Kingdom of Shadows*. It supports **formative assessment**, **differentiation**, and **intervention planning**, all aligned with **Science of Reading (SoR)** practices.

🔍 **What's Included in This Toolkit**

1. Pre-Test & Post-Test Passages
• One narrative and one informational-style passage
• Word count calibrated for 4th-grade ORF timing
• Designed to loosely reflect themes of the novel (courage, transformation, unity)

2. Vocabulary Checks
• 5 pre/post vocabulary questions drawn from novel-style usage
• Includes Tier II/III words students will encounter

3. Comprehension Questions
• 5 short-answer questions per test

- Requires text evidence, inference, and summary skills
- Rubric-aligned (0–2 point scale)

4. Oral Reading Fluency (ORF) Chart

- WCPM bands for Advanced, Proficient, Basic, and Intervention
- Space for tracking and comparison (Pre/Post)

5. Teacher Answer Key + Rubric

- Answer key for vocabulary and comprehension
- 2-point rubric for writing quality and evidence use
- Sample response variations for calibration

6. SoR Strategies Reference Guide

- Quick reference to strategies activated in each component
- Vocabulary: morphology, context clues
- Fluency: rate, accuracy, prosody
- Comprehension: inference, summarizing, cause-effect, CER

7. Fluency Tracking & Intervention Form

- Printable and repeatable
- Space to group students by fluency level and plan support
- Optional teacher reflection prompts

🗓 When & How to Use

✅ Before Chapter 1

- Administer **Pre-Test**
- Use data to group students or select fluency routines

✅ After Chapter 26

- Administer **Post-Test**
- Compare WCPM, comprehension, and vocabulary scores
- Use growth as evidence for student portfolios or reporting

✅ Optional

- Use fluency or comprehension growth for Student-Led Conferences
- Add a tracking visual to a classroom "Wall of Progress"
- Share select results with families to celebrate reading growth

Teacher Tip

This section isn't just a test—it's a mirror.

It helps us see how students evolve as **thinkers, leaders, and readers**. The best part? It's woven into a story they'll love.

APPENDIX: ASSESSMENT SUPPORT MATERIALS

Appendix: Assessment Support Materials

PRE-TEST AND POST-TEST

A. ORAL READING FLUENCY (ORF) SCORING CHART

Use this to monitor student **rate, accuracy, and fluency expression** during the 1-minute reading passages in the Pre- and Post-Test.

Words Correct Per Minute (WCPM)
Fluency Level
Instructional Action
120+ WCPM
Advanced
Extend with enrichment and deeper comprehension.

100–119 WCPM
Proficient
On grade level. Maintain current instructional pace.

80–99 WCPM
> Basic/Approaching
> Scaffold comprehension, model phrasing & accuracy.

<80 WCPM
> Below Grade Level
> Provide fluency drills, echo reading, sentence stems.

✅ **Teacher Tip:** Track both *total words read* and *words read correctly* to measure WCPM.

B. TEACHER ANSWER KEY + RUBRIC GUIDE

✅ Vocabulary Answer Keys

Pre-Test Vocabulary:
1 C
2 A
3 E
4 B
5 D

Post-Test Vocabulary:
1 B
2 C
3 A
4 E
5 D

Comprehension Rubric (Short Answer – 0–2 pts)

Score
Description

2

Accurate, complete, text-connected response with inferences or explanation.

1

Partially correct or overly brief; some text connection or vague reasoning.

0

Incorrect, off-topic, or too vague to assess comprehension.

C. SCIENCE OF READING (SOR) STRATEGIES MET

These pre/post assessments support **Science of Reading-aligned diagnostic practices** across core domains:

SoR Domain

Strategies Addressed

Phonics/Decoding

Oral Reading Fluency passage includes multisyllabic and morphologically rich words.

Vocabulary

Direct assessment of academic vocabulary (context + morphology breakdowns).

Fluency

Timed 1-minute reading measures WCPM and oral accuracy.

Comprehension

Short-answer prompts target inferencing, summarizing, and main idea extraction.

Assessment for Instruction

Results can be used to differentiate instruction and group by fluency needs.

FLUENCY TRACKING & REFLECTION FORM

Assessment Support Material – Teacher's Guide Appendix

Part A: Student Fluency Growth Tracker

Use this section to record each student's fluency growth based on their Oral Reading Fluency (ORF) pre- and post-assessment scores.

Record for each student:

• Name

• Pre-Test Words Correct Per Minute (WCPM)

- Post-Test WCPM
- Growth (Gain or Loss in WPM)
- Fluency Level (see key below)
- Notes for Intervention or Extension

Example Entry Format (for manual entry):

Student Name: _____
Pre-Test WCPM: _____
Post-Test WCPM: _____
Growth (± WPM): _____
Fluency Level: _____
Notes for Next Steps:

Fluency Level Key:

- A – Advanced (120+ WCPM)
- P – Proficient (100–119 WCPM)
- B – Basic (80–99 WCPM)
- I – Intervention Needed (<80 WCPM)

⊙ Part B: Teacher Reflection Prompts

Reflect on class trends, individual needs, and instructional decisions using the prompts below.

1. What trends did I notice in fluency growth across the class?

2. Which students need targeted fluency support?
   What strategies or tools will I use to support them?

3 Did any students exceed expectations?
   How can I extend their learning?

4. Did vocabulary or comprehension results reveal patterns or gaps?
   What adjustments will I make in future instruction?

✅ Optional Follow-Up: Small Group Planning Snapshot

Use this space to outline 3–4 instructional groups based on

fluency and comprehension needs.

Group A – Focus: Fluency phrasing
Students: _____
Strategy: Echo reading, repeated reads, fluency modeling

Group B – Focus: Vocabulary development
Students: _____
Strategy: Word-building, story-based clue connections

Group C – Focus: Comprehension inference
Students: _____
Strategy: Think-alouds, CER support, partner evidence scans

Group D – Focus: Accuracy and decoding
Students: _____
Strategy: Phonics review, whisper phones, chunking

RECIPROCAL TEACHING WORKSHEET

Instructions: Read the assigned section of the chapter with your group. As you take turns in your roles, write your thoughts in the space below.

1. PREDICTOR
What do you think will happen next in the story?
Write your prediction here:

2. CLARIFIER
List any confusing words, phrases, or ideas. Then, try to explain or define them using context clues.
Word or Phrase
What it might mean (in your own words)

3. QUESTIONER
Write two thoughtful questions about the section you just read. Try to go deeper than surface-level answers.
1.

2.

4. SUMMARIZER

Write a short summary (3–4 sentences) of what just happened in this part of the story.

What was the most important thing that happened?

Bonus Activity:

Draw what you imagine the "shimmering tear" looks like in the sky. Use the description from the text to guide you.

RECIPROCAL TEACHING ROLE CARDS

Printable Role Cards

You can print these, laminate them, and reuse them in small reading groups.

PREDICTOR
Your job is to look ahead.
Ask:
• "What do I think will happen next?"
• "What clues do I have from the title, cover, or previous chapters?"
Start with:
"I think that…" or "Based on this part, I predict…"

CLARIFIER
Your job is to clear up confusion.
Ask:
• "What words or parts are hard to understand?"
• "Can we figure them out using context clues or rereading?"
Start with:
"This part is tricky because…" or "I think this means…"

QUESTIONER
Your job is to ask deep-thinking questions.

Ask:
- "Why did the character do this?"
- "What might happen if…?"
- "How does this connect to something we've read before?"

Start with:

"What do you think…" or "Why would…"

SUMMARIZER

Your job is to retell what happened.

Ask:
- "What are the most important events or ideas here?"
- "How would I explain this part to a friend?"

Start with:

"In this part of the story…" or "So far, we've learned that…"

RECIPROCAL TEACHING ROLES ANCHOR CHART

"Four Powerful Ways to Understand What We Read!"

Predictor

"I think this will happen next…"
- Makes smart guesses using clues from the story
- Connects past events to future outcomes
- Thinks ahead like a detective!

Starter Phrases:
- I predict that…
- Based on what I read…
- I think _____ will happen because...

Clarifier

"Wait—what does that mean?"
- Finds tricky words or confusing sentences
- Looks up definitions or uses context clues
- Helps everyone understand the text better

Clarify 2–3 tricky words per reading

- I didn't understand the word _____.
- I think it means…
- Let's reread this part together.

? Questioner

"Let's go deeper…"
- Asks "why" and "what if" questions
- Looks under the surface of the text
- Makes us think about character feelings, decisions, or themes

📌 *Try one big "why" question per reading*
- Why did _____ happen?
- What does this teach us?
- How would YOU feel if…?

📝 Summarizer

"Here's what we've learned…"
- Tells what just happened in your own words
- Picks out the most important ideas
- Helps the group stay on track

📌 *Focus on the "Big 3": Who, What, and Why*
- First, _____ happened.
- Then, _____ did _____.
- In the end, we learned that…

💬 Team Reminders

☑ Everyone participates
☑ Be kind and patient
☑ Switch roles next time!
☑ Always connect to the story

▮ WEEKLY TRACKER - PLANNING & PROGRESS CHECK

| Week of: _____ | Chapters Covered: _____ |
Class/Section: _____ |

Task...Check ✔

📖 Chapters Read Aloud or Assigned

✏️ Vocabulary Taught
  (Morphology/ Word Wall)

📖 Fluency Modeled (Pacing, Tone, Expression)

🔍 Comprehension Questions Discussed

💭 Workbook Pages Completed by Students

📝 CER Worksheet Completed (if assigned)

💬 SEL Reflection/Leadership Prompts Discussed

📚 Mini Units or Extensions Used
  (Grammar, Plot, etc.)

💭 Student Participation Highlights

🖍️ "Wall of Greatness" Updates Posted

🎨 Creative or Journal Work (if assigned)

✅ Goal Tracker or Personal Growth Moments

📔 Next Week Prep Notes

   Teacher Tip: Use this to reflect on what worked well, where students needed more support, and what to adapt in upcoming lessons.

FINAL REFLECTION & PERFORMANCE RUBRIC (FOR USE WITH CER OR CREATIVE TASKS)

💬 OPTIONAL SUMMATIVE REFLECTION

Use the Final Performance Rubric in the End Matter to score student essays, journals, or creative responses. This allows for a holistic look at growth in comprehension, empathy, and mastery of novel themes.

Summative Assessment Rubric (Vellum-Optimized Version)
Vocabulary Scoring (5 points total):
- 1 point per correct answer
- Target words: *instinct, prophecy, eclipse, empathy, transformation*

✅ **Part 2: Reading Comprehension**
Reading Comprehension Scoring:
Open-ended — Use as guidance for evaluating clarity, accuracy, and use of text evidence.

1 The Three Tokens of Tariq are mystical objects that the children must find to stop the eclipse and save Wakaduo. They are hidden in symbolic places and represent courage, truth, and empathy.

2 Maya grows from being cautious and observant to showing decisive leadership. She comforts Jose, urges the group to think before acting, and steps forward first into the tear.

3 When Malik is nearly pulled into the tear, the group acts together to save him. Their teamwork and courage in that moment show their growth.

4 The tear in the sky symbolizes a call to action, a transition from childhood to responsibility, and the unknown future.

Scoring: Up to 2 points each (1 = basic understanding, 2 = accurate with support)

Total: 8 points

Each answer:
- 2 points = Strong, supported, thoughtful
- 1 point = Basic understanding
- 0 points = Incomplete or inaccurate

Claim–Evidence–Reasoning (6 points total):
- Claim (2 pts) — Clear and relevant?
- Evidence (2 pts) — 1–2 accurate, text-based examples?
- Reasoning (2 pts) — Logical explanation connecting evidence to claim?

Creative Reflection (Optional – 3 pts):
- 1 pt = Basic effort
- 2 pts = Shows creative thinking or connection
- 3 pts = Emotionally resonant or symbolically strong

Overall Assessment Total:
- **Core Sections**: 19 points
- **With Optional Reflection**: 22 points max

✅ SEL & Mastery Notes for IEP/Admin Use
Success Indicators:
✔ Vocabulary used correctly in context
✔ Comprehension includes cause-effect and inference

✔ Writing includes at least 1 example of text-based support
✔ Student shows growth in self-awareness or empathy

📊 Overall Scoring Snapshot

Section	Points Possible
Vocabulary (Part 1)	5 pts
Comprehension (Part 2)	8 pts
CER Writing (Part 3)	6 pts
Creative/SEL (Part 4)	3 pts (optional)
Total	19 pts (or 22 w/ bonus)

🗒 Rubric Summary Table for Documentation

Criteria	4 – Exceeds	3 – Meets	2 – Approaching
Vocabulary Accuracy			
Comprehension & Inference			
Use of Evidence in CER			
Reasoning Clarity in CER			
SEL Insight or Creativity			

Optional: Use checkmarks or percentages depending on reporting style.

ECOSCIENCE COMPANION: NGSS INTEGRATED MINI-UNITS (GRADES 3-5)

🌿 **EcoScience Companion: Grades 3–5**

A Science + Reading Adventure Inspired by *Unleashing Greatness: The Kingdom of Shadows*

Where science meets story—and courage meets the classroom.

NGSS-Aligned | Literacy-Enriched | SEL-Connected

📖 HOW TO USE THIS COMPANION

This companion is designed to pair with the early chapters of the novel and align with NGSS science standards for grades 3–5.

Each mini-unit includes:
- A quick science connection to the story
- Clear, grade-appropriate NGSS-aligned concepts
- Vocabulary and discussion prompts
- Simple activities and family-friendly extension options

Use it in class, at home, or as part of your reading reflections. Science is part of every story—especially this one.

Designed for Grades 3–5, these mini-units integrate NGSS, SEL (CASEL-aligned), and Science of Reading practices (vocabulary, decoding, schema-building).

🌱 MINI-UNIT 1: CONNECTIONS IN NATURE

Chapter Tie-In: Chapters 1–2
NGSS Standard:
• **3-LS4-3**: Construct an argument with evidence that in a habitat, some organisms can survive well, some survive less well, and some cannot survive at all.

🔍 **In the Story:**
When the heroes are transported into the valley of Wakaduo, they begin to notice things they've never seen before—animals, winds, light, and balance.

Maya, as Tusker, the elephant, becomes part of a natural world filled with relationships. Every creature depends on something else.

🐚 **Science Focus:**
Symbiosis and Survival
• **Mutualism:** Both organisms help each other.
• **Commensalism:** One benefits, the other isn't hurt.
• **Parasitism:** One benefits, one is harmed.

🔤 **Science Words to Know:**
Habitat, Mutualism, Predator, Prey, Survive, Balance

👋 **Try This!**
Choose one of the characters in animal form (Tusker, Henry, Ernie, or Scatter).
• Draw their habitat in Wakaduo
• Show 2 animals they might interact with
• Label if each relationship is helpful, harmful, or neutral

💬 **Family Talk Prompt:**
"Can you think of a time when two animals or people helped each other? How is that like mutualism?"

MINI-UNIT 2: ENERGY AND THE FOOD CHAIN

Chapter Tie-In: Chapters 3–5

NGSS Standard:

• **4-LS1-1**: Construct an explanation of how animals receive different types of information through their senses and process the information to guide their actions.

• **5-PS3-1**: Use models to describe that energy in animals' food was once energy from the sun.

In the Story:

Each animal character in Wakaduo plays a different role.

Scatter eats seeds.

Henry digs for food.

Ernie flies above it all.

Tusker munches on plants.

They are part of a food web.

Science Focus:

How Energy Moves Through a System

• The sun gives energy to plants

• Plants give energy to herbivores

• Herbivores give energy to carnivores

Science Words to Know:

Energy, Consumer, Producer, Food web, Trophic level, Predator

Try This!

• Make a food chain using characters from the story

• Start with the sun → go to a plant → go to an animal character

• Use arrows to show energy movement

Example:

Sun → Grass → Tusker the Elephant

Family Talk Prompt:

"Where do you think your energy came from today? What did you eat? Where did it begin?"

MINI-UNIT 3: THE POWER OF PLANTS

Chapter Tie-In: Chapters 6–9
NGSS Standard:
• **5-LS1-1**: Support an argument that plants get the materials they need for growth from air and water.
• **3-LS3-2**: Use evidence to support the explanation that traits can be influenced by the environment.

🔍 **In the Story:**

The valley of Wakaduo is filled with glowing leaves, strange flowers, and energy-charged plants. Scatter notices how even small seeds can change the course of the journey.

In science, this is called **photosynthesis**—how plants feed themselves.

🧠 **Science Focus:**
How Plants Grow and Help Life Thrive
• Plants take in air and water
• They use sunlight to make food (glucose)
• They grow, and help animals grow too

🔤 **Science Words to Know:**

Photosynthesis, Carbon dioxide, Oxygen, Trait, Seed, Root

✍ **Try This!**

Choose a plant in your neighborhood.
• Draw it
• Write where it gets water, light, and air
• Imagine what animal might need that plant

Bonus: What plant would **Scatter** use to hide from predators?

💬 **Family Talk Prompt:**

"What plants do we see every day that help animals—and us—survive? How can we take care of them?"

🌐 CLOSING THOUGHTS

In Wakaduo, nature is more than scenery—it's a living story.

Everything is connected.

Everything depends on something else.

Even the smallest choices—like helping a friend or planting a seed—can ripple out and change the world.

"To know the land is to honor it. To live with it is to understand yourself."

— *From the Elders of Wakaduo*

🔬 NGSS Standards for Grades 3–5 That Match the Themes of Unleashing Greatness: The Kingdom of Shadows

🌿 Ecosystems & Relationships

3-LS4-3: Construct an argument with evidence that in a particular habitat some organisms can survive well, some survive less well, and some cannot survive at all.

☞ (Use Wakaduo environments and transformation examples.)

3-LS4-4: Make a claim about the merit of a solution to a problem caused when the environment changes and the types of plants and animals that live there may change.

☞ (Have students design "ecological solutions" after disruptions in Wakaduo.)

5-LS2-1: Develop a model to describe the movement of matter among plants, animals, decomposers, and the environment.

☞ (Perfect for the **trophic levels**, food webs, and energy flow.)

📦 Energy & Matter Transfer

4-PS3-4: Apply scientific ideas to design, test, and refine a device that converts energy from one form to another.

☞ (You could create **simple sun-to-food energy flow posters** as a STEAM extension.)

5-PS3-1: Use models to describe that energy in animals' food (used for body repair, growth, motion, and maintaining body warmth) was once energy from the sun.

☞ (This matches the **photosynthesis → respiration** arc).

www.ingramcontent.com/pod-product-compliance
Lightning Source LLC
Chambersburg PA
CBHW051606120626
46551CB00014B/1693